THE MAGICIAN'S TABLES

First published in Great Britain in 2007 by Godsfield, an imprint of Octopus Publishing Group Ltd
Carmelite House
50 Victoria Embankment
London EC4Y 0DZ
www.octopusbooks.co.uk

An Hachette UK Company
www.hachette.co.uk

The authorized representative in the EEA is Hachette Ireland
8 Castlecourt Centre,
Dublin 15, D15 XTP3, Ireland
(email: info@hbgi.ie)

This edition published in 2026

Distributed in the US by
Hachette Book Group
1290 Avenue of the Americas
4th and 5th Floors
New York, NY 10104

Distributed in Canada by
Canadian Manda Group
664 Annette St., Toronto,
Ontario, Canada M6S 2C8

ISBN: 978-1-8418-1631-9
eISBN: 978-1-8418-1632-6

A CIP catalogue record for this book is available from the British Library.

Printed and bound in China

10 9 8 7 6 5 4 3 2 1

Publisher: Lucy Pessell
Senior Editor: Tim Leng
Designer: Isobel Platt
Assistant Editor: Samina Rahman
Production Manager: Caroline Alberti

FSC www.fsc.org MIX Paper | Supporting responsible forestry FSC® C008047

THE MAGICIAN'S TABLES

Esoteric Wisdom & Correspondences for Rituals & Spellwork

Alan Richardson

GODSFIELD

ABOUT THIS BOOK

Magic is based on correspondences – on the connections and associations between different esoteric symbols, signs and systems. In this major work, expert author Alan Richardson has fully revised and expanded the original tables drawn up by Renaissance sages to provide the definitive reference resource for the contemporary practitioner.

The Magician's Tables unlocks the secrets of magical practice by revealing the links between all the elements of esoteric wisdom. Within these pages you will find detailed tables showing the ancient mystical correspondences for symbols from the Kabbalah, signs of the zodiac, angels, the Tarot and much more.

Which runes are associated with which Tarot cards? Which colours are associated with the Kabbalah's Tree of Life? What are the herbs sacred to each month of the Egyptian astrological calendar? This book reveals all the fascinating secrets of magic and ritual based on many ancient manuscripts, some only recently rediscovered.

When it was first published, it was the first comprehensive, exhaustively researched book of correspondences for over one hundred years. *The Magician's Tables* is an essential esoteric text for everyone fascinated by magic and the world of the spirits.

Publisher's note:

The Magician's Tables contains correspondence charts taken from historical sources. The views, opinions and terminology used relate to the cultural practices, mythology and belief systems of the time in which they were written. They do not represent the views of the publisher and are included for the purposes of scholarship into magic and the esoteric arts only.

Medicinal plants included in this book should be used with care. Many of the plants listed are unsafe for human consumption and their correspondences are provided for scholarship only. The publisher cannot accept any legal responsibility for any injury sustained whilst following any of the charts herein.

CONTENTS

	Introduction	6
1	The Art of Correspondences	8
2	The Tables of Space & Time	22
3	The Kabbalah	52
4	Tarot Correspondences	76
5	The Gods & Goddesses on the Tree	86
6	The Colour Scales	98
7	Astrological Correspondences	104
8	Medical Astrology & its Correspondences	140
9	Mineral, Vegetable & Animal Correspondences	152
10	Assorted Angels & Demons	160
11	Egyptian Magic	182
12	Celtic Magic	196
13	Ogham	216
14	The Runes	220
15	The I Ching	234
16	Appendix	244
	Endnotes	256
	Index	260

INTRODUCTION

The magicians of the Hermetic Order of the Golden Dawn, founded in 1888 and containing some of the finest minds of the time, took solemn oaths to guard their occult secrets. It was believed by some that breaking the vows of secrecy would unleash a punitive and potentially deadly current.

In the decades since, however, those oaths have been broken time and again and their secrets laid bare. While the adepts who founded the GD (as it is invariably called) had good reasons for imposing such oaths, the plain fact is that in the 21st century it is almost our duty to uncover those things they once tried so ardently to conceal. As we shall see, the moment we try to do so the arcana come alive.

The Secret Art of Correspondences

Many of their secrets revolved around the art of making or discerning correspondences, which are explained at length in Chapter 1. Correspondences have never been a science; they represent humankind's intuitive, empathetic way of linking with sources of divine energy and consciousness.

In some ways they are known to us today largely because of the book entitled *Liber 777*, which Aleister Crowley published anonymously and eventually took credit for, but which rode on the greater genius of his teacher and initiator Samuel Liddell MacGregor Mathers, who had spent countless hours in the library of the British Museum translating ancient esoteric texts and distilling the occult knowledge within them.

Crowley was a genius, and his personality so large, his brilliance so odd and his infamy so attractive that his book has been regarded as unchallengeable. Yet, as we shall see, it must be challenged for correspondences to work.

The knowledge and imagery distilled by these two men, going back to Renaissance and classical sources and even further, are presented in the following pages. However, we no longer need to be in thrall to their vision or cowed by their scholarship. We no longer have to pore over dusty tomes in museums and libraries, seeking ever purer translations from Latin, Greek, Hebrew, Sumerian, ancient Egyptian, Coptic or whatever mystery tradition most concerns us. Thanks to the internet, we no longer have to rely on the vagaries of isolated individuals whom we would probably never have allowed across our doorsteps; instead we can give full rein to our own vagaries and search out our own arcana, thus creating our own mysteries.

A Modern Interpretation

For the present work I plundered (with silent thanks) the best of the Golden Dawn, the more relevant tables from Crowley, Mathers and William Wynn Westcott, the modern associations of William G Gray and, with the help of the internet, I summoned up the shades of Cornelius Agrippa, Francis Barrett and Dr John Dee – to name but a few. I also contacted old friends in the magickal business and picked their brains, while at the same time making new ones online.

That which follows gives accessible correspondences that utilize the runes, ogham, Egyptian ***neters***, Norse, Indian and Celtic deities. If you want to make talismans, summon angels, commune with faeries, invoke the raw elemental powers, create your own 'magical weapons', expand your consciousness into supernal levels and generally feel involved with the inner currents of the universe, then there are enough correspondences in the pages that follow to enable you to do so. There is no elitism involved; all you need is the urge to ask questions and the willingness to connect.

Sources – ancient and modern, historical and personal, textual and from the internet – are cited in the Endnotes. But, as we shall see, the best and most effective information will be found within your own selves and will be teased out by the art of correspondences in the simplest of ways.

How to Use This Book

Surprisingly, all you have to do to begin with is to skim through the pages. There is no need to aim for an instant grasp of the more tortuous aspects of the Kabbalah or the oddities of the *I Ching*. You don't need to appreciate it on an intellectual level until the time comes when you want to create your correspondences and explore your inner worlds.

The unconscious mind works through symbols, not academic precepts. Just leafing through the pages of this book for its images alone is tantamount to priming your unconscious, telling it that something is on its way – a new way of perceiving.

Some sections will appeal to you, some will seem deadly dull. There is no point in trying to be worthy or virtuous, and aiming for a complete and instant grasp of all the systems of correspondence. But there is every point in dipping into the text and the charts to find things that intrigue you.

Magic is not about scholarship. It is about living your life to the full at every possible level. A reader who is inflamed by the complexity of the *I Ching* might not, at first, have any empathy for the lines of the apparently simpler Ogham alphabet. Likewise, people who burn with delight at the very thought of using the elements to create magic might feel their hearts sink when they look at the philosophies attending the Tree of Life in the system known as the Kabbalah.

Eventually your intuition will prompt you towards those areas that are most important to your psyche. So in simple terms, choose what attracts you most strongly and work in that direction accordingly.

It is not a competition, it is not a race. People who attempt to be 'spiritual atheletes' – that is, self-professed all-rounders in every kind of New Age practice – rarely get very far and never have much fun.

So once you have skimmed through the book and become intrigued, sit down and read the first two chapters. This book is written so that those two chapters will give you the very essence of magic in all its most basic and potent forms. In a sense, you don't really need much more than that. Those chapters will give you a thorough grounding in how magic works, show you why it is important and guide you towards what you might want to do with the knowledge.

From there, you can launch yourself in any direction you see fit.

1

THE ART OF CORRESPONDENCES

WHAT ARE MAGICAL CORRESPONDENCES?

The theory and practice of using magical correspondences are ancient, permeate every aspect of our life and yet are almost forgotten. This is a system of insights and images that lies behind every self-improvement system that has ever existed (religious or otherwise) and can empower individuals in any direction they might choose. It is like an electrical circuit: by devising and setting out your correspondences, you can encourage a flow of energy. You can achieve marvels. It is simple, flexible and available to everyone – whether they are scholars, hands-on practical types or unrepentant daydreamers. The tables in this book are not a dry collection of words and names pinned on the board of short-term memory like dead moths: they are tools for expanding consciousness. They are a means of enabling you to link with something greater and other than yourself. We can all create our own magical correspondences.

With varying degrees of awareness, magical correspondences are used by witches, magicians, mystics, shamans, druids, alternative healers and theologians of every persuasion. They are also used by poets, artists, novelists, playwrights, doctors, psychologists, teachers (of every topic), scientists (of every discipline), lovers, haters, actors, mums and dads – by every human being who has ever used a simile or a metaphor. If, on the alphabet of experience, you can find your way from A to B with reasonable accuracy (or even from one end of the kitchen table to the other), then you can make this system work for you.

We use correspondences all the time, in simple and unconscious ways that we take for granted. When we associate the colour red with anger, for example, we are dipping the edge of one toenail into the great sea of correspondence. If we expand upon it by linking the colour red with the planet Mars and the feeling of brave, positive 'martial' responses, then we are well on the way to grasping the essence of the system.

What we learn is, in essence, a kind of 'reverse engineering'. Anyone who wanted to evoke and use the qualities of Mars would start, perhaps, by deciding to light a red candle to signify their intent, thinking of red, and wearing red; and then, in due course, with surprising ease, they would find that they could learn to channel the energies of that planet in an infinite variety of positive ways.

There is more to it than that, of course, but the essence lies within reach for us all, even now. The information in this book will provide you with the tools whereby you can:

- Feel linked with the universe
- Summon up energies
- Recreate your mundane selves
- Expand your consciousness

Who Will Use This Book?

It might be someone who, having dropped their children off at school, wants to spend a few hours doing something for themselves for once and exploring their much-neglected inner life. Or it might be a retired person with time to spare, who knows (even if no one else can see it) that they still have a powerful spark within, and who wants to go inwards and therefore upwards, but never downhill towards decay.

Magical correspondences can help us make sense of an apparently chaotic universe; they can help us develop qualities that we need in order to improve as individuals. In times of bewilderment, distress and darkness, they offer us the circuit diagrams that can enlighten us again, once we learn to find the right switches. They can wake us up.

How Is Magic Defined?

Aleister Crowley (1875–1947, see pages 17–18) – who was also known as the Great Beast, the Master Therion, Perdurabo and by other names – wrote:

> From the nature of things...life is a sacrament; in other words, all our acts are magical acts. Our spiritual consciousness acts through the will and its instruments upon material objects, in order to produce changes which will result in...new conditions of consciousness.[1]

In contrast, the magician and kabbalist William G Gray (1913–1992), who as a young boy once sat on the visiting Great Beast's knee while his anxious mother browsed through her signed copy of Crowley's *Liber 777*, commented:

> The word Magic...had root connections with greatness (*Maj*) and mastery (*Magister*), and providing this might be understood in the sense of spiritual development and self-mastery, it seemed a reasonable description of the Path I intended to follow. Orthodox religions of all descriptions rejected Magic as a dangerous rival, yet Magic was inclusive of religion...Religion was collective whereas Magic was individual, and I was all for individualism...I would find my own faith through whatever I might learn of Magic and its practical purposes.[2]

These definitions help determine something of the religious intent behind magic, but it was Crowley who also defined the actual method. 'Magic,' he wrote, 'is the art of causing changes to occur in consciousness, in conformity with one's will.' In other words, through magic you can change – expand – your consciousness from the mundane to something approaching the divine. The magician strives to do this in order to communicate with higher orders of being, and with *other* orders of being, whether these are elemental, faery, angelic or existing up there among what used to be termed the 'Masters'. And by doing so, because all consciousness is linked, the solitary magus can influence us all. And this is made possible because the subconscious[3] mind works through symbols and images, rather than reason and logic. Feed the subconscious with images, and the systems of correspondence can become primary tools for evolution.

Both Crowley and Gray used correspondences that we will look at in some depth later – correspondences that enabled them, through concept association, to expand their minds and commune with beings in other dimensions. Whether the entities were benign and with an evolutionary interest in humanity is a matter for the individual to decide. It is your own inner world that matters, and your own sense of rightness.

CONCEPT ASSOCIATION

The techniques hinge, initially, upon this notion of concept association, which is in itself profoundly necessary and utterly universal. A parent raises their finger in warning and their child (hopefully!) stops misbehaving, because they know that a certain chain of events will unfold that might cause unhappiness; that finger becomes like a magician's wand of power. Later, when the neophyte learns to use the correspondences with deliberate intent, they might choose to ritualize them with varying degrees of complexity and sophistication. But the underlying concepts are exactly the same.

In his hugely influential book ***The Golden Bough***, Sir James Frazer (1854–1941) pointed out that one of the fundamental aspects of primitive religion (and the essential principle behind 'sympathetic magic', see below) was the belief that apparently diverse and unconnected things could, and did, share a mystical connection. By finding the thread that connected everything, the seeker of enlightenment could make their way from normal consciousness towards that of the gods who ruled them. Or, viewed from a more two-dimensional perspective, the connections were like the silver thread of Ariadne, which can guide you out of the labyrinth of life, avoiding the dreaded Minotaur.

Every culture had its own systems. Preliterate societies of Celtic Britain had verbal traditions that were passed on 'from mouth to ear'. Druid training, which lasted almost 19 years – a whole ***Saros*** (lunar eclipse) cycle – was entirely oral. And although it seems that many Druids read, wrote and could speak Greek, they did not commit anything to paper, even though they did not prohibit writing. It was felt that some things were sacred and should not be written down for the profane to read. It took thousands of years before this attitude was shattered.

Even here, there were levels of awareness. The average farmer would have their own oral traditions, which would relate wheat to summer to growth to sun to gold to deity, and would organize their festivals accordingly. Millennia later we still have tiny fragments of this in the meteorological folklore that talks about 'red skies at night, shepherds' delight' and 'ne'er cast a clout till May is out'. The initiates, however, would go rather deeper.

Creating Order Out of Chaos

Despite the common perception, the use of magical correspondences was never solely the preserve of grimoires (spellbooks, see page 16), necromancers, soothsayers, witches, wizards and pagans of every kind. Any Christian who, like St Patrick, has ever glimpsed an understanding of the Holy Trinity in the three leaves of the shamrock, or has been inspired by images of lambs to understand a little more about the qualities of sacrifice, redemption and meekness, is using the same techniques. Correspondences were a means of ordering the apparent chaos of the universe. Once you could perceive the pattern, you could control it.

This was the basis of simple, 'sympathetic magic' of the sort that Frazer identified. Sympathetic magic works on the principle that 'like influences like'; some Native Americans would make a wooden image of an enemy and stick pins into it, believing that because the doll represented the enemy, harm done to the doll would harm the enemy. It was also the essence of those high magical traditions that have survived from Sumerian times, down through the temples of ancient Egypt, into Greece and Rome – and beyond.

Osiris

Whether written down in cuneiform, Hebrew, ogham (an ancient Celtic writing system) or hieroglyphics, or simply passed down the generations via oral tradition, lists of correspondences are very old and have often been zealously guarded. To name something is to have a link with it. Names have power. Gnostic books in the Nag Hammadi library – a collection of early Christian Gnostic texts discovered near the town of Nag Hammadi in 1945 – contain lists of aeons and archons (good and evil beings), correlating them to different virtues and vices. The 'First Book of Enoch' lists fallen angels and their spheres of influence. Most such knowledge has died away simply because it was not recorded in any permanent way, but we can at least pick up its tracks along the banks of the Nile.

The *Neters*: an Egyptian Concept

The ancient Egyptians had the sophisticated concept of the ***neters***. It is sometimes convenient to describe these as gods and goddesses, but the Egyptian word ***neter*** takes in rather more than is usually meant by the term 'god' and might more accurately be translated as 'spiritual powers'. If there is a quality within us that is maternal and protective, and if this quality is also found reflected in both the workings of the cosmos and the world around, then this is the ***neter*** of Isis. Isis is not, here, some external lump of divine consciousness that may have a few dim echoes within us: it is a great circle of consciousness and experience that links all the worlds equally, from the material through the emotional, mental and spiritual, in all the realms (animal, vegetable and mineral). This is the true meaning of the Hermetic axiom 'As above, so below', which is often given a diluted interpretation. The ***neters*** exist/extend through matter and energy, through space and time. So we can find the ***neter*** of Isis in a mother cuddling her child, in the strong feeling inspired by supportive words, in the protective bodywork of a well-designed car or in the raucous sound of a burglar alarm. These are also correspondences.

The Egyptians had an enormously complex system of religion, which existed over many thousands of years. The mysteries of Aunu, Memphis, Abydos and Thebes all overlap, but have distinct tones and differing correspondences. Yet an underlying and workable framework lies within the trinities of the various mystery centres (see below).

FATHER	MOTHER	CHILD
Ptah	Sekhmet	Nefertum
Amun	Mut	Khonsu
Osiris	Isis	Horus

All these ***neters*** represent energies – some dormant, others still very active – that we can link with basic symbols. The Egyptians believed that their whole land was a lower analogue of spiritual realities – an earthly expression of the universe and the human soul. If ancient Egypt had an Upper and Lower Kingdom, then this division was also to be found within the psyche of the individual; if particular gods were worshipped at particular places, then it was because this paralleled certain functions within the mind and body.

As was said to Asclepius (a Greek hero who later became the Greek god of medicine and healing) in the *Hermetica*, a category of Late Antique literature purporting to contain ancient wisdom:

Do you not know, Asclepius, that Egypt is an image of heaven, or to speak more exactly, in Egypt all the operations of the powers which rule and work in heaven have been transferred to the earth below?'

Plato (c.428–c.348 BCE) drew upon this and expressed it baldly when he talked about the microcosm and macrocosm. That is: Man (the microcosm) is an exact image of God (the macrocosm). Everything that we can find within ourselves is a lower analogue of energies and events at cosmic levels and vice versa. This was again, traditionally derived from the Hermetic axiom, which went: 'That which is above is the same as that which is below'. The fact that we now have the ability to clone whole beings from a single cell shows the inherent truth of the ancient wisdom.

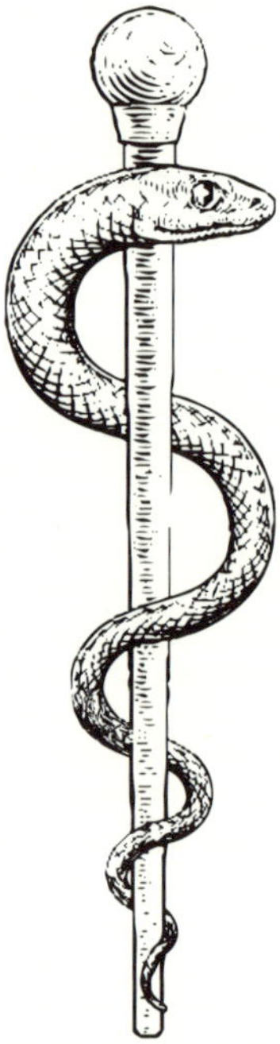

Hermeticism

The term 'Hermetic' is derived from the mysterious figure of Hermes Trismegistus, which is Greek for 'Hermes the thrice-greatest'. A syncretism of the Greek god Hermes and the Egyptian wisdom god Thoth, he was credited with a vast body of writings. Plato's *Timaeus* and *Critias* state that in the temple of Neith at Sais there were secret halls containing records that had been kept for 9,000 years. Clement of Alexandria believed that the Egyptians had 42 sacred writings by Hermes, encapsulating the sacred knowledge of Egyptian priests. He was believed to be the author of the *Emerald Tablet*, also known as the *Smaragdine Table*, *Tabula Smaragdina* or *The Secret of Hermes*, which was an ancient text purporting to reveal the secret of the primordial substance that underlies existence. In Eastern systems this substance is called *prana* or *akasha*; the Greeks called it *pneuma*; the Polynesians *mana*; and in Hebrew, *ruah*, which means 'breath of life'. Early Victorian scientists referred to the all-pervading *phlogiston*, while others preferred the term *aether*.

So it is from this ancient figure that we get the so-called Hermetic Arts. He – or It – is a kind of patron saint of all the magical practices and those tables of correspondence that make them work, and which can put us in touch with this universal energy.

The Welsh Triads

If the Egyptians had a holy trinity featuring the god Asar (Hellenized as Osiris), then so did the Welsh, centred upon Arthur. The parallels between these two figures alone are substantive enough to create an effective microsystem of correspondences in their own right – and rite. *Trioedd Ynys Prydein* were the Welsh Triads. Although these were not recorded until much later than the Egyptian material, it is believed that the Triads evolved as mnemonic devices used in the bardic schools, with pupils learning sequences by heart. In all there are some 96 triads contained in various Welsh manuscripts, many of which have strong Arthurian references that are tantalizing to us now, hinting at things that we should know, but have long since forgotten. Examples of such apparent trivia are Arthur's three great queens:

- Gwenhwyfar, daughter of Cywryd Gwent
- Gwenhwyfar, daughter of Gwythyr, son of Greidawl
- Gwenhwyfar, daughter of Gogfran the Giant

And his three mistresses were:

- Indeg, daughter of Garwy the Tall
- Garwen ('Fair Leg'), daughter of Henin the Old
- Gwyl ('Modest'), daughter of Gendawd ('Big Chin')

Their significance becomes apparent as soon as the magician starts to make connections, and then the images come alive. Gwenhwyfar is not a dreary and dead queen in the oral histories of a proud nation: the name means 'White Shadow' and is a title that is handed down, rather than a personal name. As such, it is every bit as potent as anything from the Land of Khem, as the Egyptians called their homeland.

Such links, such correspondences and such dynamic psychic contact will be achieved in several ways: from information that might be given by a teacher; from books and websites; from personal experience filtered through and understood by associative imagery; and from personal revelation derived from the very effort of making things correspond. When all these things fall into place, the mundane mind can punch its awareness through into what Carl Jung (1875–1961) termed the 'Collective Unconscious'. And then the archetypes start to talk. The reader becomes a magician. They can begin to know things – wonderful things.

The Doctrine of Signatures

In the pre-rationalist age, humankind had an inherent sense of the spiritual dimensions of our material world. Early scientists took this into account, so their concepts and explanations of the universe were steeped in mystical symbolism and deities, the basis for which can be found among the principles of astrology – the oldest science of human history. Isaac Newton (1643–1727), the greatest mind of his or perhaps any age, was first and foremost an astrologer. According to this cosmology, the planetary energies reverberated through the spheres and echoed through the four realms of existence, leaving their mark or signature in all the various aspects of the manifest and non-manifest world.

This found expression in the Doctrine of Signatures, which was so prominent in Renaissance times. It was the idea that God had marked everything with a sign – a 'signature' – that indicated its purpose. The Doctrine of Signatures was popularized in the early 1600s by the otherworldly master shoemaker Jakob Böhme (1575–1624) in the small German town of Görlitz. At the age of 25, Böhme had a profound vision in which he saw the relationship between God and humans. As a result of this vision he wrote ***Signatura Rerum: The Signature of All Things***. Although his book espoused a spiritual philosophy, it was soon adopted for its medical applications.

The Doctrine states that, by observation, one can determine from the colour of the flowers or roots, the shape of the leaves, the place of its growing or other signatures what the plant's purpose was in the divine plan. Common names of temperate plants tell us how they were once used to cure human ailments. In general, long-lived plants were used to lengthen a person's life, while plants with rough stems and leaves were believed to heal diseases that destroy the smoothness of the skin. A plant leaf shaped liked a kidney would be effective in treating kidney ailments. Plants with yellow sap were cures for jaundice, and roots with a jointed appearance were the antidote for scorpion bites.

Flowers shaped like a butterfly became cures for insect bites.

Even though the Doctrine of Signatures was a product of medieval alchemists and herbalists (see above) and influenced the development of what we now term homeopathy, a similar belief was held by Indigenous Americans and Eastern cultures, which shows the universality of the system.

The Grimoire

One other source that made an overt use of correspondences was the medieval grimoire. This word comes from the Old French *gramaire*, and is from the same root as 'grammar' and 'glamour'. The former denoted that it was a book of information and instruction; the latter that there was something otherworldly about it. Traditionally, grimoires contained lists of angels and demons, astrological secrets and correspondences, herb lore, spells and charms of every kind – particularly for the summoning of spirits – and instructions in the making of talismans (see page 68).

Notable grimoires of the late medieval period were:

- *The Book of the Sacred Magic of Abramelin the Mage*
- *The Black Pullet*
- *The Greater Key of Solomon*
- *The Lesser Key of Solomon* (also known as *The Lemegeton*)
- *The Grand Grimoire*

Some grimoires were useless, but others, particularly *The Book of the Sacred Magic of Abramelin the Mage*, are still being used today with great effect by magicians who want to touch the minds of angels and beyond. Also of this calibre were the three books written by Cornelius Agrippa (1486–1535) in 1531, and known as *De occulta philosophia*; they combined magic, astrology, the Kabbalah, theurgy, medicine and the occult properties of plants, rocks and metals.

Centuries later, in 1801, Francis Barrett's *The Magus, or Celestial Intelligencer* repeated many of Agrippa's lists and brought them forward into a world that was by now eager to embrace and develop them, though still in a comparatively covert way. So instead of thinking of grimoires as dreadful tomes containing secrets of darkness and devilry, perhaps we can coin a self-explanatory word and call them 'luminoires' instead.

Magic of this sort underwent a revival during the Renaissance, partly due to its association with a resurgent Neoplatonism, which originally flourished during the declining centuries of the Roman Empire (3rd–6th centuries CE). Neoplatonists argued that the highest stage of philosophy is attained not through reason and experience, but through a mystical ecstasy. Many later philosophers, including Nicholas of Cusa (1401–1464), were influenced by Neoplatonism.

The grimoires were thus an attempt by free-thinkers to challenge the dead hand of the all-powerful Church. They were the means by which bold individuals could attempt to summon up divine (or infernal) hierarchies for their own private ecstasies. Whether they worked or not, it was the actual trying that was important. For centuries, the very possession of a grimoire could result in torture and death for the owner. Today, you can download them for free online.

The Kabbalah

And then there was the emergence of that curious philosophy known as the Kabbalah (see Chapter 3), which comes from the root meaning 'to receive' or 'to accept' – that is, oral tradition passed on from initiate to neophyte.

The late 17th century saw an explosion of kabbalistic studies in areas as geographically diverse as Ukraine, Lithuania, Italy and Belarus. Some aspects of traditional Kabbalah are so deeply intertwined with Jewish religious beliefs and mystical practice that they are meaningless outside this context. Other aspects have been studied and practised outside Judaism for so long that they have a distinct identity in their own right, with a hybrid and very powerful existence today. In fact,

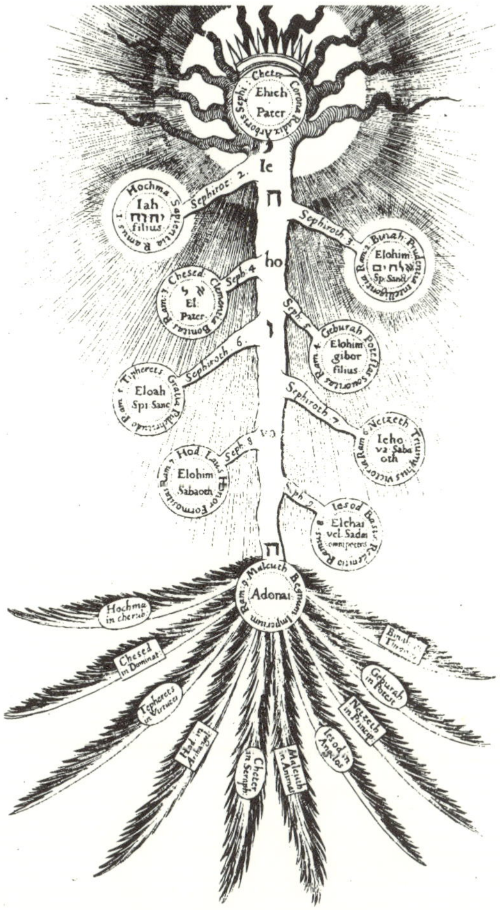

Sephirot Tree of Life, Robert Fludd, 1617

the magicians of the 19th century who seized upon Francis Barrett's work also turned their attention to the Kabbalah, and developed it accordingly, often working under the aegis of Rosicrucian aspects within Freemasonry.

By means of a simple glyph, or symbol, known as the ***otz chaim*** or Tree of Life (see page 56), the kabbalist was able to categorize every aspect of existence into a sequence of spheres and paths. By acting as a kind of filing system, the Tree enables the student to pick out one symbol and find an explosion of information from the linked material.

The Hermetic Order of the Golden Dawn

It was this that provided the framework for the magical system used within the Hermetic Order of the Golden Dawn, which was founded by three high-ranking Freemasons in 1888; its philosophies and rituals have shaped the whole of the present New Age movement in ways that are scarcely recognized. At its height, the Golden Dawn had some of the brightest and best minds of the time within its various lodges. The Nobel Prize-winning poet W B Yeats, Constance Wilde, Algernon Blackwood, Arthur Machen, J W Brodie-Innes, A E Waite, Annie Horniman, Florence Farr, Gerald Kelly and Maud Gonne were all well-known members of the society. Beyond them were physicians, surgeons, coroners, artists, generals, engineers, novelists, poets, explorers – and William Peck (1862–1925), the Astronomer Royal. There was a persistent rumour that E A Wallace Budge (1857–1934), who was in charge of Egyptology at the British Museum, was also involved and that the basement of the museum was used for rituals, although this has never been verified.

Aleister Crowley

Once branded the 'Wickedest Man in the World', Aleister Crowley is now being rediscovered and reinterpreted as one of the most inspiring of these modern mages. In his youth he had been a world-class mountaineer and had conquered some of the highest peaks in the Himalayas; he also did much the same on spiritual levels. He summoned angels and demons. He was a chess master, a renowned poet (although much of his poetry has not stood the test of time), a tireless explorer, hunter, trickster, bully, traitor, novelist, prolific writer of some of the most influential occult books of the 20th century, socialite, sponger, one of the greatest conversationalists of his generation, libertine, drug addict and Logos of the Aeon (prophet of the new religion expressed by Crowley's ***Book of the Law***). He was the occult world's equivalent of a rock star, 60 years before rock music appeared, and he created that dense tome known as ***Liber 777***.

Liber 777

He was a genius, he was a scoundrel. He was – at his height – a very powerful magician. And he wrote a book called *Liber 777*, which had an enormous influence on many of the magicians who came after him. In fact, the history of magical correspondences is so tied up with the legend of Crowley and his seminal book that the assumption is often made that he devised them.

In his notorious autobiography *Confessions* he implies that he wrote the book in a few days of inspiration in Bournemouth. In fact, about 90 per cent of the details were taken directly from the teachings of the Hermetic Order of the Golden Dawn, in which he was an initiate – more specifically from the inner order of the *Rosæ Rubeæ et Aureæ Crucis* (RR et AC). Most of the Hebrew correspondences, the four colour scales, and the order and attribution of the Tarot trumps are exactly as taught in that order. Yet the real genius behind the GD (as it was invariably called) and the awesome range of its teachings was Samuel Liddell MacGregor Mathers (1854–1918), whom the poet William Butler Yeats (also an initiate) described as half-lunatic, half-knave – like a walking flame.

Mathers's translations of such books as *The Book of the Sacred Magic of Abramelin the Mage*, *The Kabbalah Unveiled*, *The Key of Solomon the King* and *The Lesser Key of Solomon*, while often criticized by later scholars, were responsible for making what had been obscure and inaccessible material widely available to the non-academic English-speaking world. Without naming Mathers, Crowley attacked him in the introduction to *Liber 777* for his fondness for whisky, implying that his teachings were skewed because: '...Daath got mixed with Dewar, and Beelzebub with Buchanan'. Even so, despite the unnecessary dig at his teacher and initiator, no one had shown the correspondences so boldly before. This was partly because the neophytes within the Golden Dawn swore oaths never to reveal the teachings, and partly because no one who was not privy to the occult systems of the Kabbalah would have the slightest idea what the tables were about (and were hardly likely to be interested anyway). Young Aleister confessed that he had stopped worrying about the secrecy of centuries that had kept all such information hidden, and wrote refreshingly: 'All this secrecy is very silly.'

Although he concluded a later edition of *Liber 777* with the apparently modest words 'None of the editors claim to possess even the smallest degree of scholarship', his intention was always to impress and even to browbeat. Crowley's trick was to use enough classical and Hebrew scholarship, with smatterings of Arabic, to try to make his intellect unchallengeable. In such circumstances obscurity can seem like profundity, and the reader who is not gifted in languages tends to follow meekly. For generations, people have been in awe of Crowley's writings.

FINDING YOUR OWN CORRESPONDENCES

Yet the response is simple. There is no need to challenge Crowley's scholarship head-on or try to absorb it. We can just walk around him. We can – and must – make our own *magical tables*. As soon as we start to think for ourselves, and link our own insights and experiences with the major concepts and keys, we will come alive. We can do this with a notepad while sitting in a cafe; we can trawl the local library; or we can sit in front of our computers surfing for information.

There is a belief in almost all spiritual systems in what has been called the Akashic Records. This is an otherworldly location or level of consciousness in which all knowledge, all experience, from all time can be tapped. You might simply think of it as a cosmic library. Today there is a virtual manifestation of the Akashic Records in the shape of the internet. Everyone with access to the internet can find information on just about anything, with varying degrees of quality, and all filtered through the style and approach of its creators. Anyone intrigued by names, items, associations or links can go online and check them out instantly. The moment they do this – the moment they ask *why* – is the moment the correspondences will start working.

Liber 777 consists of some 200 columns, with each row corresponding to a specific *sephirah* or path on the Tree of Life (see page 56), for a total of 35 rows. The columns cover the art of *gematria* (or sacred numbers), gods and goddesses, animals, colour scales, spices, plants and astrology. It is a daunting book and an inspiring one. Everything you might need in order to make contact with otherworldly energies can be found within. It has been regarded as the *ne plus ultra* of books on correspondences. But all too often it takes the student more on a tour of Mathers's dense but uncertain scholarship and Crowley's heroin-riddled psyche than it does through the clear white light of the aether.

Nevertheless, it is an invaluable source book, though one that should be used with caution. Knowledge of Hebrew, ancient Greek and Latin are no longer prerequisites for the study and use of correspondences – if indeed they ever were. If that seems absurdly cavalier, then consider this: from late medieval times onwards, the subject of rhetoric was considered indispensable in every university curriculum. A graduate whose rhetoric was considered weak was a second-class graduate. Who studies rhetoric today? Obviously things have changed since. And the same is true within the magical curricula.

When Crowley visited William G Gray and left the boy's mother with that inscribed copy of his tome, the Old Master would never have dreamed that within a week the boy would have copied it by hand and found much of it lacking. Or that the mother, Christine Gray (née Logie), would destroy the original, believing it to have been 'magnetized' (as they said then) for unscrupulous and malign reasons. What young Bill did was create his own correspondences, based upon his own learning and experience, using Crowley's lists as items for debate and discussion – but never regarding them as God-given dogma.

The plain fact is that endless rows of tabulated information are more expressions of the formulator's scholarship than they are accessible keys to the inner worlds. Any book of correspondences is only ever one step away from becoming a necronomicon

– a Book of Dead Names. The endless charts and tables become statements of authority rather than welcoming signposts. Reading *Liber 777* a century after it was written, you can almost glimpse young Crowley in his hotel room, with blanks on the tables that had him stumped, and which he eventually filled in with a 'That'll have to do' flourish. Although passionate Crowleyans invariably bristle when the Logos of their Aeon is challenged, some of what he offered is no longer relevant to the 21st century.

The Tables in This Book

You must bear this in mind as you approach the tables in this book. There was a temptation to try to produce a sort of *Compleat Book of Correspondences*, outdoing every other in sheer size and comprehensiveness. But this would be self-defeating. Life moves too quickly, and so do our concept associations. Those bold souls who want to explore the obscure Enochian Aires – according to Crowley and John Dee, the spiritual levels of existence that block the Earth from the star, and which can be explored by the magician – will find this complex information from a myriad of other sources. What is given here are the basic tables that the ordinary person (strapped for time and money) may need in order to make effective contact with inner sources of light and energy. In this respect there is no place for the awesome paraphernalia of the medieval ceremonial magician.

So these correspondences are carefully researched. They are based on long experience and practice. They do not require classical learning or a grasp of Hebrew or Sanskrit. They will take you, step by step, towards an understanding, and they will all work.

However, everything within is there to be challenged. This is the most crucial thing of all. In fact, as soon as readers do so, they will sing! The tables are not there to burden you with rote learning: they are there to end the stasis, or stagnation. The silver thread of Ariadne that will lead you from the labyrinth will also take you back into it – if you dare. And there, in the centre,

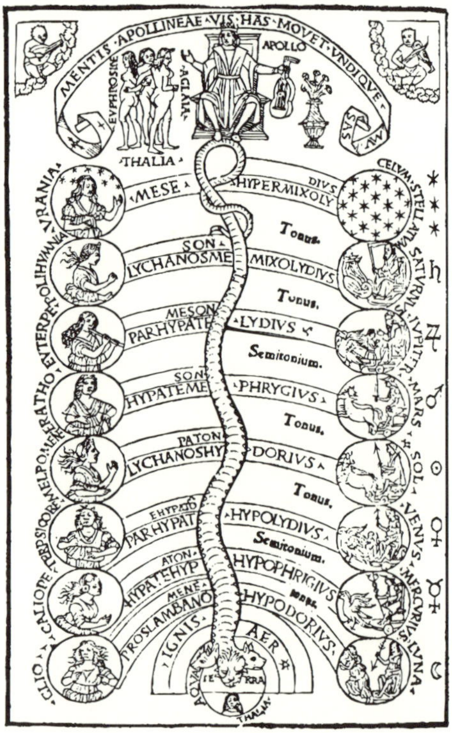

Franchinus Gaffurius's correspondences of the celestial choir. From Practica Musicae

you will find that the roaring, partly formed human in the darkness, which has worried you for so long, is actually your own self, waiting to be set free.

What is Magic?

Some people are afraid of the very mention of magic. They have grave concerns revolving around the notions of black and white magic, which is understandable given the lurid presentations of both in modern novels and movies. And they can feel it is by definition anti-Christian and anti-goodness. So why should they involve themselves in learning such a dubious art?

Well, is there such a thing as white magic or black magic? Remember that the clergy of the Inquisition, who tortured and murdered anyone they suspected of even the slightest heresy, honestly and earnestly believed that they were working for the Light of Jesus. Likewise, there are some modern 'mystical' New Age cults that simply involve commerce and coercion or just plain brainwashing. There is a simple rule to follow: if they're after your money, forget it. If they have hierarchies, then cut and run.

It's all double-edged and two-way though, and it should be remembered that magic was actually a fundamental part of Christianity even in the late medieval period. When pagans berate Christians and go on about the 'old ways' as if there was once a golden age of peace, love and light, they are ignoring the fact that the matriarchal goddess-worshipping pre-Christian pagans were, in fact, head-hunters and into human sacrifice. And, by the same token, when Christians lambast the neo-pagans as if they are involved in infanticide and public orgies, they can't see that all they are really into is a kind of eco-mysticism and concern for the planet.

The motto of real magicians has to be: 'I desire to Know, in order to Serve'. It all has to be for the improvement of our fellow humankind. Of course there are idiots in this field, just like any other, who want nothing more than power, but that is just the way of the world. If the Devil existed and really wanted to rule the world, he wouldn't waste time with pagans trying to draw down the moon in cornfields, he'd whisper in the ears of the captains of industry, of the armaments manufacturers and the politicians...

The point is that by creating your own system of correspondences you become your own teacher, your own guru and create your own inner light.

Creating Your Own Magick

By means of the correspondences given in this chapter alone, you will be able to achieve self-initiation into the realms of Magick. You will be able to 'travel in the spirit vision', as they once said, summon elementals and learn to work earth Magick. By making contact with inner sources of energy and awareness, you simultaneously make subtle links with those spiritual realms that intermingle with our own. But it cannot be stated too often that everything is there to be challenged – every time you issue a challenge, you make the foundations of your own Magick more solid.

2

THE TABLES OF SPACE & TIME

KEY CONCEPTS

The moment you start to use any table of correspondences, you define yourself in space and time. You create a universe around yourself, in which you are the centre. This is not a matter of megalomania, but a simple act of creating order from chaos. As magicians, using our correspondences and absorbing the energies inherent in myth and symbol, we become our own *axis mundi*, our own *omphalos*. We will look at these two concepts now, paving the way for the work to come.

The *Omphalos*

Omphalos means 'navel' in Greek. According to legend, the god Zeus sent out two eagles to fly across the world and they met at its centre, at the 'navel' or *omphalos*. The various oracle centres in the Mediterranean lands – most notably Delphi – all had sacred *omphalos* stones, which were held to allow direct communication with the gods. Some people feel that this concept originated from the 'stone of splendour' associated with the Canaanite god Baal, but it is more likely to have derived from the even older Benben stone of ancient Egyptian religion. There is a panel in the *Book of the Dead* showing an *omphalos* stone that was believed to enable a human to speak with Sokar, the god of the afterlife.

The *Axis Mundi*

Axis mundi (world axis) is the notion of the world centre, and the connection between heaven and earth. Every culture on Earth has this concept, and it is especially strong in those whose cultures are derived from, or still use, shamanic practices involving the world tree concept or animist belief systems. In the former, the shamanic healer traverses or climbs the *axis mundi* to bring back knowledge from the Otherworld. There is a direct reflection of this in the rod of Asclepius, the symbol of medicine and the well-known image of the caduceus: a staff entwined with serpents; the staff is the axis itself, and the serpents (or serpent) are the guardians or guides to the other realm.

When the magician takes up the wand of fire, they are (whether they realize it or not) creating their own world axis; wherever they live, they are themselves the *omphalos*, the centre of their own universe. So the *axis mundi* provides a path between heaven and earth. It is commonly represented as a tree, rope, vine, ladder, staff or pillar, among other things.

All cultures have specific places that are sacred and considered to be meeting points between the worlds. They are invariably hills, mountains or pyramids. Some of them have only local appeal and will be unknown to anyone but mystics and magicians of the area; others are known globally, such as the Black Hills of the Sioux; Uluru or Ayers Rock of the Indigenous Australians; Mount Kailasa; the Dome of the Rock, where Muhammad was raised to and lowered from heaven; the shrine at Mecca for the followers of Islam; Mount Olympus; Glastonbury Tor for the English...the list is long and their histories even longer.

This passion for the sacred hill as an *axis mundi* or *omphalos* is reflected in the actual structures of religion, the most notable examples being the pyramids of Egypt and the ziggurats of Mesopotamian civilizations. Mount Meru is echoed in the *stupas* or sacred monuments of Hinduism, and later of Buddhism. The upright bar of the Calvary cross is sometimes seen as representing a world axis, while the steeple of a church or the minaret of a mosque indicates a place where the earthly and divine meet. Structures such as maypoles in pre-Christian Europe, which are linked to the *Irminsul* – the solar-phallic pillar used in religious practices by early Anglo-Saxons – and totem poles among Indigenous Americans also formed local or temporary world axes.

In addition, plants (which will figure largely in the later tables) were regarded or used as world axes or world trees. In some Pacific island cultures, the banyan tree is the abode of ancestor spirits. The Bodhi tree is the name given to the tree under which Gautama Siddhartha, the historical Buddha, sat on the night he attained enlightenment. Other examples include *Yggdrasil* of Norse mythology, *Jievaras* of Lithuanian mythology, the pre-Christian Germanic people's Thor's oak, the sephirothic tree of Judaism, the chakras that are common to many Eastern religions, and the Trees of Life and Knowledge of Good and Evil in the Garden of Eden. Conscious-expanding plants known as entheogens, such as the fly agaric mushroom among the Evenks of Russia, are often considered to be the *axis mundi*.

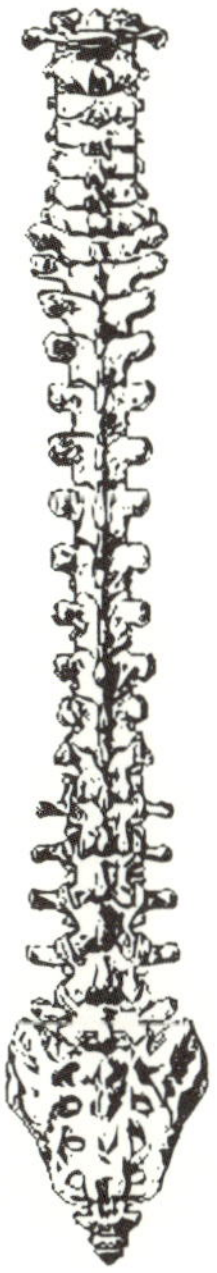

In a sense, the true *axis mundi* with which we have to concern ourselves is our own spine. It is the spine that makes us upright beings. It is connected with the chakras or energy centres, and with the occult channels known as the *ida* and *pingala nadis* and the central *sushumna nadi*, up which roars *kundalini* energy. This itself is also symbolized within the caduceus. So when you stand upright and begin to use your correspondences to invoke your gods, the primary *axis mundi* is to be found as your spine – the still centre of a turning world.

The Magic Circle

The magician forms their magic circle and uses it rather as a surgeon uses an operating theatre – that is to say, it is a purified area in which work of a highly specialized nature takes place. When you perform, say, the 'lesser banishing ritual of the pentagram' (see page 40), you are actually doing something that has an effect on your inner levels. The ritual itself is simply a prelude to other work. The great adept W E Butler (1898–1978) wrote:

> When you tread your magic circle in the lodge or temple and you are all walking solemnly in procession, psychic vision can actually see those lines of force formulating...The curious thing is that although you're forming your magic circle on one level, you are actually building a sphere (those lines of force go, in equal distance, beneath as well as above).[4]

In most Western magical traditions there is the concept of the Seven Directions: north/east/south/west/above/below/within. This is sometimes also thought of, or visualized, as the Cube of Space. More usually it is simplified to the four quarters of the magical circle used by anyone with ritual intent, whether they are Hermeticists or Wiccans (adherents of the modern interpretation of witchcraft known as Wicca, a form of nature religion). The practical effect, on psychic levels, is to create a sphere of light.

When Aleister Crowley received his initiation into the magical Order of the Golden Dawn he complained that he was given no more than a few astrological symbols and trivial details that he already knew. Yet that is all any genuine group can possibly give. The importance is not in accumulating endless tables of information, but in working through them, linking imagery with your own understanding and experience. A young person may build up a collection of love poems and anecdotes about the beauty of falling in love; they may reach puberty knowing all the symptoms and effects of being in love, but the knowledge crumbles beside the reality. Similarly you may – by analysis of the symbolism connected with, say, Hermes – gain a good idea of what a particular god is like, but until you actually make some sort of contact with that god you will not ***really know***.

So the beginning of the correspondences is the beginning of knowledge, which may – just may – lead to wisdom.

BALANCING THE ELEMENTS

To start this exercise, you face east and should be aware of the other directions around you. Facing east in this instance has nothing to do with Mecca or Jerusalem (or any other holy city); it is simply the place where the sun rises and the day begins. You visualize the sun rising before you, then follow its apparent orbit to reach its zenith in the south, to your right; its setting in the west behind you; and then have a sense of the darkness of midnight to your left.

In the traditional system of correspondences we start with four simple items:

East
South
West
North

1. They are in this sequence so that the magician will turn ***deosil*** (as witches term it) – that is to say, sunwise. Feel a sense of these four directions now. You are about to create your own cosmos and become its very centre. Your spine will be the ***axis mundi***.
2. The next awareness is logical and self-evident:

East	Sunrise
South	Noon
West	Sunset
North	Midnight

These might seem trivial perceptions and attributions, but they are fundamental to the way we create and arrange our universe. So be aware of these four directions, the rising and setting of the sun, and the darkness of midnight to your left. Have a sense of being at the centre of the universe; a sense of the excitement of spirit caused by the rising sun. Imagine a cool breeze flowing towards you, and try to sense a great being sending you new ideas.

3. Turn to the south and feel the warmth of the sun at noon. The great being in that quarter gives you an inner radiance. You burn with excitement; you are alive, on fire with inspiration.
4. Turn to the west and visualize the setting sun, the coolness, and have a sense of the being of the west giving you a blessing of pure joy.
5. Turn to the north and sense the darkness that is also necessary to this world, wherein things are growing and are ready to reveal themselves in the fullness of time; feel contentment. Then turn back to the east and feel that your inner circuit is completed and that the elements are balanced.

Elemental Attributions

That is all very simple, but the act of trying is crucial: it is the first step in putting yourself in touch with your elemental nature. It is not so much what you do as the fact that you are doing something – something that is different and filled with intent. As you expand upon the list of correspondences and add the words of power, utilize the colours and identify the deities, and then perhaps build and use your own 'magical weapons', you will be able to pick up one symbol and find that it is charged with a mass of associations that will help push your mind to other levels of consciousness.

In almost every Western system, the next four elemental attributions are inevitably linked as follows:

East	Sunrise	Air
South	Noon	Fire
West	Sunset	Water
North	Midnight	Earth

There is a notion in Magick (the spelling used by Crowley to distinguish the art from the mere conjuring magic) that unless you can work with the elemental forces, the rest of your efforts will misfire or be ineffective. To this extent the elemental tables *must* precede any other.

To the ancients, the human being comprised the four elements, and in a physiological sense they are exactly right: the element of Earth is found in our flesh and bones; the element of Water is in all the bodily fluids that are so necessary; the element of Air is obviously fundamental to our need to breathe; while Fire is that bodily heat which shows we are alive. If we were to give it a modern gloss, we might add another section and think in terms of the table below.

There is a fifth element, of course, which goes under many names, depending on tradition, but is usually referred to as ***prana*** – the all-pervading and underlying vital (primordial) substance of the universe (also see page 14). The Greeks called it ***pneuma***, the Polynesians ***mana*** and in Hebrew it was ***ruah***, which means 'breath of life'. Early Victorians referred to the all-pervasive ***phlogiston***, while others used the term ***aether***. It has many parallels with the modern idea of zero-point energy. It can be expressed graphically in the famous image of the pentagram.

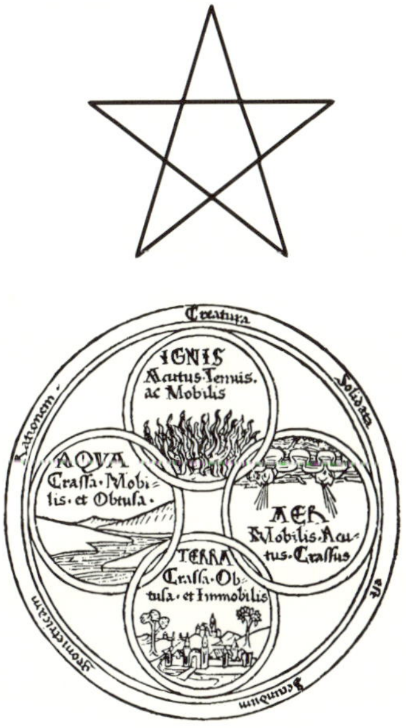

The pentagram and the four classical elements

Table of the Quarters

DIRECTION	TIME	ELEMENT	PHYSICAL STATE
East	Sunrise	Air	Gases
South	Noon	Fire	Radiations
West	Sunset	Water	Liquids
North	Midnight	Earth	Solids

OTHER FOURFOLD PATTERNS

Whether in the fields of Magick, medieval medicine or modern transformative psychology, there is a fundamental (and elemental) need to order both our psyches and the universe that we inhabit. According to the Hermetic doctrine of 'as above, so below' (see page 13), the individual psyche and the infinite universe are one and the same.

The fourfold arrangement is thus a natural, intuitive response to our sense of space and how it is interpreted by time; the four directions are inseparable from sunrise/noon/sunset/midnight. There is also a sense in which all Magick is for healing. It deals with 'dis-ease' and seeks to make whole. Early physicians were just as keen to arrange their systems in fourfold patterns.[5] Hippocrates' (c.460–c.370 BCE) system of humours can be seen in the table opposite.

His influence filtered down through two generations to Aristotle (384–322 BCE) and Galen (129–216 CE). Aristotle, without linking it with the elements, identified four sources of happiness, whereas Galen offered four temperaments (see opposite). Even today, 1,800 years on, we still use those terms to describe individuals.

On the other hand, Plato (c.427–c.347 BCE) gave a slightly different slant with his own correspondences (see opposite).

Paracelsus

Then came the great Paracelsus (1493–1541), who was an alchemist, physician, astrologer and all-round magus, and who went a step further and named the orders of elemental spirits (see the table opposite). Nearly five hundred years later, magicians are still using the Parcelsian model.

Hippocrates' System of Humours

HUMOUR	BLOOD	YELLOW BILE	BLACK BILE	PHLEGM
Season	Spring	Summer	Autumn	Winter
Element	Air	Fire	Earth	Water
Organ	Heart	Gall bladder	Spleen	Brain/lungs
Characteristics	Brave, amorous	Volatile	Despondent, sleepless	Calm, unemotional

Aristotle's Four Sources of Happiness

Happiness	Hedone (sensuous pleasure)	Propraitari (acquiring assets)	Ethikos (moral virtue)	Dialogicke (logical investigation)

Galen's Four Temperaments

Temperaments	Sanguine	Melancholic	Choleric	Phlegmatic

Plato's Correspondences

FIRE	AIR	WATER	EARTH
Brightness	Darkness	Darkness	Darkness
Thinness	Thinness	Thickness	Thickness
Motion	Motion	Motion	Quietness

Paracelsus's Order of Elemental Spirits

	AIR	FIRE	WATER	EARTH
Totem Spirits	Sylphs (Air) Curious	Salamanders (Fire) Changeable	Undines (Water) Inspired	Gnomes (Earth) Industrious

TWENTIETH-CENTURY ANALYSES

The psychologists of the early 20th century – particularly Carl G Jung, who was more magician than physician – were fully aware of the need to create similar analyses of their own. In a very real sense they were following on from the pre-Christian and medieval paradigms.

According to Jung, the Ego – the 'I' or self-conscious faculty – has four inseparable functions, four different fundamental ways of perceiving and interpreting reality, and two ways of responding to it. Accordingly, he divided people into Thinking, Feeling, Sensation and Intuition types, but added the qualities of introvert and extrovert to modify each of them. This matches the elemental scheme exactly. So we might see the individual as being composed of: Sensation (Earth), Feeling (Water), Thinking (Air) and Intuition (Fire). Or, put another way: Doing, Feeling, Thinking and Being.

Jung was not alone in this. From the beginning of the 20th century we can find are a wide range of categorizations (see below).[6]

Not all of these fit neatly into the fourfold elemental system, but even the merest analysis and slightest attempt to make them do so ensure that the correspondences become energized.

Magical Weapons

Where Jung and his peers, rivals and descendants would work with these qualities through what might broadly be termed psychoanalytic methods, the magician would seek to use and control the elemental forces by means of what they would term 'magical weapons'. These are:

- Sword – Air
- Spear – Fire
- Cup – Water
- Pentacle – Earth

When the magician picks up the Sword, by a chain of associations the energies and awareness of that quarter can be manipulated. The reasons for these associations are as seen on the next page.

Different World Views

Adicke's world views	Innovative	Traditional	Doctrinaire	Sceptical
Spränger's value attitudes	Artistic	Economic	Religious	Theoretic
Kretchmer's character styles	Hypomanic	Depressive	Hyperaesthetic	Anaesthetic
Fromm's orientations	Exploitative	Hoarding	Receptive	Marketing
Myers's cognitive function types	Sensory perception	Sensory judgement	Intuitive feeling	Intuitive thinking
Keirsey's temperaments	Artisan	Guardian	Idealist	Rationalist

Earth, Air, Water and Fire according to 15th-century alchemist, Basil Valentine

The Sword

The Sword was originally an arrow (which is a flying sword), hence its association with Air. It associates with hearing, speech and smell. Our tongues are swords, in that they can be cutting or healing, and they express our intelligence.

The Spear or Rod

The Spear or Rod was associated with Fire because it could keep the camp fire in check without being burned, and was a means of carrying it from one place to another. We can link it with matches, candles, torches, tapers and light switches.

The Cup

The Cup is a depression that can be found in caves, wombs, wells, hollows and so on, and holds Water. It is associated with love in that it holds, pours out, comforts and cheers. It is linked with grails and with the blood, and thus with fertility and germination. Symbolized as a horn, it is both female and male.

The Pentacle

The Pentacle, which means 'all-keys', is essentially any kind of surface that can scrape the earth. It can represent a spade, trowel, coin, blackboard or mirror – 'a medium for translating thoughts into things or the reverse'.[7] It is also known as a Shield because it protects and deflects. It is a means of communicating with the inner world by placing some pattern on it that is understandable to both human and higher types of intelligence.

Elemental Correspondences

ELEMENT	DIRECTION	SEASON	TIME	TOOLS	MAGICK	COLOUR	RULES
Air	East	Spring	Dawn	Sword, athame (dagger), censer, incense	Healing (hurts and wounds), divination, concentration, prophecy, visualization, invocation	White, yellow, lavender, grey	Life, intellect, knowledge, philosophy, teaching, instruction, telepathy, memory, analysis, wind, breath, speech, hearing, new beginnings, sudden revelation
Fire	South	Summer	Noon	Wand, candles	Healing (diseases), candle, storm, sun magic, cleansing	Red, gold, crimson, orange, brilliance	Illuminative change and passion, light, energy, sexuality, authority, purification, sun, blood, destruction, creativity, courage, strength, physical exercise, self-knowledge, power
Water	West	Autumn	Dusk	Chalice, cauldron, mirror	Love magic, magic of the sea, snow or ice, moon magic, cleansing and purification	Blue, blue-green, green, grey, indigo, aquamarine	Emotions, feelings, love, the unconscious mind, dreams, the womb, friendship, happiness, sleep, menstruation, fertility, cleansing, purification, psychic ability
Earth	North	Winter	Night	Pentacle, salt, images, stones, gems	Gardening, touch, grounding, magnetic ability, image, stone, tree, knot, binding	Citrine, olive, russet, black	The body, growth, money, creativity, material gain, rocks, trees, animals, manifestation, materialization, crystals, metal, empathy, employment, stability, success, strength

KABBALISTIC ASSOCIATIONS

Instead of linking the elements in the circular sequence of the quarters, we can also look at them 'vertically', so to speak. In this way we can see a distinct staging process of increasing density from Fire downwards. This relates to the so-called 'Four Worlds' of the kabbalists:

- Atziluth – Emanation
- Briah – Creation
- Yetzirah – Formation
- Assiah – Action

There is a certain amount of dispute about the position of the elemental attributes in the order of descent, but the traditional Golden Dawn system gives:

- Fire – Atziluth
- Water – Briah
- Air – Yetzirah
- Earth – Assiah

Other magicians prefer a different ordering:

- Fire – Atziluth
- Air – Briah
- Water – Yetzirah
- Earth – Assiah

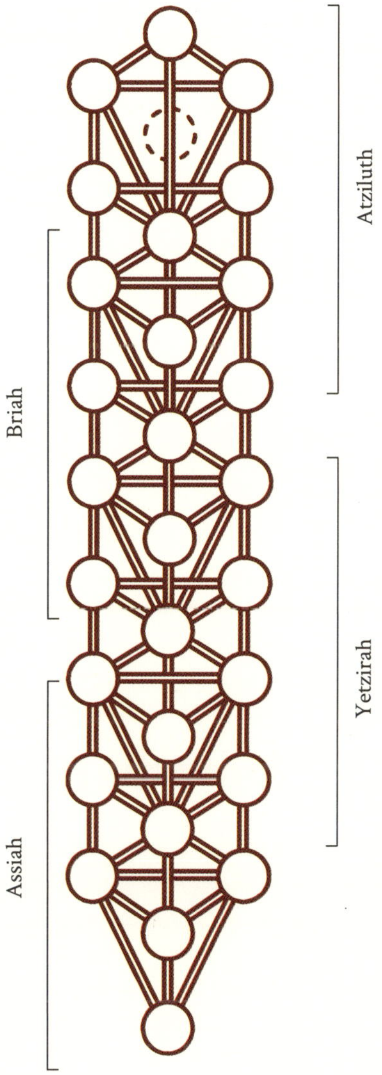

Elemental Correspondences and the Kabbalah

WEAPON	ELEMENT	SEASON	TIME	ZODIAC SIGN	REPRESENTS	COLOUR	QUALITY
Sword	Air	Spring	Dawn	Aquarius	Life	Yellow	Thought
Rod	Fire	Summer	Noon	Leo	Light	Red	Intuition
Cup	Water	Autumn	Dusk	Scorpio	Love	Blue	Feeling
Shield	Earth	Winter	Night	Taurus	Learning	Citrine, olive, russet, black	Sensation

There are strong arguments to be made for both the circular and 'vertical' systems, but the important thing to note is that both work. The student must choose for themselves.

You can see the sequence of the Four Worlds at work in the urge to paint a picture. A spark (Emanation) is stuck within the artist's psyche and is nearly imperceptible, in the realms of unmanifest thought. Yet it gradually expands into vague but powerful impulses to paint (Creation), which eventually begin to shape themselves into specific designs (Formation) and are brought to fruition after much physical effort (Action).

This shows that the elements can also be used to refer to the most subtle and intangible aspects of our thoughts. They refer, then, to the four bases of our physical and spiritual worlds. If we were to make a list of elemental correspondences so far, it might look like the table above. The list can be extended infinitely, and later on we will add more attributions. But there is sufficient there to show that the actual physical elements are worthless in themselves.

Instead of thinking in this tabulated form, however, you must see it as a genuine magic circle, with yourself as the axis. The important thing is that when you stand facing one of the quarters of the magic circle, there will be a vast range of concepts in your mind relating to that particular quarter, creating an impact within you. When a magician takes up the Wand (or Rod or Spear) and holds it aloft in a particular way, it is a signal to the unconscious to unleash the vast hoard of Wand-qualities within the magician's psyche.

DRUIDIC & OTHER SHAMANIC SYSTEMS

Modern druidry has a different take on the system of elements. This system is known as ***Duile***, which means 'leaf' in Gaelic. In the first table below there is no mention of Fire, which is regarded here as a manifestation of a deity, a living entity in its own right. What makes this system unique is that it is composed of nine elements, which the Celts believed were necessary for life. Take any of these elements away and life would cease. This threefold system includes an internal, external and a 'directional' point of view – there being nine elements in each of the three categories.

In contrast, the Indigenous American tradition, which shares the shamanist background of the very earliest 'druidic' systems, uses a variety of medicine wheels, and their allocation of the elements differs from the Wiccan system.

But the magician is not just dealing with themselves. They are attempting to guide their consciousness from the mundane towards the divine and to link with other orders of existence. They are attempting to contact the gods. And in order to do so, they often start working with archangelic forces first.

The Duile

INTERNAL	EXTERNAL	DIRECTION
Face	Sun	South
Mind	Moon	Inwards
Blood	Sea	West
Breath	Wind	East
Head	Sky	Above
Hair	Green world	Outwards
Flesh	Land	Below
Bones	Stone	North
Spirit	Clouds	Through

Indigenous American Elemental Correspondences

ELEMENT	DIRECTION	TIME	SEASON	ANIMAL
Fire	North	Night	Winter	Bison
Earth	East	Morning	Spring	Eagle
Air	South	Midday	Summer	Coyote
Water	West	Evening	Autumn	Bear

FOUR GOD-FORMS

Traditional magic uses the images of four archangelic figures placed at the quarters of the circle-cross: they are Raphael, Michael, Gabriel and Auriel. These are often, for convenience, known as 'god-forms'. Those who might feel uncomfortable with such Judaeo-Christian figures can easily substitute them with imagery from whatever tradition most appeals to them, for example Celtic or Egyptian dieties.

There are two main theories concerning what these god-forms actually do. First, by energizing these figures (which are personifications of qualities within our own psyches) with the highest aspects of ourselves, we are in effect sending out a signal to the inner worlds. At a certain point this signal will be answered by specialized, evolved inner entities, who can judge by the quality of the signal that they might want to associate with and help us. The god-forms are thus seen as points of contact between this and the Otherworld, and are used by the entities as vehicles, for the duration of the working.

The second theory holds that these god-forms push through into the collective unconscious, and what comes through are selected aspects of the group-mind. It is as though we can tap those parts of the genetic structure that contain all of our unconscious inherited learning.

The traditional archangels of the four quarters and the objects they carry can be seen on the next page.

By adding these otherworldly beings into the correspondences, you are (in more ways than one) giving them another dimension. In the most basic terms, when you stand in your magic circle facing south and use a match (Wand) to light a candle (Fire), while visualizing the mighty archangelic figure of Michael, you are effectively connecting with that being, even if there is no immediate dramatic response.

Although for convenience the masculine gender is used for all of these essentially asexual god-forms, it is clear that the gods themselves must react with goddesses. So Gabriel and Auriel might be given feminine qualities – being a young and mature woman respectively, perhaps. It is up to the reader to determine what *feels* right. Those who prefer working with what might be termed the Native British tradition might choose the following associations (see opposite).

The Four God-Forms

GOD-FORM	DESCRIPTION	CARRIES
Raphael	A yellow-orange figure, young and with sharp intelligent eyes, he wears a short Grecian-style tunic for ease of movement (in another guise he is Mercury, god of travel)	Large sword; emblazoned on his cloak is a caduceus
Michael	Clad in the colours of Fire, he is golden-haired, strong and radiant; he wears a breastplate emblazoned with a lion's head	Spear or wand of Fire
Gabriel	He wears long robes in shades of blue and violet; his face is pale with deep-set features	Silver goblet
Auriel	He is dressed in the colours of nature: his long robes are olive-green, brown, citrine and russet	Shield, representing a portion of the Earth's curvature

Native British Associations

DIRECTION	PERSONA
East	Merlin
South	Arthur
West	Vivienne
North	Morgana

Archangels of the Quarters

ARCHANGEL	TOOL	DIRECTION
Raphael	Sword	East
Michael	Rod	South
Gabriel	Cup	West
Auriel	Shield	North

POSTURE

One of the least well-known aspects of correspondences lies in the notion and practice of posture. Shamanic traditions worldwide have their own series of physical postures, which facilitate trances and the direction of vision. Freemasonry has its own highly structured and formalized system of signs and movements, some of which involve just the arms and head, and others whole-body movements; so do Tai Chi and yoga. Any form of psychodrama involves use of the body in expressing ideas and energy. By connecting posture with the internal chain of associations, the magician learns to weave with light.

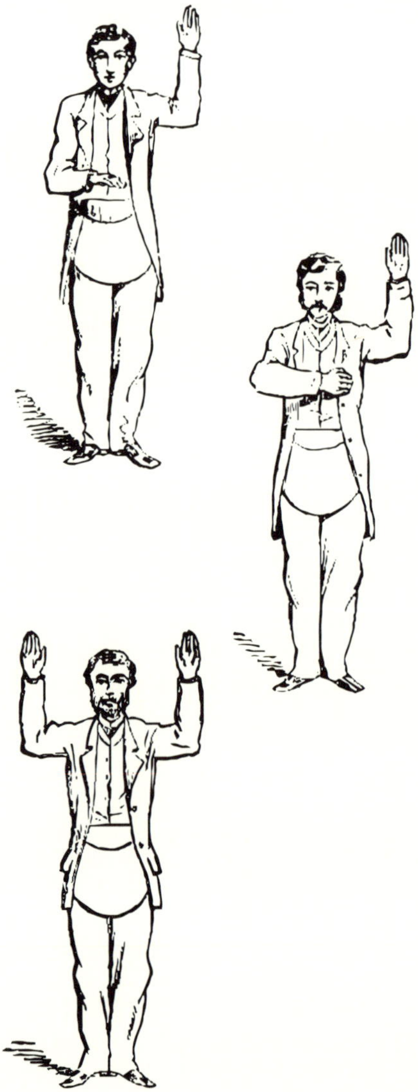

The ancient Egyptians had a symbol to represent something known as the ***ka***. In simple terms, the ***ka*** was a symbol of the reception of life powers from the gods; it was the source of these powers and also the spiritual double that resides within every human. It is akin to what might be termed the 'lower soul', containing all of an individual's personality, potential and energies. Among other things, the two arms represent the way in which we control and manipulate the material world, and the way we express ourselves. The ancient Egyptians also had the ***ka*** posture.

Try this posture: it involves no more than standing with your feet together and your arms raised as shown opposite. When done in a spiritless fashion, the ***ka*** posture is an empty exercise, but you can fill it with great energy with surprising ease. By simple and subtle alterations of your hands (making them clenched or open, facing upwards or forwards, straight or tilted) you can make the ***ka*** posture express rage or victory, supplication or surrender.

Masonic gestures as described in **Duncan's Masonic Ritual and Monitor,** *1866*
(from top to bottom)
1. Sign of an entered apprentice
2. Duegard of a fellow Craft mason
3. Grand hailing sign of distress

Athletes constantly (and unconsciously) express the ***ka*** posture when they have won an event and are in the throes of exultation. With only the simplest changes, the same gesture is used by soldiers who are surrendering. Someone who has had great and unexpected luck will often glance upwards and fling the arms in a ***ka*** posture.

The Ka posture

Try a variety of such postures, varying the angle and inclination of the arms and body, adopting the appropriate mannerisms for each emotion. At the same time try to feel the emotion concerned: triumph or delight, pleading, yearning or perhaps even divine submission to a will greater than your own. Actors and magicians do this sort of thing all the time, for the two crafts are closely linked. All great actors are good magicians; all great magicians are decent actors. With practice and the power of the correspondences behind you, you can be a bit of both.

Whatever signs and symbols we look at later, from the areas of Freemasonry, Hermetic magic, Wicca and so on, all are far less potent than those everyday gestures from parents and lovers that pass non-verbal communication across space from one soul to another. So yet again it is important to emphasize the one great and obvious secret behind all magical correspondences: the power lies not in learning word lists by heart and reciting them by rote; but in making the words come alive by drawing on your own experience and creating your own correspondences.

All this is reminiscent of the famous account by the French writer Marcel Proust (1871–1922), who was triggered into remembrance of things past by the taste of little cakes known as madeleines. All of us have in our backgrounds the equivalent of this madeleine. Think of an object now; summon it up. Try not to look just at the visual image, but to feel the emotional response. It does not have to be any kind of occult or mystical symbol; it could be an old toy or a lover's keepsake. And then think of your own – perhaps quirky – equivalents of the ***ka*** posture. Can you tie them together in any natural way?

If simple items and gestures can have such evocative power, imagine the possible impact when deities become involved. No longer will you be drawing on the poignancy of your own history; you will be summoning up gods and goddesses, with all their energies, their blessings and trials. What you are doing is stepping out from the herd: you are initiating yourself. You do not need anyone else.

LESSER BANISHING RITUAL OF THE PENTAGRAM

You could think of this as an entry-level ritual. It is quirky, yet effective, even though it is well over a century old. In many ways it is the perfect first ritual, using much of what you have learned so far. The purpose of banishing rituals is not so much to get rid of unwanted spirits as to create a sterile atmosphere in and around the operator. It is no more than a surgeon would do before commencing work. This ritual, from the Hermetic Order of the Golden Dawn is still regarded by many (if not most) magicians as the standard technique.

1. Start by standing facing east. Then raise your hands with a sweeping movement to your brow, placing your hands together as in prayer. Forcefully 'vibrate' (state powerfully and resonantly out loud) the word 'Ateh'. Now perform what is known as the 'kabbalistic cross':

- Hands together to chest or heart –
  Vibrate 'Malkuth'
- Hands to right shoulder –
  Vibrate 'Ve Geburah'
- Hands to left shoulder –
  Vibrate 'Ve Geburah'
- Hands crossed over breast –
  Vibrate 'Le-Olahm'
- Hands clasped together as in prayer –
  Say 'Amen'

2. Next, with a forefinger, wand or dagger, trace a full-size banishing pentagram (above) of Earth in the air before you. That is, start at the point of Earth and trace up towards Spirit, and so on. The two lower points are roughly outside the left and right hips, the apex is level with the crown of your head, and the other two points are outside the left and right shoulders. As you point towards the centre, vibrate 'Yod He Vau He'. (Do not lower the point of your tool throughout the ritual; visualize the circle you are tracing in light.)

Now do the following:

- Turn to the south and draw the pentagram –
  Vibrate 'Adonai'
- Turn to the west and draw the pentagram –
  Vibrate 'Eheieh'
- Turn to the north and draw the pentagram –
  Vibrate 'Agla'

3. Complete the circle and stand in the Tau posture, with your arms extended so as to make a ***ka*** posture T-cross with your whole body, facing east. Now visualize the archangels and say: 'Before me Raphael, behind me Gabriel, on my right hand Michael, on my left hand Auriel. For around me flames the pentagram, and above me shines the six-rayed star!' Repeat the kabbalistic cross as at the beginning.

Every gesture you make should be visualized as having an effect upon the inner worlds. You should see yourself in a column of light, with a six-rayed star both above you and at your feet, and brilliant pentagrams at every quarter. Visualize the archangelic figures beyond them, and have a sense of their qualities. As Crowley wrote about this ritual:

> You are thus standing in a column which is protected by microcosmic invocation. The consequent result, being macrocosmic response, is that without any effort on your part the hexagram or sixfold star appears both above you and below you. In this way you are completely shut off from the outer and Qliphotic [unbalanced] parts of the Universe.[8]

WICCAN ADAPTATIONS

Wiccans have adapted this ritual by using their own god- and goddess-forms, substituting an outward spiral for the pentagram. Study the tables in the rest of this book and try to create your own version.

William Gray, who had an enormous impact on the burgeoning craft of Wicca, both as an individual and as a writer (even though his own path was Hermetic and kabbalistic), gave the following table of correspondence, which, if used correctly, can provide all anyone needs in order to perform effective magic.[9] This ostensibly simple table contains the very essence of magical practice.

Working the Circle[10]

ACTION	DIRECTION			
Move on and stop	East	South	West	North
Breathe in and out	Inhale	Hold	Exhale	Exclude
Call name	Ooooay	Eeeooo	Hoooah	Hayeeee
See the	Sunrise	Noon	Sunset	Midnight
Think of the moon as	New	Full	Old	Dark
Feel the	Spring	Summer	Autumn	Winter
Greet Archangel	Raphael	Michael	Gabriel	Auriel
Experience the element of	Air	Fire	Water	Earth
Feel	Pure	Radiant	Flowing	Fertile
Feel as if	Flying	Burning	Swimming	Walking
Take and use the	Sword	Rod	Cup	Shield
Emote	Sorrow	Excitement	Joy	Contentment
Use magnetism to	Repel	Control	Attract	Hold
Decide to	Will	Work	Want	Wait
Have	Perception	Power	Purpose	Patience
Dedicate	Mind	Spirit	Soul	Body

ASTROLOGICAL ASSOCIATIONS

We can add some basic astrological associations to what we've learned at this point and expand upon them later (see Chapter 7). In the tables below, the cardinal sign represents the birth of the element; the fixed sign its life; and the mutable sign its passing over towards the ideal form proper to it – that is, towards spirit.

FIRE (ASTROLOGICAL RULERS: SUN, MARS, JUPITER)

ZODIAC SIGN	QUALITY	ELEMENT	ENERGY	MANIFESTATION
♈ Aries	Cardinal	Fire of Fire	Lightning	Swift violence of onset
♌ Leo	Fixed	Air of Fire	Sun	Steady force of energy
♐ Sagittarius	Mutable	Water of Fire	Rainbow	Fading spiritualized reflection of the image

AIR (ASTROLOGICAL RULERS: MERCURY, JUPITER)

ZODIAC SIGN	QUALITY	ELEMENT	ENERGY	MANIFESTATION
♎ Libra	Cardinal	Fire of Air	Wind	Swift onset (note the idea of balance, as in trade winds)
♒ Aquarius	Fixed	Air of Air	Clouds	Steady conveyors of water
♊ Gemini	Mutable	Water of Air	Vibrations	Bulk unmoved, spiritualized to reflect mind

Water (astrological rulers: Venus, Moon)

ZODIAC SIGN	QUALITY	ELEMENT	ENERGY	MANIFESTATION
♋ Cancer	Cardinal	Fire of Water	Rain, springs	Swift passionate attack
♏ Scorpio	Fixed	Air of Water	Sea	Steady force of putrefaction
♓ Pisces	Mutable	Water of Water	Pool	Stagnant, spiritualized reflection of images

Earth (astrological rulers: Venus, Saturn)

ZODIAC SIGN	QUALITY	ELEMENT	ENERGY	MANIFESTATION
♑ Capricorn	Cardinal	Fire of Earth	Mountains	Violent pressure (due to gravitation)
♉ Taurus	Fixed	Air of Earth	Plains	Steady bearing of life
♍ Virgo	Mutable	Water of Earth	Fields	Quiet

Putting all this together, we can give a more comprehensive table of elements (see pages 44–45). There is now enough material for readers to become self-initiated into the realms of elemental magic – the basis of modern Wicca and the foundation of all Hermetic systems.

Complete Table of Elements

	AIR	FIRE	WATER	EARTH
Alchemical symbol	🜁	🜂	🜄	🜃
Qualities	Hot, moist; light, active	Hot, dry; light, active	Cold, moist; heavy, passive	Cold, dry; heavy, passive
Astrological rulers	Mercury, Jupiter	Sun, Mars, Jupiter	Venus, Moon	Venus, Saturn
Feminine aspect	Maiden	Mistress	Mother	Crone
Goddesses	Arianrhod, Aradia, Athena	Brigid, Hestia, Vesta, Freya	Aphrodite, Isis, Morgana, Tiamat	Ceridwen, Ceres, Demeter, Gaia, Persephone, Rhea, Rhiannon
Gods	Mercury, Hermes, Shu, Thoth	Vulcan, Ra, Agni, Horus	Manannan, Osiris, Neptune, Poseidon	Cernunnos, Herne, Marduk, Tammuz, Adonis
Direction	East	South	West	North
Hour	Dawn	Noon	Dusk	Midnight
Season	Spring	Summer	Autumn	Winter
Colours	Yellow	Red, orange	Blue	Black, russet, citrine, olive
Weapons	Sword, athame	Wand, rod	Cup	Shield, stone, pentacle
Animals	Eagle, human, birds of any kind	Lion, dragon, phoenix	Marine life	Bull, bear, ox
King of the elements	Paralda	Djin	Niksa	Ghob

	AIR	FIRE	WATER	EARTH
Angel of the elements	Chassan	Aral	Taliahad	Phorlakh
Ruler of the elements	Ariel	Seraph	Tharsis	Kerub
Spirits	Sylphs	Salamanders	Undines	Gnomes
Demon king	Oriens	Paimon	Ariton	Amaimon
Sense	Hearing, smell	Sight	Taste	Touch
Nature	Sky, clouds, winds	Sun, stars, volcanoes, comets	Oceans, rivers, ponds, lakes	Sacred mountains, fields, gemstones, forests, megaliths
Key concept	Life	Light	Love	Law, learning
Part of the soul	Ruach	Chiah	Neshamah	Nephesh
Virtues	Communication, intelligence, persuasion	Courage, passion, virility	Compassion, sensitivity, tenderness	Strength, endurance, stability
Vices	Gossip, boastfulness, untruthfulness	Ruthlessness, greed, vengefulness	Moodiness, delusions, cowardice	Inertia, melancholy, stagnation
World	Briah – Creation	Atziluth – Emanation	Yetzirah – Formation	Assiah – Action
Secret name of the Four Worlds	Seg	Aub	Mah	Ben
Emotions	Analysis	Intensity	Loving kindness	Solidity

THE CHINESE ELEMENTS

The Eastern concepts and definitions that we now take for granted – Masters, karma, reincarnation, yoga and the chakras – entered the West in a modified and/or diluted form via Madame Blavatsky (1831–1891) and the Theosophical Society, which was founded in New York in 1875. The TS, as they called it, had enormous influence in the esoteric world for the next 50 years. The ideas and practices they espoused were further developed by adepts within the Golden Dawn (many of whom were members of the Theosophical Society), and were fine-tuned to appeal more to the Western psyche. Nevertheless, these technical terms (often of Hindu origin) have taken root in the English language and have grown with their own vigour. Just as there are few intelligent westerners today who are unaware of Chinese systems relating to alternative medicine and spirituality, so anyone seeking to work with the elements should look at the approaches used by other cultures.

The Five Elements of Chinese Tradition

The essence of Chinese medicine is that the opposing forces of yin and yang, besides exerting their dualistic nature, are also subdivided into five elements: Metal, Water, Wood, Fire and Earth. These elements are in constant motion, reacting and relating to each other. The cycle can be shown clearly in table form (see below right).

These correspond in turn with the seasons (see below left).

Any mystical or magical work involving these qualities would necessarily take into account the fundamental concept of 'when'. You would work best with the element of Earth, for example, on a humid day in late summer. Or, put another way, when you feel hot and humid during late summer, you can be sure that the elemental beings of Earth are speaking to you and, with the right correspondences, can make stronger contact.

The Elements and Seasons

ELEMENT	SEASON	CLIMATE
Metal	Autumn	Dry
Water	Winter	Cold
Wood	Spring	Windy
Fire	Summer	Hot
Earth	Late summer	Humid

The Cycle of Elements

ELEMENT	DESTROYS	CREATES
Metal	Wood	Water
Water	Fire	Wood
Wood	Earth	Fire
Fire	Metal	Earth
Earth	Water	Metal

The Chinese Elements and Associations

ELEMENT	METAL	WATER	WOOD	FIRE	EARTH
Direction	West	North	East	South	Centre
Season	Autumn	Winter	Spring	Summer	Change of seasons
Climate	Dry	Cold	Windy	Hot	Humid
Planet	Venus	Mercury	Jupiter	Mars	Saturn
Colour	White	Black	Green or blue	Red	Yellow
Virtue	Righteousness	Wisdom	Benevolence	Propriety	Faith
Mythological animal	Tiger	Tortoise	Dragon	Phoenix	Ox
Organ (yin)	Lung	Kidney	Liver	Heart	Spleen/ Pancreas
Organ (yang)	Large intestine	Urinary bladder	Gall bladder	Small intestine	Stomach
Sense	Smell	Taste	Hearing	Sight	Touch
Digit	Thumb	Little finger	Ring finger	Middle finger	Index finger
Orifice	Nose	Tongue	Ears	Eyes	Mouth
Sound	Weeping	Groaning	Shouting	Laughing	Singing
Odour	Rotten	Putrid	Rancid	Scorched	Fragrant
Flavour	Spicy	Salty	Sour	Bitter	Sweet
Emotion	Grief	Fear	Anger	Joy	Sympathy

The Buddhist Elements and Associations

ELEMENT	VOID	WATER	EARTH	FIRE	AIR
Buddha	Vairocana	Aksobhya	Ratnasambhava	Amitâbha	Amoghasiddhi
Shakti (feminine power)	Âkâsha-dhâtu	Locanâ	Mâmakî	Pândarâ	Târâ
Bodhisattvas (male)	–	Maitreya	Âkâshagarbha	Avalokiteshvara	Vajrapâni
Bodhisattvas (male)	–	Ksiti-garbha	Samatabhadra	Mañjushrî	Dîpanî
Bodhisattvas (female)	–	Lâsyâ	Mâlâ	Gîtâ	Gandha
Bodhisattvas (female)	–	Pushpâ	Dhûpa	Âloka	Naivedya
Buddha function	Buddha-nature approach	Wisdom to realize, raising	Condition to practise, cultivating	Fruit of Bodhisattva	Fruit of Nirvana
Wisdom	Dharma-realm	Great perfect mirror	Non-discrimination	Subtle observation	Accomplishment
Family	Buddha	Thunderbolt (*vajra*)	Gem/Jewel (*ratna*)	Lotus (*padma*)	Action (*karma*)
Emblem	Stupa	Five-pronged	Gem/Jewel	Lotus	Three-pronged *vajra, vishvavajra*
Jewel	Sapphire	Diamond	Gold	Ruby	Emerald
Bright colour	White body, blue light	Blue body, white light	Yellow	Red	Green

ELEMENT	VOID	WATER	EARTH	FIRE	AIR
Soft colour	White	Smoky	Blue	Yellow	Red
Direction	Centre	East	South	West	North
Shape	Almond	Sphere	Square	Triangle	Crescent
Seedword	*Kha* (void)	*Vaktva* (word)	*Anutpâda* (unborn)	*Raja* (dust)	*Hetva* (origin)
Mudra (hand gesture)	Teaching	Earth-touching	Giving	Meditation	Fearlessness
Mantra	Om	Hûm	Tram	Hrîh	Âh
Throne	Lion	Elephant	Horse	Peacock	Garuda
Bodily constituent	Crown	Navel	Knee	Chest	Brow
Organ	Mind	Ears	Eyes	Nose	Tongue/Body
Objects	–	Sounds	Sights	Smells	Tastes, textures
Vices	Delusion	Anger	Pride	Lust	Envy
Vices	Ignorance	Hatred	Envy	Craving	Pride

ELEMENTS, GEMSTONES & PLANTS

Although the correspondences relating to gemstones and plants are dealt with in more detail later (see pages 154–157 and 246–255), the associations in the tables below will set the tone for basic magical work involving the elements.

Elements and Their Gemstones

Fire	Bloodstone, garnet, lava, quartz crystal, ruby, carnelian, tiger's eye, agate, red jasper
Air	Topaz, aventurine, mica, fluorite, amethyst, blue or yellow stones
Water	Amethyst, aquamarine, blue tourmaline, pearl, coral, blue topaz, blue fluorite, lapis lazuli, sodalite
Earth	Emerald, peridot, rock crystal, onyx, azurite, royal azute, tourmaline

Elements and Their Plants

Fire	Basil, cacti, cinnamon, garlic, hibiscus, juniper, mustard, nettle, onion, red pepper, poppy, thistle, allspice
Air	Anise, acacia, aspen, benzoin, clover, dill, frankincense, lavender, myrrh, pine, primrose, vervain, yarrow
Water	Aloe, apple, catnip, chamomile, fern, gardenia, lemon, lettuce, lilac, lotus, passion flower, seaweed, thyme, water lily, willow tree
Earth	Cedar, cypress, comfrey, honeysuckle, ivy, magnolia, primrose, sage, nuts, oak

THE *TATTWAS* & THEIR SYMBOLS

EARTH | WATER | AIR | FIRE | SPIRIT

There are some simple keys to accessing the above energies/areas of consciousness, and they can be found in the *tattwas*.

In the Vedic tradition of India, *tattwas* are the five elements or states of being, namely: Water, Air, Earth, Fire and Spirit. Each of these elements has a simple symbol that can be used to evoke their energies and/or explore the actual realms in a visionary sense (see the illustrations at the top of this page).

According to modern science, five forces govern the universe. These are:

- Electromagnetism
- Gravity
- Weak force governing nuclear structure
- Strong force governing nuclear structure
- Hypercharge

Centuries before this structure was determined, the system of the *tattwas* likewise identified five forces known as Prithivi, Apas, Tejas, Vayu and Akasha – or Earth, Water, Air, Fire and Spirit respectively. These symbols (fundamental to the magical systems devised by the Golden Dawn) are among the simplest and most effective means for getting in touch with the energies that exist both within you and within the universe itself.

Working With the *Tattwas*

Choose which element you want to explore, then draw the relevant *tattwa* symbol on a card in any colour. Sit comfortably and gaze at the symbol until you have thoroughly absorbed it. The edges of the symbol will appear luminous after several minutes, as the flashing (or complementary) colour (see page 103) appears on your retina. This complementary colour is considered to be the astral counterpart of the actual colour. While meditating on your chosen *tattwa*, you should also 'feel' the attributes of the associated element, using the correspondences given earlier, letting your consciousness be filled with the appropriate sensations. Concentrate on how this might affect your other senses. Smell burning; hear the crackling of the flame.

Once the symbol has been completely assimilated, set aside the card and close your eyes. The *tattwa* symbol should now appear in its flashing colour. This symbol serves as an astral portal through which you travel. When entering through the symbol, you should feel yourself pass through a 'veil' or membrane. Once on the other side, take a moment to adjust to your new surroundings and make a note of them, no matter how fuzzy or vague they might seem at first.

Mentally summon up a guide. Ask it to explain what you are seeing. Treat your guide with respect, and when the journey is finished, give thanks to it and bid farewell. Go back to your original entry point, and step back through the portal. And *always* visualize the portal closing behind you. Write down what you have seen and felt.

3

THE KABBALAH

THE PHILOSOPHY

The Kabbalah can also be spelled Qabalah or Cabala, or written simply as QBL (there are no vowels in Hebrew). The name is derived from the root word *Qibel*, meaning 'to receive', which is sometimes written as ***k-b-l*** (***kuf-beit-lamed***). This refers to secret oral teachings, passed on from one initiate to the next, from generation to generation. Although the Kabbalah's origins are Hebrew, it has been altered (purists might say debased) and developed (some might say corrupted) to such an extent that it forms the foundation stone of the Western esoteric tradition. Almost every Western spiritual system in modern times can trace its origins to the single glyph known as the kabbalistic ***otz chaim***, or Tree of Life.

The origins of this philosophy are unclear. Legend, which is often more potent than mere history, credits Isaac the Blind (c.1160–c.1236) as being the father of the Kabbalah, in that he put it on a scholarly footing. But there are clear Egyptian, Greek and Chaldean influences dating back to the 1st century CE and before.

The early Jewish mystics insisted that Kabbalah was taught to Adam by God himself, who passed it to Noah and thence to Abraham, who took the knowledge into Egypt, where it was developed still further and disseminated in the Mystery Schools there. There then followed an unbroken line of initiates – Solomon and David being the most adept – and no one dared write it down until Schimeon Ben Jochai, who lived at the time of the destruction of the Second Temple in 70 CE. After his death, his son Rabbi Eleazar and his secretary Rabbi Abba, as well as his disciples, collated Schimeon Ben Jochai's treatises and from them composed the celebrated work known as ZHR or the *Zohar* ('Splendour'), which is the grand storehouse of kabbalism.

The Kabbalah is usually classed under four headings:

1. The practical Kabbalah
2. The literal Kabbalah
3. The unwritten Kabbalah
4. The dogmatic Kabbalah

Of these, we need only concern ourselves with the first two. The practical Kabbalah is the means by which we will use the correspondences. The literal Kabbalah is the area that so concerned Aleister Crowley in his *Liber 777* (see page 18), and we should dispose of it now. The literal Kabbalah was divided into three parts: Gematria, Notariqon and Temura. The crucial thing to know is that there are no separate numerical characters in Hebrew. Each letter has its own peculiar numerical value. In simple terms, every word is a number, and every number is a word.

Left-To-Right Ordering

In this respect, words with similar numerical values can say things about each other. For example, the letter Shin ש has a number value of 300. This is the same value as the letters of the words RVCH ALHIM, *Ruach Elohim*, which means 'the spirit of Elohim', for R = 200, V = 6, Ch = 8, A = 1, L = 30, H = 5, I = 10, M = 40: totalling 300. Therefore, Shin ש is a symbol of the spirit of Elohim.

Another example is that of ACHD (*Achad*) meaning 'unity', and AHBH (*Ahebah*) meaning 'love'. Both share the value of 13, so one can look for meanings in that.

The Kabbalah was therefore an esoteric doctrine passed on from initiate to initiate – a mystic lore said to be capable of explaining the secrets of the heavens above and the earth beneath. The *Zohar* or 'Book of Splendour' and the *Sepher Yetzirah* or 'Book of Creation' were further developed by Moses de Leon in the 13th century.

The theoretical Kabbalah contains elements from ancient Egyptian, Babylonian and Greek philosophies, spiced with the mysticism of the early Christian Gnostics, with the doctrines of reincarnation, transmigration and the enduring realities of Good and Evil, Light and Darkness thrown into the mix. Truly, all human and non-human life can be found here.

Spiegel der Kunst und Natur, in Alchymia,
Stephan Michelspacher, 1615

Values of the Hebrew Alphabet

VALUE	1	2	3	4	5	6	7	8	9
Value x 1	א Alef	ב Bet	ג Gimel	ד Dalet	ה He	ו Vav	ז Zayen	ח Het	ט Tet
Value x 10	י Yod	כ Kaf	ל Lamed	מ Mem	נ Nun	ס Samekh	ע Ayin	פ Pe	צ Tzadi
Value x 100	ק Qof	ר Resh	ש Shin	ת Tau					

THE TREE OF LIFE

If all this proved irresistible to the mystics, then the practical Kabbalah proved itself ***manna*** to the magicians. And it is the diagram known as the ***otz chaim***, or Tree of Life, that provided the framework upon which all else was hung. One commentator described it as the 'Mighty and All-embracing glyph of the Universe and the soul of Man'. And, despite the bombast, it is exactly that. Crowley explained in his introduction to *Liber 777*:

Many columns will seem to the majority of people to consist of mere lists of senseless words. Practice, and advance in the magical or mystical path, will enable them little by little to interpret more and more.[11]

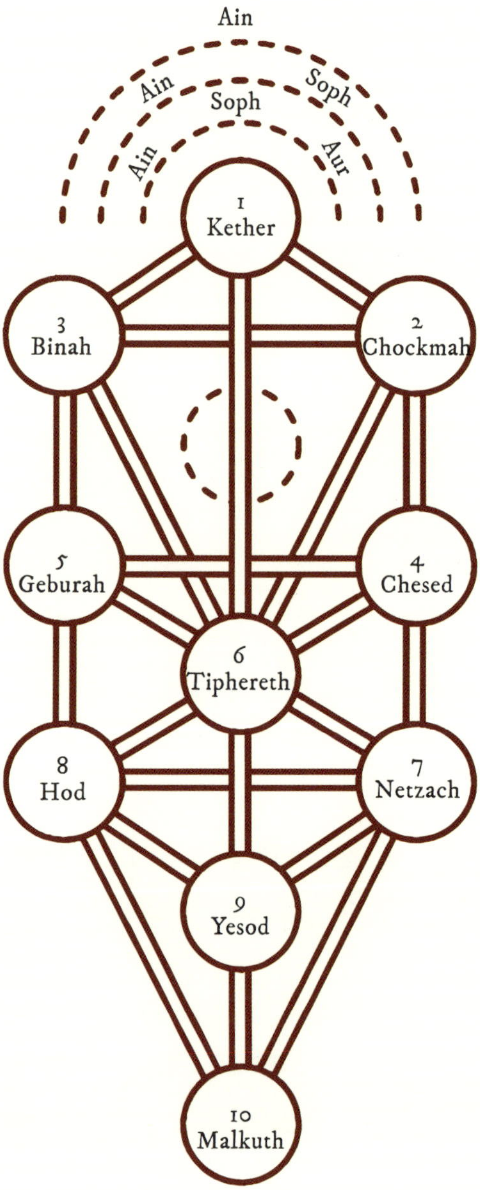

Origins

According to the revelation, all life proceeded via a series of emanations, beginning from the *Ain*. This is a complete void and vacuum; not simply 'nothing', but not even the existence of 'nothing' – absolute and incomprehensible. Then came *Ain Soph*. If *Ain* is the idea of Infinity, then *Ain Soph* is Infinity or Limitlessness. For convenience, *Ain Soph* is known as the Waters. Then *Ain Soph* 'moved' and created the Limitless Light, known as *Ain Soph Aur*.

From the limitless ocean of that Absolute Nothingness came the single point of pure and condensed white light known as Kether, which is the state of consciousness that we might crudely (very crudely) describe as God. It was from this first sphere, or *sephirah*, that the universe began to manifest itself in the numerical sequence shown, so that Kether (1) is at the level of absolute spirit, and Malkuth (10) is the realm of densest matter. It is in Malkuth, the earth-sphere, that we find ourselves. The Tree provides us with a ladder by which we can attempt to climb back up to our Source.

The Pillars

The spheres (or *sephiroth*, plural of *sephirah*) are clearly arranged on three columns known as pillars. All the positive, upbuilding energies in the universe are linked with the right-hand column, and all the negative, breaking-down forces are placed on the left. In this sense, however, 'negative' was never regarded as evil in itself, any more than it is evil to knock down buildings (or psychological edifices) that are dangerously decayed. It is wrong to associate Good with positive and Evil with negative. Always being positive, always saying 'yes', can create just as much evil within the world as its unbalanced opposite. The balance, therefore, is represented by the middle pillar.

Within these columns we can resolve the universe for ourselves, if we are uncompromising enough: yes/no/maybe, white/black/grey. Sometimes, as all magicians know, the best way to deal with the world is to retreat to the basics. By analysing the spheres, however, we can add some subtleties to the way these three qualities express themselves.

We can best imagine the Tree as a kind of filing system that is divided into ten compartments, and into which everything – *everything* – can be placed. Our initial problem is simply that of having the exact nature of this system explained to us, because after that it begins to explain itself.

Had there been 26 compartments, this would present no problem at all, for it would be based on the Roman alphabet. Into the compartment L, for example, would go leopards, lemurs, light, locusts and love. While it would be simplicity itself to store such data, the exercise would be meaningless on any spiritual level: it is no good looking for love and finding lice, lugworms and loquaciousness. But with the system used by the Tree, we can not only store away our own experiences in a particular area – intellectual, emotional or spiritual – but we can also use to it to lead us into the collective experience of humankind as a whole.

The Spheres

Each of the spheres upon the Tree of Life has some basic attributions (as do the paths linking them). To understand how we can use each of these as keys into areas of consciousness, we can codify them in sequence.

1. **Kether** The Crown; the point within the circle; a pinpoint of pure white light that contains All.
2. **Chockmah** Archetypal male energy; the first cosmic laugh; force; all phallic symbolism.
3. **Binah** Archetypal female energy; form; the Great Mother; all yonic symbolism (relating to female genitalia).
4. **Chesed** Benevolence, generosity, philanthropy; all stable, civilizing influences.
5. **Geburah** Purifying, scourging energies; destroying in order to create.
6. **Tiphereth** Harmony; the resolution of opposites; the sacrificed gods.
7. **Netzach** Romance; quickening impulses; arts and emotions; victory or achievement.
8. **Hod** Intellect; reason and logic; communication; glory or splendour.
9. **Yesod** Moon and the unconscious mind; instincts; foundation.
10. **Malkuth** Kingdom; the material world; the four elements.

Tree of Life Sphere Associations

	Sphere	Archangel	Divine Name	Colour	Magical Image
1	Kether	Metatron	Eheieh	Brilliance	The face of an old man, in profile
2	Chockmah	Ratziel	Jehovah	Brilliance	A masculine, bearded face, full-on
3	Binah	Tzaphkiel	Jehovah Elohim	Blackness	A mature woman
4	Chesed	Tsadkiel	El	Blue	A wise king, on his throne
5	Geburah	Khamael	Elohim Gibor	Red	A warrior king, on his chariot
6	Tiphereth	Michael	Jehovah Eloah va Daath	Rose pink	A child, priest king, sacrificed god
7	Netzach	Auriel	JHVH Tzavoos	Emerald	A beautiful naked woman
8	Hod	Raphael	Elohim Tzavoos	Orange	An intersex person
9	Yesod	Gabriel	Shadai el Chai	Violet	A naked man, very strong
10	Malkuth	Sandalphon	Adonai ha Aretz	Olive	Mother Nature, on her throne

Sequence of the Spheres

As you can see from the diagram, the spheres of the Tree are joined by paths, which might be regarded as blending points. Thus the path between Yesod and Netzach represents that area within our consciousness that rises from pure blind instinct and leads into the glow of more romantic considerations: where having sex turns into making love. And the path connecting Hod and Netzach represents the careful balance we must all sometimes strike between soulless intellect and brainless passion.

Learning to Use the Tree

You can begin to see how this unique filing system of the Tree of Life can work. Like a novice secretary, the neophyte will handle the system clumsily at first, often putting things into the wrong holes; but, with rapidly increasing assurance, the peculiar patterns and interrelationships between the spheres will begin to teach of their own accord.

For example, all those gods related to the intellectual 'Hermetic' arts would be equated with the sphere of Hod: Thoth, Hermes, Merlin and so on; while all those figures of romance and enchantment will go into Netzach: Nimue, Nephthys, Freya and so on. There is no dogma attached to this (or shouldn't be): you are quite welcome to reverse the polarities and adapt them to your own vision of the universe. As long as the neophyte makes their own efforts in determining the correspondences for each sphere, that process known as 'Building the Tree into the aura' will take place. It is when this happens that the filing system starts to become more akin to a super-computer of spiritual possibilities.

In fact, the magicians of the Golden Dawn and the Fraternity of the Inner Light, a magickal organization founded by Dion Fortune when she broke away from the Hermetic Order of the Golden Dawn, would have done exactly that – building the Tree into the aura (that is, fixing it in the unconscious) by visualizing it as shown in the illustration. They would ritualize it by touching the top of the head (the crown) and intoning the word *Eheieh*, while attempting to experience the qualities of Kether, or the 'pure white light', within. Then to the right temple, the left, and down the body in the order of manifestation, doing all of the above while also visualizing each sphere in its associated colour. In time – in a surprisingly short time – the magician will have a marked sense of the reality of these spheres. It is as though the amorphous mass of their psyche has been moulded into a particular pattern, and highly specific areas of their consciousness begin to interact in the same way as the spheres upon the Tree. When they come to work on their correspondences (which involves no more than associating items of experience, symbols and impulses with the patterns of the spheres), then they will find links, parallels and suggestions springing into their mind that will be altogether surprising (and never less than illuminating).

For example, a magician who feels that they have been unfairly dealt with might use kabbalistic magic to seek justice. They would wear red clothes, light five red candles, intone the words ***Elohim Gibor*** in a fivefold rhythm and even ***think*** red, before addressing their complaint to the Archangel Khamael, visualized as a great, winged, darkly red figure wielding a flaming sword and wearing a pentagram upon his chest. This would not, however, be any kind of 'revenge magic'. Geburah (Mars) cannot be used for that. Their plea would be: 'If these events are right and proper, if it is part of my karma to suffer this, then so be it. But if it is not, and I am being unfairly treated, then please redress the balance, bring justice back into my life.'

The actual words are less important than the intention, but the supplicant should be very strong in their belief that they are being wronged, for if such suffering is part of their karma, or nothing more than their own stupid fault, then the effect of such an invocation is to bring all the energies to a head sooner than usual, with all the intensified suffering that might ensue. On the other hand, they may well find that balances ***are*** made in their favour, ways made smooth and burdens lifted.

TAPPING INTO THE COLLECTIVE UNCONSCIOUS

The forces on the Tree are all perfectly balanced with one another. It is impossible to 'trick' these energies into giving something for nothing. There are always prices to be paid, harmonies that must be maintained. And when the Tree is built into the aura, it becomes a device that enables us to connect our own limited consciousness with the unlimited consciousness of the universe. Whatever changes we affect within ourselves ultimately affect the whole of existence. We become part of the great cosmic balancing act and must accept a grave responsibility for an inward kind of decency and honesty.

But in purely magical terms this means that, in time, the magician will be able to pick up one symbol – an ***ankh*** (symbol of life), for example – and that single glyph will give them access not only to the huge store of their own ideas, but also to the infinite experience of the collective unconscious. By lifting this simple device from the altar of their conscious mind, with ritualistic intent, they are potentially in touch with the experience of every Egyptian worshipper of Isis, every latter-day hippie, every astrologer who has ever marvelled at Venus and every Roman who has ever adored that goddess as she rose from the sea. It becomes simpler with practice: like driving a car, or handling complex machinery, it becomes almost automatic. In time, you can forget about it all with your conscious mind, because it propels you inwards from unconscious levels. And then, as so many other magicians have learned to do, you can sit down in a quiet place, summon up your gods, goddesses or guides and start to perform real magic.

The Nativity, Christ Blessing the Virgin, Christ on the Cross *(c. 1480) by Martin Schongauer*

Magical Images

Meditating on the interlinked magical images for, say, Tiphereth – child, priest king and sacrificed god (see page 58) – will enable the magician to understand and access some of the solar-god qualities of that *sephirah*. For example, using the Christian scheme, Jesus (the very centre of the Mystery) is born as divine child, becomes priest king and ends on the cross as sacrificed god. The same pattern can be seen in the myth of King Arthur, Odin and other solar-hero figures across the globe.

In one of the Golden Dawn Knowledge Papers, Samuel Mathers also gives a list of magical images for each path. Those described in the table on pages 62–63 are valuable keys for tapping into the energies of each sphere. The magical images for each path may be thought of as convenient forms enabling the explorer's mind to make contact with the otherworldly intelligence ruling it (see page 36).

Mathers warns that using these images is a serious business:

Now there is also a mode whereby, combining the letters, the colours, the attributions and their Synthesis, thou mayest build up a telesmatic Image of a Force. The Sigil shall then serve thee for the tracing of a Current, which shall call into action a certain Elemental Force. And know thou that this is not to be done lightly for thine amusement or experiment, seeing that the Forces of Nature were not created to be thy plaything or toy. Unless thou doest thy practical magical works with solemnity, ceremony and reverence, thou shalt be like an infant playing with fire, and thou shalt bring destruction upon thyself.[12]

The Spheres and Paths of the Tree of Life

UNMANIFEST	HEBREW NAME	ENGLISH NAME
	Ain	Nothingness
	Ain Soph	Limitlessness
	Ain Soph Aur	Limitless Light
SPHERE		
1	Kether	Crown
2	Chockmah	Wisdom
3	Binah	Understanding
4	Chesed	Mercy
5	Geburah	Strength
6	Tiphereth	Beauty
7	Netzach	Victory
8	Hod	Splendour
9	Yesod	Foundation
10	Malkuth	Kingdom

UNMANIFEST	HEBREW NAME	ENGLISH NAME
PATH		
11	Aleph	Ox
12	Beth	House
13	Gimel	Camel
14	Daleth	Door
15	He	Window
16	Vau	Nail
17	Zain	Sword
18	Cheth	Fence
19	Teth	Serpent
20	Yod	Hand
21	Kaph	Palm
22	Lamed	Ox goad
23	Maim	Water
24	Nun	Fish
25	Samekh	Prop
26	Ayin	Eye
27	Pe	Mouth
28	Tzaddi	Fish-hook
29	Qoph	Back of head
30	Resh	Head
31	Shin	Tooth
32	Tau	Tau cross

Magical Images Associated With the Paths

PATH	NAME	IMAGES
11	Aleph	Spiritual; wings generally; epicene (both male and female), but rather more male than female; rather thin type
12	Beth	Active and slight; male
13	Gimel	Grey, beautiful yet changeful; feminine; rather full face and body
14	Daleth	Very beautiful and attractive; feminine; rather full face and body
15	He	Fierce, strong, rather fiery; feminine
16	Vau	Steady and strong; rather heavy and clumsy; masculine
17	Zain	Thin, intelligent; masculine
18	Cheth	Full face, not much expression; feminine
19	Teth	Rather strong and fiery; feminine
20	Yod	Very white and rather delicate; feminine
21	Kaph	Big and strong; masculine
22	Lamed	Well-proportioned; feminine
23	Maim	Reflective, dream-like; epicene, but rather more female than male
24	Nun	Square determined face; masculine; rather dark
25	Samekh	Thin, rather expressive face; masculine
26	Ayin	Rather mechanical; masculine
27	Pe	Fierce, strong, resolute; feminine
28	Tzaddi	Thoughtful, intellectual; feminine
29	Qoph	Rather full face; masculine
30	Resh	Proud and dominant; masculine
31	Shin	Fierce, active; epicene, rather more male than female
32	Tau	Dark, grey; epicene, rather more male than female

The Four Worlds

The Kabbalah's Four Worlds of manifestation (see also page 33) can be seen in the structure of the Tree, and in each of the *sephiroth* 'descending' the Tree. These are perhaps more easily visualized as increasing densities of manifestation, comparable to, say, a drop of water condensing from steam.

The Four Worlds On the Tree

WORLD	SPHERE
Atziluth (Emanation)	Kether
Briah (Creation)	Chockmah, Binah
Yetzirah (Formation)	Chesed, Geburah, Tiphereth, Netzach, Hod, Yesod
Assiah (Action)	Malkuth

The Four Worlds and the *Sephiroth*

SPHERE	ATZILUTH – DIVINE NAME	BRIAH – ARCHANGEL	YETZIRAH – ANGELIC CHOIR	ASSIAH – MATERIAL WORLD
Kether	Eheieh	Metatron	Chioth ha Qodesh	Primum Mobile
Chockmah	Yahweh	Ratziel	Auphanim	Zodiac
Binah	Yahweh Elohim	Tzaphkiel	Aralim	Saturn
Chesed	El	Tzadkiel	Chasmalim	Jupiter
Geburah	Elohim Gibor	Khamael	Seraphim	Mars
Tiphereth	Yahweh Eloah ve Daath	Michael	Malakim	Sun
Netzach	Yahweh Tzabaoth	Auriel	Elohim	Venus
Hod	Elohim Tzabaoth	Raphael	Beni Elohim	Mercury
Yesod	Shaddai el Chai	Gabriel	Ashim	Moon
Malkuth	Adonai ha Aretz	Sandalphon	Kerubim	Earth

The Tree and the Elements

The basic elements also have traditional correspondences with the spheres of the Tree of Life, and the modern Kabbalah expands on this to provide an updated version.

As scholars, the adepts within the Golden Dawn were good examples of what the public-school system of Victorian Britain could produce. They did their best to translate obscure tomes without any belief that they would get financial reward. Their work was always there to be developed. So we can now add to our understanding by diverging from the traditional Golden Dawn attributions and expanding on the insights expressed by William G Gray.

To this can be added the vowel sonics for use with the elements (see right). These are what might be thought of as the 'names of power'. Instead of the Hebrew god-names for each quarter, Gray suggested that by using these simple vowel sounds, at the same time as meditating upon the archangels and attributes of the quarters, a great deal of energy could be invoked.

Writing a few years before Gray was born, Samuel Mathers commented on the same topic:

Then formulate the letters of the Name required in your heart, in white, and feel them written there. Be sure to formulate the letters in brilliant white light, not merely in dull whiteness as the colour of the Apas *tattwa*. Then, emitting the breath, slowly pronounce the Letters so that the sound vibrates within you, and imagine that the breath, while quitting the body, swells you so as to fill up space. Pronounce the Name as if you were vibrating it through the whole Universe, and as if it did not stop until it reached the further limits.[13]

The *Sephiroth* and the Elements

SPHERE	ELEMENT	DIRECTION
Kether	Root of Air	–
Chockmah	Root of Fire	–
Binah	Root of Water	–
Chesed	Water	West
Geburah	Fire	South
Tiphereth	Air	East
Netzach	Fire	South
Hod	Water	West
Yesod	Air	East
Malkuth	Earth	North

Vowel Sonics

DIRECTION	VOWEL SOUNDS	TONE
East	EEEEEEEEEE EEEEEEEEEE	(toning to EI)
South	IIIIIIIIIIIIIII IIIIIIIIIIIIIIII	(toning to IO)
West	OOOOOOOO OOOOOOOO	(toning to OA)
North	AAAAAAAAA AAAAAAAAA	(toning to AE)

An Updated Version of the *Sephiroth* and the Elements

SPHERE	ELEMENT	QUALITY	SENSE	PHYSICAL
Netzach	Fire	Feelings	Sight	Solar plexus
Yesod	Water	Instincts	Taste	Genitals
Hod	Air	Thoughts	Smell	Head, throat, shoulders
Malkuth	Earth	Senses	Touch	Hands, arms, legs, feet

The Modern Kabbalah

NUMBER	SEPHIRAH	CONSCIOUSNESS	MANIFESTING	QUALITY
0	Nil	The Unconscious	(I AM NOT)	Essence
1	Summit	Being	(The I AM)	Will
2	Wisdom	Knowing	(This from That)	Gnosis
3	Understanding	Feeling	(I and They)	Compassion
4	Compassion	Attraction	(Loving, wanting)	Courage
5	Severity	Repulsion	(Hating, rejecting)	The Self
6	Beauty	Stabilizing	(Equanimity, normality)	Feeling
7	Victory	Increasing	(Gaining amount of awareness)	Thinking
8	Glory	Improving	(Quality gain of awareness)	Instinct
9	Foundation	Constructing	(Arrangement of awareness)	Bodily senses
10	Kingdom	Continuity	(Memory)	–

Astral Portals

One of the useful aspects of the Hebrew letters was as astral portals, although we can just as effectively use runes, ogham or *tattwa* symbols. The magician would visualize a portal or astral gateway bearing the particular symbol of the path he wanted to explore. Making the appropriate gestures of opening the door or curtain and stepping through it, he would activate the 'spirit vision'. The traditional technique derived from the Golden Dawn was to visualize the Hebrew letter for a particular path, then imagine yourself stepping into it. Thus the seer who wanted to explore the realm of the 32nd path connecting Malkuth with Yesod would use the letter TH. The letters thus became markers on the inner planes. Anyone travelling them in a body of light would use them to find their way.

However, instead of slavishly accepting the Hebrew attributions, Gray anglicized the Kabbalah to an astonishing and liberating degree, assigning English letters to the paths of the Tree of Life, as shown here.

The Kabbalah, as used by magicians of the West, is not a religion. It is more akin to an infinitely flexible, self-programmable computer that will enable you to rearrange and file the entirety of your experience and find out things you never knew were lurking inside you.

Gray's Anglicization of the Tree of Life

PATH	ENGLISH LETTER
11	B
12	C
13	D
14	F
15	G
16	H
17	J
18	K
19	L
20	M
21	N
22	P
23	Q
24	R
25	S
26	T
27	V
28	W
29	X
30	Y
31	Z
32	TH

TALISMANIC MAGICK

One of the arts that can bring all of the previous together, and enable you to create a tangible object that will express all your inner energies and affect the outer world, is talismanic Magick. A talisman is a device that has been made for a particular purpose, consecrated accordingly and – as magicians say – 'magnetized'.

Talismans

Some of the earliest artefacts of human civilization are talismans, and the most popular example was the ***ankh*** (a hieroglyphic symbol for life), as favoured by the ancient Egyptians. Amulets featuring ***ankhs*** were worn by both the living and the dead. The symbol was felt to offer protection and guidance. Early talismans often featured symbols of sacred geometry, such as mandalas, pentagrams, hexagrams and spirals. Spirals were particularly popular in prehistoric western Europe, and can be found in prominent holy sites such as Newgrange in Ireland, and in 'cup and ring' markings throughout Britain.

The oldest examples of talismans consist of symbols scratched into stones, sometimes with a hole cut for a cord, enabling the object to be worn as a pendant. This is something that all lovers do, in one form or another, and on an emotional level the power of such simple Magick is unforgettable.

In the early medieval period, magicians would inscribe intricate designs on flat pieces of metal, which would be worn as amulets. The designs were usually derived from grimoires or spellbooks (see page 16). They invariably included charts that combined geometric structures with 'words of power', such as the Tetragrammaton ('word with four letters') of YHVH: the name of God, which was actually the Hebrew root for Yahweh. Many ancient talismans of the Christian era featured the Tetragrammaton.

Talismans could ward off evil, attract love, protect from illness, command spirits or bring wealth – whatever the magician created it for. They were held to be objects of real power, and were constructed of certain materials at particular times of the day or month, in order to attract the necessary planetary influences. And they can be created today with relative ease, their effectiveness depending upon the maker's attitude and – above all else – quality of effort.

Magic Squares

The seven planets traditionally used for making talismans are those found on the Tree of Life. Each of these planets was equated with a 'magic square' (***kamea*** in Hebrew). The numbers are arranged in each square so that the sum of any column is the same as the sum of any row and the sum of the diagonals. The ***kamea*** of Saturn, for example, which is the third sphere, has three rows and columns, each totalling fifteen. From the sequence of numbers, a geometric diagram can be devised that will represent the guiding entity known as the Intelligence of the planet.

The *Kamea* of Saturn

4	9	2
3	5	7
8	1	6

The *Kamea* of Jupiter

4	14	15	1
9	7	6	12
5	11	10	8
16	2	3	13

The *Kamea* of Mars

11	24	7	20	3
4	12	25	8	16
17	5	13	21	9
10	18	1	14	22
23	6	19	2	15

The *Kamea* of Sol (Sun)

6	32	3	34	35	1
7	11	27	28	8	30
19	14	16	15	23	24
18	20	22	21	17	13
25	29	10	9	26	12
36	5	33	4	2	31

The *Kamea* of Venus

22	47	16	41	10	35	4
5	23	48	17	42	11	29
30	6	24	49	18	36	12
13	31	7	25	43	19	37
38	14	32	1	26	44	20
21	39	8	33	2	27	45
46	15	40	9	34	3	28

The *Kamea* of Mercury

8	58	59	5	4	62	63	1
49	15	14	52	53	11	10	56
41	23	22	44	45	19	18	48
32	34	35	29	28	38	39	25
40	26	27	37	36	30	31	33
17	47	46	20	21	43	42	24
9	55	54	12	13	51	50	16
64	2	3	61	60	6	7	57

The *Kamea* of Luna (Moon)

37	78	29	70	21	62	13	54	5
6	38	79	30	71	22	63	14	46
47	7	39	80	31	72	23	55	15
16	48	8	40	81	32	64	24	56
57	17	49	9	41	73	33	65	25
26	58	18	50	1	42	74	34	66
67	27	59	10	51	2	43	75	35
36	68	19	60	11	52	3	44	76
77	28	69	20	61	12	53	4	45

Signs and Sigils

The magician also devises signs and sigils (often a seal or signet) by reducing the name of a particular deity – or even of themselves – to a geometrical form. This simple glyph will evoke all the qualities the magician might want, not only in their own psyche, but in the universe at large, with which they are interconnected.

So a talisman of Venus that aims to invoke the highest emotions for the health and protection of their beloved would ideally be made of copper, although any copper-coloured material would do. It would be made and consecrated at the hour/day/feast relevant to Venus and would have upon it the symbols invoking the powers of Venus. The magician might also reduce their lover's name to a sigil by using the number/letter chart of the modern numerologist (see below) as follows.

The name RUTH on the *kamea* of Venus might be sigilized thus, using the numbers 9328.

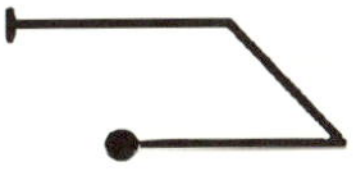

There is no need to be too pure about the construction of these: there is no 'wrong' way. This is the difference between a talisman crafted with the best skills you have, expressing your highest impulses, and a mass-produced 'lucky charm'.

It is simply a question of focusing an impulse through the lens of a particular *kamea* and recording the result. The sigils no more command the spirits than road signs directly control those mental and physical responses that cause the driver to slow or stop. The sigils, and the energies behind them, come alive when we use our imagination combined with effort. With experience, the magician can dispense with them entirely. Each person must build upon the work of their predecessors, otherwise the correspondences remain dead wood.

Number/Alphabet Correspondences

1	2	3	4	5	6	7	8	9
A	B	C	D	E	F	G	H	I
J	K	L	M	N	O	P	Q	R
S	T	U	V	W	X	Y	Z	

The Fourth Pentacle of Jupiter.—It serveth to acquire riches and honour, and to possess much wealth. Its Angel is Bariel. It should be engraved upon silver in the day and hour of Jupiter when he is in the Sign Cancer.
Editor's Note. —Above the Magical sigil is the Name IH, Iah. Below it are the Names of the Angels Adoniel and Bariel, the letters of the latter being arranged about a square of four compartments. Around is the Versicle from Psalm cxii. 3: —"Wealth and Riches are in his house, and his righteousness endureth for ever."

The Key of Solomon the King,
S Liddell MacGregor Mathers, 1888

Symbols of the Planets

PLANET	INTELLIGENCE	SPIRIT	SEAL
Saturn	 Agiel	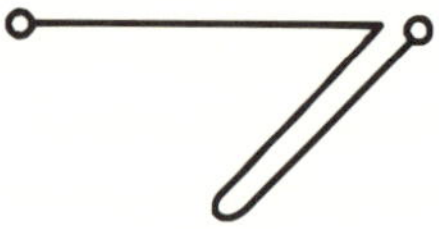 Zazel	
Jupiter	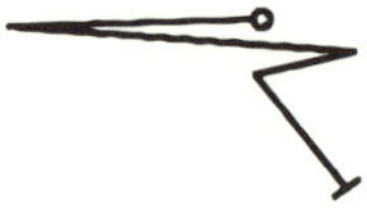 Yophiel	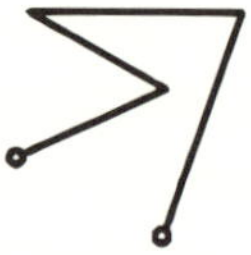 Hismael	
Mars	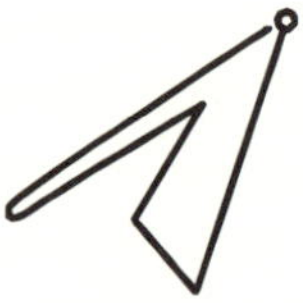 Graphiel	 Bartzabel	
Sun	 Nakhiel	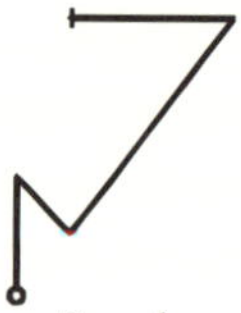 Sorath	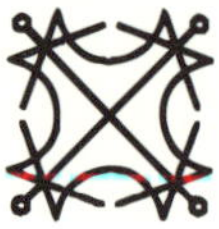
Venus	 Hagiel	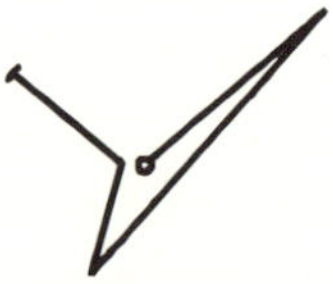 Kedemel	
Mercury	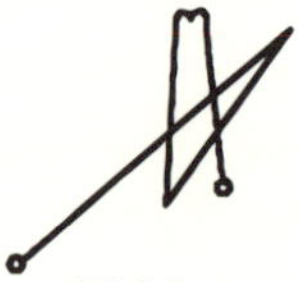 Tiriel	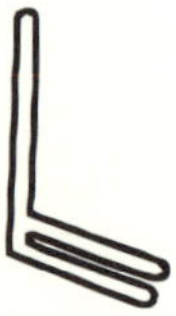 Taphthartharath	
Moon	 Scharthathan	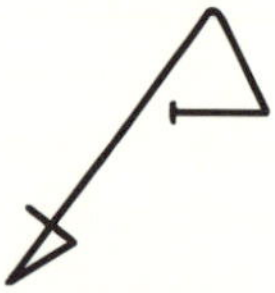 Chashmodai	

The Flying Rolls

As useful additions, Flying Roll XXXII (one of the Knowledge Papers circulated among members of the Golden Dawn) gives the 'Theban alphabet' (see below), as found in Francis Barrett's ***The Magus***; and in Flying Roll XIV Mathers himself, writing as Frater D D C F, gives a complete table of all the talismanic figures classed under the planets and signs (see pages 74–75).

You do not ***always*** need to have a complete grasp of the rationale; sometimes the sheer glamour of such scripts can have a real effect and enable you to create your own attractive talismans.

Mathers adds:

The mode of using these Talismanic Characters drawn from the Talismanic Figures in the construction of a Talisman or Pantacle, is to take those formed by the figures under the Planet required, and to place them either at the opposite ends of a wheel of eight radii as shown, or to place them in the compartments of a Square. A versicle suitable to the matter is then to be written within the double line.[14]

He then gives a neat and workable example of this in the illustration below.

Mather's Talisman Figures in a Square and Circle

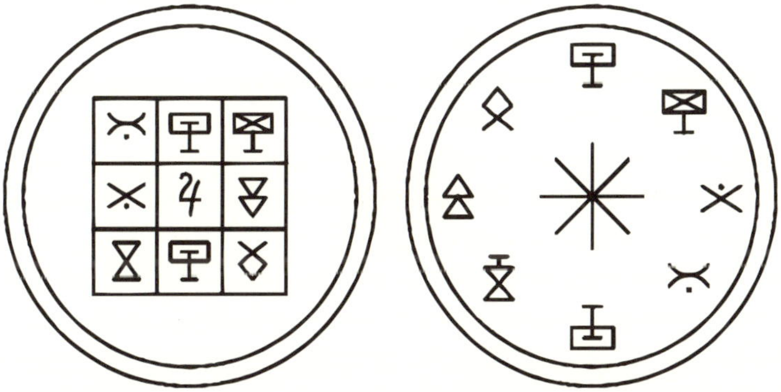

The Theban Alphabet

The Rosicrucian Cross

One of the most famous images in Western Magick is that of the cross that adepts had to make when they achieved a certain level of initiation. The 22 petals of the rose, each coloured differently, correspond to the 22 letters of the Hebrew alphabet – 'three mothers, seven doubles and twelve simple' – and the 22 paths of the Tree of Life. From these petals a geometrical figure representing any named spiritual force can be obtained; the name is first transliterated into Hebrew letters, and then a figure is drawn that would connect up all the letters of that name if it were drawn upon the rose. In the middle of the petals is a Calvary cross, symbolic of death and spiritual rebirth. The rose itself lies upon the four-armed cross of nature, symbolic of the physical elements that the adept has to transmute into pure gold in the ***athanor*** (furnace) of their heart. The pentagrams on the cross show the symbols of four physical elements plus the fifth or quintessence; the hexagram below the rose shows the moon and five planets, centred on the sun. In its own way, this Rosicrucian symbol was an explanation of all human life – and of some of the non-human orders, too. William G Gray offered a similar device in his ***Magical Ritual Methods.***[15]

The Rosicrucian Cross

Talisman Figures Under the Planets and Signs

The characters of Saturn and Zazel taken from Carcer equals Capricorn

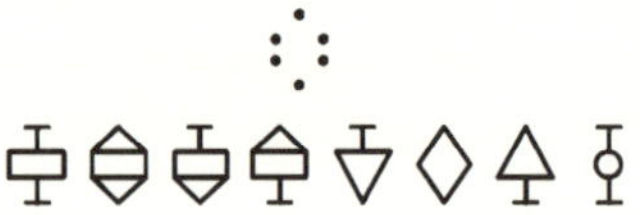

The characters of Saturn and Zazel taken from Tristitia equals Aquarius

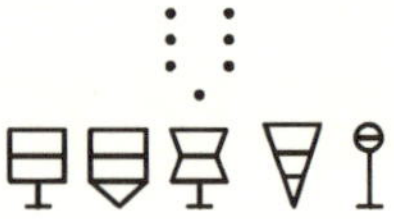

The characters of Jupiter and Hismael taken from Acquisitio equals Sagittarius

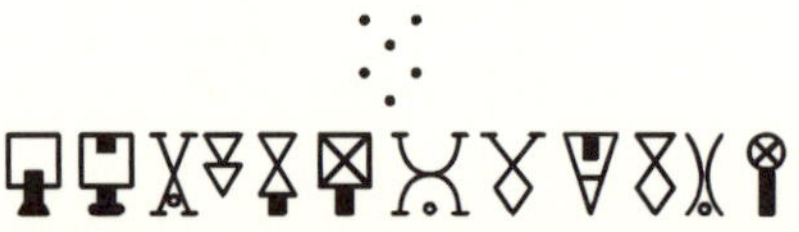

The characters of Jupiter and Hismael taken from Laetitia equals Pisces

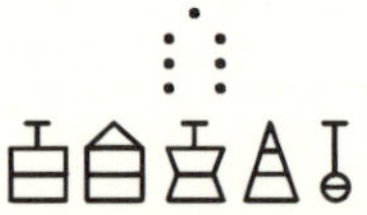

The characters of Mars and Bartzabel taken from Rubeus equals Scorpio

The characters of Sol and Sorath taken from Fortuna Major equals Leo

The characters of Venus and Kedemel taken from Amissio equals Taurus

The characters of Mercury and Taphthartharath taken from Albus equals Gemini

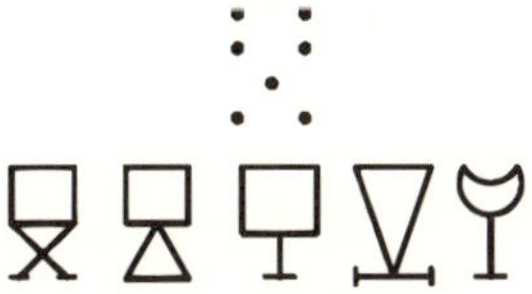

The characters of Luna and Chasmodai taken from Populus equals Cancer

The characters of Caput Draconis are:

The characters of Mars and Bartzabel taken from Puer equal Aries

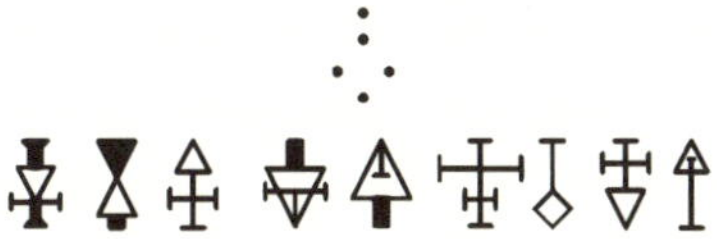

The characters of Sol and Sorath taken from Fortuna Minor equals Leo

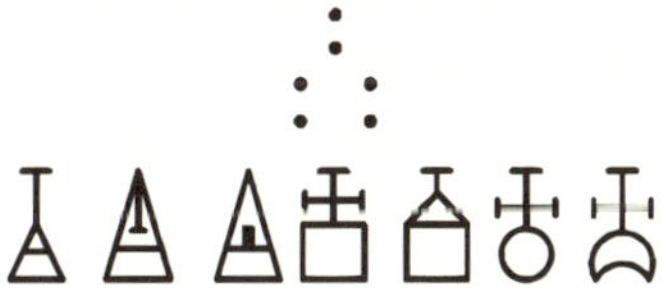

The characters of Venus and Kedemel taken from Puella equals Libra

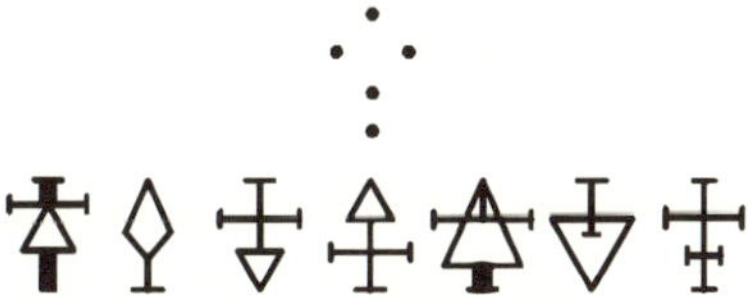

The characters of Mercury and Taphthartharath taken from Conjunctio equals Virgo

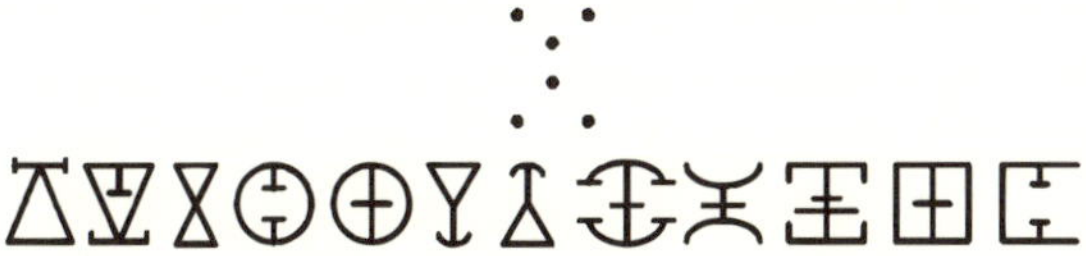

The characters of Luna and Chasmodai taken from Via equals Cancer

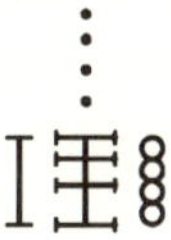

The characters of Cauda Draconis are:

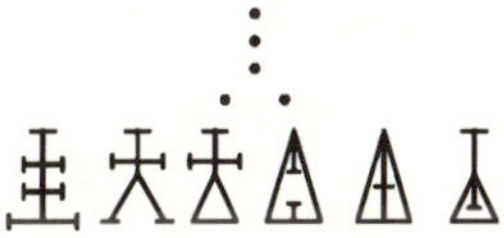

4

TAROT CORRESPONDENCES

TAROT ASSOCIATIONS

The felicity of the Tarot and the Tree of Life is that the 22 Tarot cards of the Major Arcana (the trump cards) were a natural match with the 22 paths between the *sephiroth*. The original correspondences involved no more than putting the first Tarot card, The Fool, on the first path and working downwards. Although there were later minor alterations by Aleister Crowley, the overall scheme held.

William Gray ignored the numbering of the cards and instead went for their sense, matching the positive Tarot cards with the right-hand pillar of the Tree, the negative cards with the left-hand pillar and putting the Moon, Sun and Star on the middle pillar.[16] The pillars were conjoined by Judgement, Justice and the Wheel of Fortune, which are three different levels of energy equating with the wisdom that comes from mature life assessment, the changes that occur through karmic events, and the happenstance of everyday luck (good and bad).

Another formidable magician and kabbalist who was not intimidated by Crowley was Charles Stansfield Jones (1886–1950), who, under the name of Frater Achad, wrote some influential analyses of his mentor's work and devised his own system. We can thus compare the attributions of these three magicians and note the differences between them (see the table opposite).

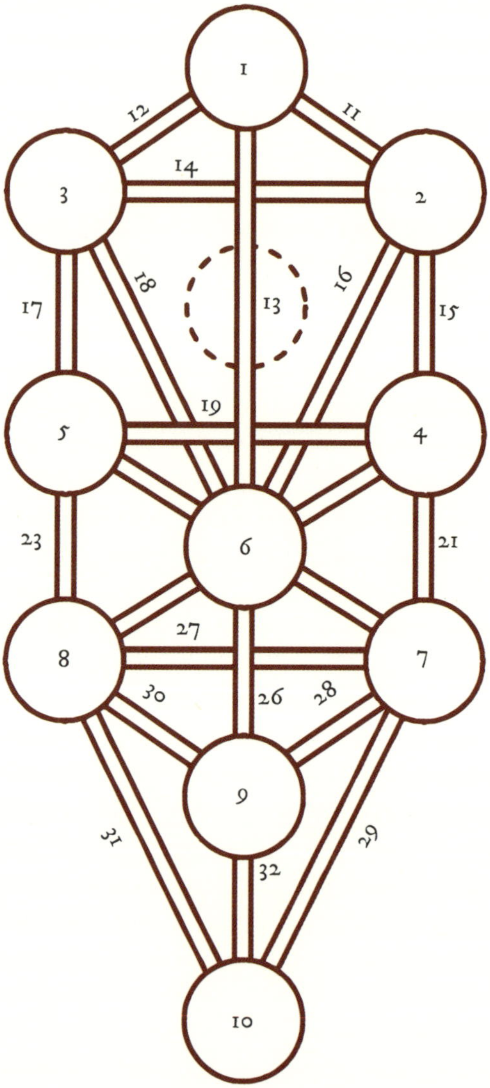

The Paths and Spheres

Crowley's attributions for the entire pack of Tarot cards – including the 22 trumps of the Major Arcana and the four suits (Wands or Rods, Cups, Swords and Shields) of the Minor Arcana (78 cards in all) – links them as shown in the table below. Meanwhile Gray showed a way in which you could do without images entirely, unless you wanted to draw your own. For the purpose of rapid comprehension, he codified each card with a single concept (see page 81).

As a final exposition of Gray's system, the chart on page 82 can give depth to the existing concepts, showing the Tarot's validity and impact through time, space and property. However, often the sheer weight of such tabulation can be counter-productive and it may be best to sit quietly, pick up a card, look at it and effectively say to it: 'What is your meaning?'

Differing Path Attributions

PATH	CROWLEY'S ATTRIBUTIONS	GRAY'S ATTRIBUTIONS	ACHAD'S ATTRIBUTIONS
11	The Fool	The Hierophant	Wheel of Fortune
12	The Juggler	The Hermit	Universe
13	The High Priestess	The Star	Last Judgement
14	The Empress	Judgement	The Star
15	The Emperor	The Emperor	Temperance
16	The Hierophant	Temperance	The Sun
17	The Lovers	Death	The Tower
18	The Chariot	The Hanged Man	The Devil
19	Strength	Justice	Death
20	Hermit	Strength	The Moon
21	Wheel of Fortune	Empress	Justice
22	Justice	Tower	The Emperor
23	The Hanged Man	The Devil	The Hermit
24	Death	Lovers	Strength
25	Temperance	Chariot	The Lovers
26	The Devil	The Sun	The Hanged Man
27	The House of God	Wheel of Fortune	The Hierophant
28	The Star	High Priestess	The Chariot
29	The Moon	The World	The Empress
30	The Sun	The Magician	High Priestess
31	Last Judgement	The Fool	The Magician
32	The Universe	The Moon	The Fool

Crowley's Attributions for the Tarot Pack

SPHERE	PATH NAME OF THE SEPHER YETZIRAH	TAROT ATTRIBUTION
1	Hidden Intelligence	The 4 Aces
2	Illuminating Intelligence	The 4 Twos – Kings or Knights
3	Sanctifying Intelligence	The 4 Threes – Queens
4	Cohesive Intelligence	The 4 Fours
5	Radical Intelligence	The 4 Fives
6	Intelligence of the Mediating Influence	The 4 Sixes – Emperors or Princes
7	Occult Intelligence	The 4 Sevens
8	Absolute or Perfect Intelligence	The 4 Eights
9	Pure or Clear Intelligence	The 4 Nines
10	Resplendent Intelligence	The 4 Tens – Empresses or Princesses
11	Scintillating Intelligence	The Fool – Swords Emperors or Princes
12	Intelligence of Transparency	The Juggler
13	Uniting Intelligence	The High Priestess
14	Illuminating Intelligence	The Empress
15	Constituting Intelligence	The Emperor
16	Triumphal or Eternal One	The Hierophant
17	Disposing One	The Lovers
18	Intelligence of the House of Influence	The Chariot
19	Intelligence of all the Activities of Spiritual Being	Strength
20	Intelligence of Will	Hermit
21	Intelligence of Conciliation	Wheel of Fortune
22	Faithful Intelligence	Justice
23	Stable Intelligence	The Hanged Man – [Cups] Queens
24	Imaginative Intelligence	Death
25	Intelligence of Probation	Temperance
26	Renovating Intelligence	The Devil
27	Exciting Intelligence	The House of God
28	Natural Intelligence	The Star
29	Corporeal Intelligence	The Moon
30	Collecting Intelligence	The Sun
31	Perpetual Intelligence, Last Judgement	[Wands] Kings or Knights
32	Administrative Intelligence	The Universe

Gray's Attributions for the Suits

SPHERE	RODS	CUPS	SWORDS	SHIELDS
1	Fire	Water	Air	Earth
2	Choice	Liberty	Uncertainty	Change
3	Intention	Affection	Suffering	Effort
4	Magnanimity	Hope	Truce	Reward
5	Retribution	Grief	Defeat	Adversity
6	Balance	Happiness	Safety	Benefit
7	Ability	Amusement	Deceit	Attention
8	Expediency	Enthusiasm	Danger	Skill
9	Endurance	Satisfaction	Misfortune	Means
10	Responsibility	Friendship	Disaster	Opportunity

Gray's Attributions for the Court Cards

CARD	FIRE / RODS	WATER / CUPS	AIR / SWORDS	EARTH / SHIELDS	ELEMENT
King	Incisive	Magnanimous	Severe	Reliable	Fire
Queen	Capable	Affectionate	Serious	Practical	Water
Knight	Astute	Idealistic	Aggressive	Ambitious	Air
Page	Diligent	Cheerful	Troublesome	Amenable	Earth

Gray's Expanded Associations

LETTER	TRUMP	TIME-TYPE	SPACE-TYPE	PROPERTY
B	Hierophant	Incarnation	Outer	Pressure
C	Hermit	Excarnation	Inner	Inertia
D	Star	Aeons	Cosmos	Cohesion
F	Justice	Evolution	Height	Velocity
G	Emperor	Epoch	Large	Mass
H	Temperance	Peacetime	Plane	Equilibrium
J	Death	Cessation	Void	Vacuum
K	Hanged Man	Fateful moments	Small	Density
L	Judgement	Decisive times	Breadth	Hardness
M	Strength	Power periods	Line	Force
N	Empress	Happy times	Curve	Softness
P	Tower	Adverse times	Separation	Repulsion
Q	Devil	Testing times	Edge	Friction
R	Lovers	Love life	Junction	Attraction
S	Chariot	Travel time	Distance	Propulsion
T	Sun	Years	Universe	Illumination
V	Wheel of Fortune	Intervals	Length	Elasticity
W	Priestess	Devotional time	Range of soul	Dispersion
X	World	Lifetime	Planet	Gravity
Y	Magus	Thinking time	Range of mind	Concentration
Z	Fool	Now	Proximity	Incidence
TH	Moon	Months	Locality	Reflection

THE TAROT & PATHWORKING

Two women within the Golden Dawn took a slightly different approach, using the Tarot cards in the same way as the ***tattwa*** symbols (see page 51).

The actress Florence Farr (1860–1917), known by the initials of her magical name as S S D D (*Sapientia Sapienti Dona Data*), and Elaine Simpson, known simply as F (for *Fidelis*), learned to step into the cards entirely. In a working dated 10 November 1892 they gave clear directions as to how the Tarot cards might be used:

Justice and The Moon from the Tarot of Marseilles, Claude Burdel, 1751

Secure for an hour or for longer absolute freedom from interruption...Remain in silence and contemplation for several minutes.

Rise, and perform the Qabalistic Cross and prayer. Then proceed to contemplation of some object, say a Tarot Trump: either by placing it before you and gazing at it, until you seem to see into it; or by placing it against your forehead or elsewhere, and then keeping the eyes closed; in this case you should have given previous study to the Card, as to its symbolism, colouring, analogies, etc.

In either case you should then deeply sink into the abstract ideal of the card; being in entire indifference to your surroundings. If the mind wanders to anything disconnected with the card, no beginner will succeed in seeing anything spiritually.

Consider all the symbolism of the Tarot Card, then all that is implied by its letters, number, and situation, and the paths connected therewith.

The vision may begin by the concentration passing into a state of reverie; or with a distinct sense of change, something allied in sensation to a faint, with a feeling urging you to resist, but if you are highly inspired, fear not, do not resist, let yourself go; and then the vision may pass over you.

If you have anything occur or disturb you, you will come to readily enough – or as from a doze; otherwise the vision ends of itself, or some can check it by will, at any stage, others can not, at first, at any rate.[17]

By this means Farr and Simpson were able to get a great deal of unusual information from the attendant reverie/vision. This is similar to what is now termed 'pathworking': an exploration of inner landscapes (which are very real) by means of the active imagination. In more modern terms there is a simple scheme that anyone can use.

Imagine that you are stepping into or through the card of, say, The Moon (which Gray places on the path between 9 and 10, Malkuth and Yesod on the Tree of Life, see pages 56 and 78) with the intention of exploring the Hidden Valley. For the best results this should be done in partnership with a narrator for the journey and another person simply taking a passive role and listening. In practical terms, the apparently passive listener more often than not acts as a kind of battery, providing energy for the joint vision. Everyone who does this for the first time is astonished that all those involved start to 'see' the same things and get an awareness that the inner landscapes are – in some way – real.

This can be more potent when the pathworkings use mythological imagery, tapping into the collective subconscious. To this extent there are some suggestive correspondences derived from the Arthurian tradition, which has, in recent decades, come back into its own – as though the sleeping king has indeed been awakened (see opposite).

By reading the stories and involving yourself in the emotions behind the figures, it is possible to key into the aggregates of consciousness that they represent, even if there is little historical substance behind them.

Pathworking Associations

SPHERE	ASSOCIATION
Kether	The Holy of Holies
Chockmah	The Starry Sky
Binah	The Great Ocean
Chesed	The Temple of Love
Geburah	The Temple of Power
Tiphereth	The Temple of the Sun
Netzach	The Secret Garden
Hod	The Lodge
Yesod	The Hidden Valley
Malkuth	The Meadows of Asphodel

The Arthurian Tradition

SPHERE	ARTHURIAN IMAGERY
1	Avalon
2	Round Table
3	Morgan le Fay
4	Guinevere
5	Lancelot, Mordred
6	Arthur
7	Nimue, Vivienne
8	Merlin
9	Holy Grail
10	Camelot
11	Sword and Spear
12	Cup and Shield
13	Quest
14	Attainment of the Grail
15	Galahad and the Siege Perilous
16	Final Penitence in Holy Orders
17	Sir Bruce sans Pitié
18	The Dying King
19	Guinevere's Trial
20	Gawaine
21	Royal Marriage
22	Joyous Gard
23	The Old Order
24	The Lovers
25	Merlin's Vision
26	Knighthood
27	Coronation
28	Lady of the Lake
29	Lady of Shalott, Elaine
30	Fisher-King
31	Lancelot's Madness
32	Training

5

THE GODS & GODDESSES ON THE TREE

GREEK & ROMAN DEITIES

Greek and Roman deities have long been invoked by magicians of all traditions. Aleister Crowley gained a certain notoriety by invoking the great god Pan in a Paris hotel room, although that notoriety was more a reflection of contemporary attitudes than a comment on the supposedly demonic force of Pan. In fact, Pan can be the most good-natured of gods, as long as the earth ways are respected.

You can summon Greek and Roman gods by name, using the appropriate planetary correspondences, but only after spending some time researching their qualities and deliberately building up a 'telesmatic' (magical) image of what they would look like, to enable your own mind to link with that of the archetype or model of the god.

The major Greek and Roman deities are given below, first in association with the spheres of the Tree of Life, and then in greater detail in alphabetical order (see opposite page), without linking them to the Tree.

Tree of Life Associations

SPHERE	GREEK DEITY	ROMAN DEITY
1	Zeus	Jupiter
2	Athena	Minerva
3	Demeter, Rhea, Hera	Cybele, Juno, Hecate, Ceres
4	Poseidon	Neptune
5	Ares, Hades	Mars
6	Apollo, Adonis	Apollo
7	Aphrodite	Venus
8	Hermes	Mercury
9	Artemis	Diana
10	Persephone, Psyche	Proserpina

Wider Associations

GREEK NAME	DESCRIPTION	ANIMAL	PLANT	SYMBOL	ROMAN NAME
Amphitrite	Queen of the sea	Dolphin, fish, seal	Seaweed	Dolphin, fish, pinched fingers	Salacia
Aphrodite	Aphrodite, the goddess of love; born of the blood of Uranos and the foam of the sea	Turtle dove, sparrow, goose, hare	Apple tree, rose, myrtle, myrrh tree, anemone, lettuce	Eros (winged godling), apple, dove	Venus
Apollon	Apollon, the son of Zeus and Leto; brother of Artemis (Apollo, Apollon, Phoibos Apollon, the Striker from Afar)	Swan, raven, mouse, wolf	Laurel, larkspur	Lyre, laurel wreath or branch, bow and arrows	Apollo
Ares	Ares, the god of war; the son of Zeus and Hera (Ares, Aries, Mars, god of war)	Serpent, vulture, woodpecker, eagle-owl	Manna ash	Helmet, spear	Mars
Artemis	Artemis, Diana, goddess of the hunt and the Moon	Deer, bear, wild boar, guinea fowl, quail	Cypress, walnut, amaranth flower	Bow and arrows, hunting spears, lyre, deer	Diana
Asclepius	God of medicine	Serpent	Herbs (healing)	Serpent-entwined staff	Aesculapius
Athena	Athene, the goddess of wisdom; the daughter of Zeus and Metis; the virgin goddess of intellect and invention (Athene, Athena, Pallas Athene, Tritogeneia, Glaukopis, Minerva)	Little owl, crow	Olive tree	Greek helmet, *aigis* (breastplate), spear	Minerva
Circe	Circe, the dread goddess; the daughter of Helios and mistress of potions and spells	–	Enchanter's nightshade	–	Saturn

GREEK NAME	DESCRIPTION	ANIMAL	PLANT	SYMBOL	ROMAN NAME
Cronos	Kronos, the Titan; father of the Olympians (Kronos, Cronos, Cronus, Saturn)	–	–	–	–
Demeter	Demeter, the goddess of the Harvest; the daughter of Cronos and Rhea (Demeter, Ceres)	Serpent, swine, gecko	Wheat, barley, poppy, mint	Grain sheaf, lotus, staff, torch, horn of plenty	Ceres
Dionysus	God of: wine, drunkenness, madness and the afterlife	Leopard, lynx, tiger, serpent, bull, goat, donkey	Grapevine, ivy, bindweed, silver fir	Thyrsus (pinecone-tipped staff), grapes, ivy wreath, leopard	Liber, Bacchus
Eileithyia	Goddess of childbirth	Weasel (*Ichneumon*)	–	Raised hands	Lucina
Erinyes	Erinys, the mist-walking and kindly one; punisher of the unfaithful (Erinyes, Erinys, Furiae, Furies, Tisiphone, Megaera, Alecto, Alekto)	Poisonous serpent, screech owl	Elm tree	Serpentine hair, poisonous serpents, wings, whip	Furiae
Eros	Eros, the god of love; using arrows of gold and lead, he wounded the hearts of mortals and immortals alike	Hare	Apple, rose, myrtle	Wings, bow and arrows, torch, myrtle wreath	Cupid
Hades	Hades, lord of the Underworld; the son of Cronos and Rhea	Screech owl	Asphodel, mint, white poplar	Cornucopia, bird-tipped staff	Pluto
Hecate	Goddess of witchcraft and ghosts	Dog, weasel, polecat	Herbs, asphodel	Twin torches, triple body	–

GREEK NAME	DESCRIPTION	ANIMAL	PLANT	SYMBOL	ROMAN NAME
Helios	Helios, the sun; the son of Hyperion and Eryphaesa; he sees everything that his light touches	Rooster, white horse	Heliotrope, frankincense	Aureole	Apollo, Sol
Hephaistos	Hephaistos, the god of the smith; the son of Hera and artificer of the Olympians (Hephaistos, Hephaestus, Vulcan)	Donkey, crane	Fennel	Hammer, tongs, anvil, donkey, crane-head	Vulcan
Hera	Hera, the daughter of Cronos and Rhea; wife to Zeus; the most beautiful of the immortals	Cuckoo, peacock, crane, hawk, cow (heifer), lion	Chaste Tree, pomegranate	Lotus staff, crown, lion	Juno
Herakles	Herakles, the ultimate hero; the son of Zeus and Alkmene (Hercules of the 12 Labours)	Lion	White poplar	Lionskin cape, gnarled club	Hercules
Hermes	Hermes, the wing-shod messenger of the Olympians; the son of Zeus and Maia (Hermes, Mercury, Argeiphontes)	Tortoise, sheep, cattle, hawk	Crocus, strawberry tree	*Kerykeion* (herald's rod), traveller's cap, winged boots	Mercury
Hestia	Hestia, the virgin goddess of the hearth and humble domestic joy	Swine	Chaste tree	Chaste-tree branch, head veil, kettle	Vesta
Kheiron (Chiron)	Kheiron, the most righteous of the Centaurs; powerful master of many arts and sciences (Cheiron, Kheiron, Eurytion)	–	–	–	–
Leto	Leto, the consort of Zeus and mother of Apollon and Artemis	Rooster, weasel (*Ichneumon*)	Date palm	Head veil	Latona

GREEK NAME	DESCRIPTION	ANIMAL	PLANT	SYMBOL	ROMAN NAME
Muses	The Muses attend the festivals on Olympus and entertain and inspire the other gods with their wit and charm (Mousai)	Dove	–	Lyre (cithara and barbiton), laurel wreath, scroll-chest, scroll	Musae
Orai, The Hours	Orai, the three sisters – Eunomia (Harmony), Dyke (Justice) and Eirene (Peace) – assist the Olympians by organizing the seasons and adding balance to nature (Hours, The Hours, Eunomia, Dyke, Eiren, Horae, The Horae, Orai)	–	Fruit trees	Branches of fruit and blossoms, basket of fruit, cornucopia	Horae
Pan	Pan, the goat-god; he prances through the fertile countryside in the company of nymphs, playing his seven-reed pipe in wild abandon (Pan, Faunus, horned god)	Goat, sheep	Pine tree, reeds	Pan-pipes, goat legs, horns	Faunus
Persephone	Persephone, the daughter of Demeter and Zeus; wife of Hades and queen of the Underworld	Screech owl	Wheat, narcissus, black poplar, mint, asphodel	Eleusinian torch or torches, wheat sheaves	Proserpina
Poseidon	Poseidon, the lord the sea; the son of Cronos and Rhea	All sea creatures	Seaweed, coral	Trident	Neptune
Prometheus	Prometheus, the rebel god; in defiance of Zeus, he gave fire and other comforts to the mortals on Earth	–	–	–	–
Rhea	Rhea, the wife of devious Cronos (and mother to the Olympians)	Lions	Silver fir	Turret crown	Ops
Zeus	Zeus, the Olympian; the son of Cronos and Rhea; lord of the sky (Zeus, Jupiter)	Golden eagle, wolf	Oak, celery	Lightning bolt, lotus staff, eagle, oak wreath	Jupiter

EGYPTIAN & HINDU DEITIES

The sephiratic correspondences as given by Crowley for the major Egyptian and Hindu deities are also worth looking at. The Egyptian gods correspond to the sophisticated concept of the ***neters*** (see page 187), a deeper and more all-embracing term than is suggested by the word 'deity'.

In looking at Crowley's attributions for the paths, it seems that many of them are notional and idiosyncratic, and readers of ***Liber 777*** should allow themselves to suspend their uncritical admiration of Crowley, the Logos of the Aeon, and remember that he was also Aleister, the young genius who was taking drugs, challenging his superiors in the Golden Dawn and trying a little too hard at times to fill in the gaps and impress.

A more modern approach to such ancient arcana has been taken by the Belgian Wim van den Dungen (b. 1961), with separate tables for Hindu and ancient Egyptian correspondences (see pages 95–96). He extends this to analyses of Buddhist correspondences, too (see page 97).

Wondrous though the Tree of Life is when it comes to arranging correspondences, it is not applicable to all systems. Celtic deities, for example, fit only begrudgingly – if at all; they are like quicksilver. And the Egyptian ***neters*** are so multilayered, and their meanings change so profoundly over vast periods of time, that any attempt to place them on the Tree should be done in the spirit of lively speculation, rather than that of dogma. And there are some systems that should never be compared directly in that sense; it would be like comparing the northern cities of England with the northern cities of Japan and trying to get a cosmic patterning and wisdom – it would, by any standards, be a fruitless exercise.

Crowley's Correspondences For Major Egyptian and Hindu Deities

SPHERE	EGYPTIAN DEITY	HINDU DEITY
1	Ptah	Parabrahm
2	Isis (as Wisdom)	Shiva
3	Nepthys	Bhavani (all forms of Sakti), Prana (as Force), Yoni
4	Amoun	Indra, Brahma
5	Horus	Vishnu (Varuna Avatar)
6	Ra	Vishu-Hari-Krishna-Rama
7	Hathor	Bhavani
8	Thoth	Hanuman
9	Shu	Ganesha, Vishnu (Kurm Avatar)
10	Osiris	Lakshmi
11	Mont	The Maruts
12	Thoth	Hanuman, Vishnu (as Parasa-Rama)
13	Chomse	Chandra
14	Hathor	Lalita (sexual aspect of Sakti)
15	Isis	Shiva
16	Osiris	Shiva (Sacred Bull)
17	The twin Merti	Various twin and hybrid deities
18	Hormakhu	Krishna
19	Horus	Vishnu (Nara-Singh Avatar)
20	Heru-pa-Kraath	The Gope girls, the Lord of Yoga
21	Amoun-Ra	Brahma, Indra
22	Maat	Yama
23	Asar	Soma
24	Hammemit	Kundalini
25	Nepthys	Vishnu (Horse Avatar)
26	Set	Lingam, Yoni
27	Horus	Krishna
28	Nuit	The Maruts
29	Anubis	Vishnu (Matsya Avatar)
30	Ra	Agni, Yama
31	Mau	Surya
32	Sobek	Brahma

Van Den Dungen's Hindu Correspondences

SPHERE	DIMENSION	TANTRA: LOKA	TANTRA: KOSHA	LIMBS OF YOGA	HINDU DEITY
0	10				
00	9	Parârûpa	Purusha	Dharma megha samâdhi	Nirguna Brahman
000	8				
1	7	Satya		Viveka-khyati	Ishvara
2	7	Tapar	Hiranya	Asamprajñâta samâdhi	Vishnu
3	7			Samprajñâta samâdhi (subtle)	Shiva
4	6	Janar	Vijñana	Samprajñâta samâdhi (crude)	Varuna
5	6	Mahar	Atima	Dhyâna	Indra
6	6				Krishna
7	5	Svar	Mano	Dhâranâ	Lakshmi
8	5			Pratyâhara	Hanumat
9	5	Bhurvar	Kâma	Prânâyâma	Ganesha
10	4,1	Bhur	Prânâ	Asana	Kundalini
10	4,1		Anna	Yama/Niyama	

Van Den Dungen's Egyptian Mysteries

Sphere	Dimension	Cosmogony (Origin)	Parts of Man	Sacred Architecture	Mystical Theologies	Deity
0	10			–		
00	9	Pre-creation	Akhu of deities	–	Heliopolitan, Nun and Atum, Hermopolitan, Ogdoad, Memphite, Ptah-Nun	Nun, Atum
000	8			–		
1	7	Atum-Re		Cult statue		Atum-Re Ptah
2	7	Retinue of Re	Akh Kha	Sacred barque	Cosmogalactic imperishables, solar illumination, cult of Re	Shu
3	7	Sky of Re		Naos		Tefnut
4	6					Amun-Re
5	6	Akhet	Ba turns, Akh	Sanctuary	Eastern horizon, transformation, temple cults	Horus-Seth
6	6					Re
7	5	Sky of Duat				Isis, Nephthys
8	5		Ba	Hypostyle halls	Lunar, moon judgement and resurrection, Osirian cult, cult of Thoth	Thoth
9	5	Duat				Osiris
10	4, 1	The two lands	Ka, Ib Khaibit	Great court	Terrestrial, two lands, royal cult	Geb, Pharaoh
10	4, 1		Khat	Pylons		

Van Den Dungen's Buddhist Correspondences

SPHERE	DIMENSION	TYPES	STATES	PRACTICES	PATHS
0	10	Dharmakâya		Dharma	
00	9	Sambhogakâya	Buddha-dhatu svâbhâvika kâya	Buddha-fields	Timeless, permanent, a dual featureless Buddha-nature
000	8	Nirmânakâya		Incarnation of Buddha	
1	7	Boddhisattva	Buddhahood	Buddha	The way of Lord Buddha
2	7	Pratyeka Buddha		Community	
3	7	Asekha		Generosity	Perfect view
4	6	Arhat	Vipassana insight	Death	Perfect resolve
5	6	Anâgâmin		Discipline	Perfect conduct
6	6	Pure self-possession		Heavenly beings	Perfect concentration
7	5	Tranquil joylessness		Peace	Perfect mindfulness
8	5	Concentration	Samatha, tranquillity	Teaching	Perfect speech
9	5	Tranquil detachment		Inhaling, exhaling	Perfect effort
10	4/1			Body	Perfect livelihood

6

THE COLOUR SCALES

COLOUR SCALES & THE TREE OF LIFE

Colour is one of the most powerful influences upon our lives, and this has been recognized in many esoteric systems. If the Tree of Life is a schematic representation of the universe and the soul of human beings, then it is apparent that colour must find a place within the system.

The colour of the Tree's spheres and paths represents the way the energies are perceived on the inner planes, at varying levels of manifestation. Astral travellers and people who have had near-death experiences have all commented on the sheer intensity of colours on the other side. Artists, using their right-brain perceptions, have always known this.

In the Kabbalah, the colours are codified as the King, Queen, Emperor and Empress scales, and their equations are simple enough:

- King = Atziluth
- Queen = Briah
- Emperor = Yetzirah
- Empress = Assiah

When colouring the *sephiroth*, the colours 1–10 of the Queen scale are frequently used. The King scale is generally used to define the paths. When performing magical operations that aim for tangible effect, the colours of the Queen scale or Briah level are generally chosen. Thus operations involving the sphere of Jupiter – Chesed (see page 58) – would necessarily use blue: blue robes, blue candles and so on.

While these are the traditional colours as determined by the seers of the Golden Dawn, caution should be applied and individual discernment encouraged. It has been suggested by later commentators that the scales only worked because the seers got it right at the levels of Briah and worked from there accordingly. Nevertheless, people who work along the lines of colour healing insist that, for example, blue light will have quite distinct and measurably different effects upon a person than red light. They state that this is objective not subjective.

As ever, give the traditional correspondences a try, but never be afraid to substitute your own when you feel confident.

Colours of the King and Queen Scales

SPHERE	KING SCALE (ATZILUTH)	QUEEN SCALE (BRIAH)
1	Brilliance	White brilliance
2	Pure soft blue	Grey
3	Crimson	Black
4	Deep violet	Blue
5	Orange	Scarlet red
6	Clear rose pink	Yellow (gold)
7	Amber	Emerald
8	Violet purple	Orange
9	Indigo	Violet
10	Yellow	Citrine, olive, russet, black
11	Bright pale yellow	Sky blue
12	Yellow	Purple
13	Blue	Silver
14	Emerald green	Sky blue
15	Scarlet	Red
16	Red orange	Deep indigo
17	Orange	Pale mauve
18	Amber	Maroon
19	Yellow	Deep purple
20	Greenish yellow	Slate grey
21	Violet	Blue
22	Emerald green	Blue
23	Deep blue	Sea green
24	Green blue	Dull brown
25	Blue	Yellow
26	Indigo	Black
27	Scarlet	Red
28	Violet	Sky blue
29	Crimson	Buff, flecked silver white
30	Orange	Gold yellow
31	Glowing orange scarlet	Vermilion
32	Indigo	Black

Colours of the Emperor and Empress Scales

SPHERE	EMPEROR SCALE (YETZIRAH)	EMPRESS SCALE (ASSIAH)
1	White brilliance	White, flecked with gold
2	Blue pearl grey, like mother-of-pearl	White, flecked with red, blue and yellow
3	Dark brown	Grey, flecked with pink
4	Deep purple	Deep azure, flecked with yellow
5	Bright scarlet	Red, flecked with black
6	Rich salmon	Gold amber
7	Bright yellow green	Olive, flecked with gold
8	Red russet	Yellowish brown, flecked with white
9	Very dark purple	Citrine, flecked with azure
10	Citrine, olive, russet, black, all flecked with gold	Black, rayed with yellow
PATH		
11	Blue emerald green	Emerald, flecked with gold
12	Grey	Indigo, rayed with violet
13	Cold pale blue	Silver, rayed with sky blue
14	Early spring green	Bright rose, rayed with pale green
15	Brilliant flame	Glowing red
16	Deep warm olive	Rich brown
17	New yellow leather	Reddish grey inclined to mauve
18	Rich bright russet	Dark greenish brown
19	Grey	Reddish-amber
20	Green grey	Plum colour
21	Rich purple	Bright blue, rayed with yellow
22	Deep blue green	Pale green
23	Deep olive green	White, flecked with purple, like mother-of-pearl
24	Very dark brown	Livid indigo brown, like a black beetle
25	Green	Dark vivid blue
26	Blue black	Cold dark grey approaching black
27	Venetian red	Bright red, rayed with emerald
28	Bluish mauve	White, tinged with purple
29	Light translucent pinkish brown	Stone colour
30	Rich amber	Amber, rayed with red
31	Scarlet, flecked gold	Vermilion, flecked with crimson and emerald
32	Blue black	Black, rayed with blue

FLASHING COLOURS

The colours are particularly useful when making talismans. Frater Sapere Aude (the magical name of W Wynn Westcott, who was one of the original founders of the Golden Dawn) wrote:

> A talisman is a magical figure charged with the force which it is intended to represent. In the construction of a Talisman, care should be taken to make it, as far as is possible, so to represent the Universal Forces that it should be in exact harmony with those you wish to attract, and the more exact the symbolism, the more easy it is to attract the force – other things coinciding, such as consecration at the right time, etc.
>
> A symbol should also be correct in its symbolism, but it is not necessarily the same as a Talisman.
>
> A flashing tablet is one made in the complementary colours. A flashing colour, then, is the complementary colour which, if joined to the original, enables it to attract, to a certain extent, the Akashic current from the atmosphere, and to a certain extent from yourself, thus forming a vortex which can attract its flashing light from the atmosphere.[18]

This is not as esoteric as it sounds. We have all seen patterns of tightly grouped colours and shapes (usually dots) on items as mundane as clothes, furniture and carpets, which seem to 'flash' and can cause acute discomfort. This flashing is caused by the effect upon the eye of the complementary colours, as follows:

- White is complementary to black and grey
- Red is complementary to green
- Blue is complementary to orange
- Yellow is complementary to violet
- Olive is complementary to violet
- Blue green is complementary to red orange
- Violet is complementary to citrine
- Reddish orange is complementary to greenish blue
- Deep amber is complementary to indigo
- Lemon yellow is complementary to red violet
- Yellow green is complementary to crimson.

Judicious use of these colours when making talismans, as described in Chapter 3, can make those magical devices come alive in a purely visual sense, with an accordingly potent effect upon the unconscious.

Frater Sapere Aude goes on to say:

> A flashing tablet should be carefully made charged, and consecrated, and then each morning the Adeptus should sit before it and practise clairvoyance, endeavouring to go through it to the plane it represents, and then to invoke the power and ask for strength to accomplish the matter desired, which will be granted if it be a lawful and laudable operation.[19]

By making use of simple attributions for the major colours, you can proceed to see the world in a different way: every item, every colour will offer you a message. By deliberate use of colour, you can create 'messages' in return.

7

ASTROLOGICAL CORRESPONDENCES

THE ORIGINS OF ASTROLOGY

If any body of occult knowledge can be said to be vital in order to 'energize' all the information given so far, it can be found in astrology. It was Crowley who penned the phrase: 'Every Man and Woman is a Star'. The occult tradition is that humankind's true home is among the stars. Tribal cultures in every epoch have venerated particular stars or whole constellations as the home of their ancestors, and thus the place their souls would return to after death. Societies throughout the developed world have felt that stars could in some way influence people at every level, whether this was physical, emotional, mental or spiritual.

There were practical reasons for star-watching and time measurement: societies revolved around agrarian and breeding cycles (both human and animal), which depended upon a precise knowledge of ***when***: when to plant; when to put bull to cow; when to conceive the next king; when to marry; when to sail. The Pleiades, for example, were often thought of as the mariner's stars because their rising and setting marked the calmer times to set sail upon the great beast that is Ocean.

It is generally accepted that astrology originated with the Chaldeans, in Babylon in Mesopotamia (now Iraq) around the fourth millennium BCE, where it was a fundamental part of their religious worship. The earliest Babylonian zodiac of which we are aware had 18 constellations: 10 of the 12 that we still use, plus the Pleiades, Hyades, Orion, Perseus, Auriga, Praesepe and the southern and northern Fish. These are described in the Mul.Apin Tablets from the royal libraries of Assyria (now in the British Museum) as 'constellations which stand in the path of the Moon, and into the region of which the moons pass monthly, and which they touch'.

The major planets of the Babylonians' pantheon were as follows:

- Sun – Shamash
- Moon – Sin
- Mercury – Nebo
- Venus – Ishtar
- Mars – Nergal
- Jupiter – Marduk
- Saturn – Ninib

Babylonian knowledge is thought to have spread to Egypt around the third millennium BCE, because the first records of its use by Egyptian rulers as a predictive tool for agricultural events are dated to this time. However, more recent research shows that Egyptian knowledge of the heavenly bodies may well predate that of their near neighbours, as hinted by the arrangement of the principal monuments at Giza to form an accurate terrestrial 'map' of the three stars of the constellation Orion's belt, as these appeared in the sky in 10,500 BCE.[20] More startling yet is the deeply researched thesis of Christopher Knight and Robert Lomas in their book ***Uriel's Machine***,[21] where they argue that the megalithic sites in Britain were actually early-warning systems to detect comets, following major and devastating comet impacts on Earth in 7640 BCE, and then again in 3150 BCE, which were responsible for the global legends of the Flood. They argue that such knowledge was actually transferred ***eastwards***, from the circle-builders of western Europe, who used their megaliths as predictive devices to warn about comets.

EGYPTIAN ASTROLOGY

Certainly the first clearly preserved example of the zodiac that we know today was found in the Temple of Hathor at Denderah, which was dated to the Late Ptolemaic Period, which lasted from around 300 BCE until the early Christian era. This round zodiac ceiling shows the whole sky as it was understood by both Greek and Egyptian cultures, with the familiar constellations associated with the Greek astrological signs, along with a number of other figures. The disk is supported by the goddesses of the four cardinal points and by eight falcon-headed gods. Around the edge of the circle there is a procession of 36 figures representing the spirits of the 36 'decan stars', one corresponding to each of the Egyptians' ten-day weeks.

The Egyptians used 36 bright stars that rose in the east just before sunrise to mark the start of their weeks; a new star rose about every ten days. The outer ring of decans is meant to show the concordance of the decan stars with the Greek astrological zodiac. It has been argued that there was a parallel between the constellations and celestial figures shown at Denderah with the Egyptian townships or ***nomes*** (see page 191). The sequence of the ***nomes*** parallels the sequence of the zodiac, and this relationship confirms that the Egyptians conceived of a celestial-terrestrial coordination between the stars and precise places on the land.

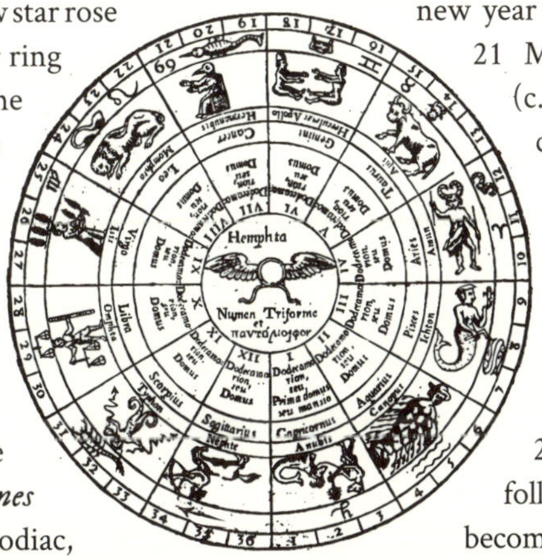

Unlike the Greeks, however, the Egyptians did not use their constellations for natal astrology. Instead, their birth signs were determined by the Egyptian months of the year. At the time of the Old Kingdom (c.2600–c.2030 BCE), the new year began on the Spring Equinox, 21 March. The Middle Kingdom (c.2030–c.1650 BCE) saw it coincide with the heliacal (solar) rising of Sirius (or Sothis, as the Egyptians termed it). When the New Kingdom arrived in the 16th century BCE, the new year was determined by the inundation of the Nile on 29 August. Because calendars following a strictly lunar system become slightly skewed, five extra or 'epagomenal' days were added between 14 and 18 July to bring the calendar back into line – in much the same way as we now have leap years. These extra days were given a special magical significance and were equated with major deities.

Egyptian Extra Days

DATE	ASSOCIATED DEITY
14 July	Osiris (Asar), Lord of the Underworld, the first Green Man
15 July	Horus the Elder, the hawk-headed one, god of light
16 July	Set, god of chaos and darkness
17 July	Isis (Aset), great in Magick, wife of Osiris
18 July	Nepthys, the shape-shifter, wife of Set and mother of Anubis (by Asar)

Correspondences For the Monthly Signs of Egyptian Astrology[22]

DEITY	DATE	HERB	STONE	TREE	ANIMAL	FLOWER
Thoth	29 August–27 September	Thyme	Carnelian	Quince	Ibis	Marigold
Horus	28 September–27 October	Rosemary	Citrine	Acacia	Falcon	Carnation
Wadjet	28 October–26 November	Mustard	Amethyst	Ash	Serpent	Hyacinth
Sekhmet	27 November–26 December	Pepper	Tiger's eye	Sandalwood	Lioness	Poppy
Sphinx	27 December–25 January	Coriander	Quartz	Almond	Lion	Lily
Shu	26 January–24 February	Lemon balm	Moonstone	Silver birch	Swallow	Iris
Isis	25 February–26 March	Tarragon	Lapis lazuli	Sycamore	Cat	Rose
Osiris	27 March–25 April	Basil	Moss agate	Cedar	Scarab	Violet
Amun	26 April–25 May	Sage	Turquoise	Oak	Ram	Bluebell
Hathor	26 May–24 June	Fennel	Jasper	Elm	Cow	Cowslip
Phoenix	25 June–24 July	Nutmeg	Amber	Alder	Lyrebird	Daffodil
Anubis	25 July–28 August	Savory	Obsidian	Yew	Jackal	Foxglove

THE WESTERN ZODIAC

Western horoscopic astrology is based on an exact moment in time, such as a person's birth, in which various planetary and stellar bodies are said to have an influence. Most Western astrologers use the tropical zodiac, beginning with the sign of Aries at the northern hemisphere's Vernal Equinox, which occurs on or around 21 March each year. However, some Western astrologers use the sidereal zodiac, which is aligned with actual star positions.

A horoscope or chart is based on a specific moment in time and shows where planets and various other cosmic bodies are positioned in relation to each other at that moment. The most prominent of these features is the position of the sun in relation to the signs of the zodiac. These signs, as used in Western astrology, are based on the tropical zodiac and therefore cosmic bodies are not in the actual constellation. From these planetary positions astrologers draw conclusions about the moment, and magicians can seize the moment for their own invocations.

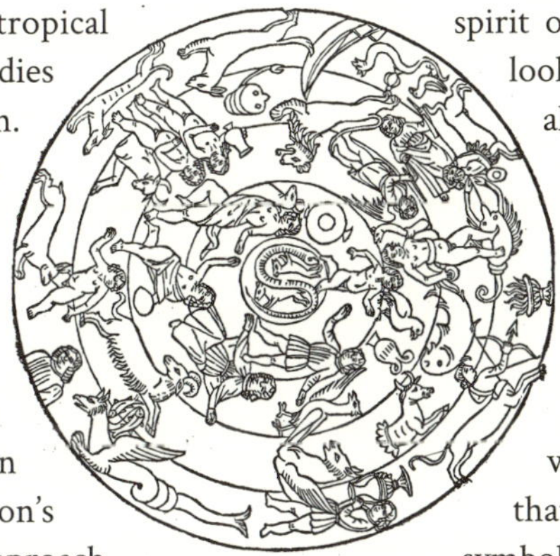

The groupings of signs are regarded as having certain 'qualities', which describe a person's attitudes in life and the way they approach projects. The three qualities are known as cardinal, fixed and mutable. The modern Western codification of the zodiac follows on page 110: these are the basic signs and symbols from which all else develops. It can then be broken down further into the planetary symbols.

Judy Hall (1944–2021), a pupil of the late Christine Hartley (1897–1985), a senior adept within the Golden Dawn), gave a more detailed and unusual set of correspondences in her book, *The Astrology Bible.*[23] Intriguingly (and very much in the spirit of 'things Egyptian' that we will look at later in Chapter 11), she also gave a list of the places to which each sign might be linked (see pages 114–115). Even if you are not an astrologer as such, you can pick out which correspondences seem most relevant to you. You might want to create a pathworking that uses the animal/colour/crystal symbolism of a particular sign, and visit the temple of the appropriate deity to ask for guidance. You can back this up on the outer level by using related incense, music and lighting.

Zodiac Signs

NAME	GLYPH OR SYMBOL
Aries	♈
Taurus	♉
Gemini	♊
Cancer	♋
Leo	♌
Virgo	♍
Libra	♎
Scorpio	♏
Sagittarius	♐
Capricorn	♑
Aquarius	♒
Pisces	♓

Planetary Symbols

PLANET	SYMBOL
Sun	☉
Moon	☽
Earth	⊕
Mercury	☿
Venus	♀
Saturn	♄
Mars	♂
Jupiter	♃
Neptune	♆
Uranus	♅
Pluto	⯓

Wider Associations

SIGN	MEANING	BRIGHTEST STAR	ELEMENT	QUALITY	RULING PLANET
Aries	Ram	Alpha Arietis	Fire	Cardinal	Mars
Taurus	Bull	Aldebaran	Earth	Fixed	Venus
Gemini	Twins	Pollux	Air	Mutable	Mercury
Cancer	Crab	Beta Cancri	Water	Cardinal	Moon
Leo	Lion	Regulus	Fire	Fixed	Sun
Virgo	Virgin	Spica	Earth	Mutable	Mercury
Libra	Scales	Beta Librae	Air	Cardinal	Venus
Scorpio	Scorpion	Antares	Water	Fixed	Pluto/Mars
Sagittarius	Archer	Epsilon Sagittarii	Fire	Mutable	Jupiter
Capricorn	Horned goat	Delta Capricornii	Earth	Cardinal	Saturn
Aquarius	Water bearer	Beta Aquarii	Air	Fixed	Uranus/Saturn
Pisces	Fish	Eta Piscium	Water	Mutable	Neptune/Jupiter

Hall's Metal, Animal and Gemstone Correspondences

SIGN	METAL	ANIMAL	BIRTHSTONE	CRYSTALS
Aries	Iron	Dragon, sheep, tiger	Ruby, diamond	Amethyst, aquamarine, aventurine, bloodstone, carnelian, citrine, fire agate, garnet, iron pyrite, jadeite, jasper, kunzite, magnetite, pink tourmaline, orange spinel, spinel, topaz
Taurus	Copper	Cow, elephant	Emerald	Aquamarine, azurite, black spinel, boji stone, diamond, emerald, kyanite, kunzite, lapis lazuli, malachite, rhodonite, rose quartz, sapphire, selenite, tiger's eye, topaz, tourmaline, variscite
Gemini	Mercury	Magpie, small birds, parrot, monkey, butterfly	Tourmaline, agate	Apatite, apophyllite, aquamarine, blue spinel, calcite, chrysocolla, chrysoprase, citrine, dendritic agate, green obsidian, green tourmaline, sapphire, serpentine, tourmalinated and rutilated quartz, tiger's eye, topaz, variscite, ulexite, zoisite
Cancer	Silver, copper	Crab, frog	Moonstone, pearl	Amber, beryl, brown spinel, carnelian, calcite, chalcedony, chrysoprase, dendritic agate, emerald, fire agate, moonstone, moss agate, opal, pink tourmaline, rhodonite, ruby
Leo	Gold	Lion, domestic cat, lynx	Cat's eye, ruby	Amber, boji stone, carnelian, cat's eye, chrysocolla, citrine, danburite, emerald, fire agate, garnet, golden beryl, green and pink tourmaline, kunzite, larimar, muscovite, onyx, orange calcite, petalite, pyrolusite, quartz, red obsidian, rhodochrosite, ruby, tiger's eye, topaz, turquoise, yellow spinel

SIGN	METAL	ANIMAL	BIRTHSTONE	CRYSTALS
Virgo	Mercury, copper	Mouse, insects, cat, bee	Peridot, sardonyx	Amazonite, amber, blue topaz, carnelian, chrysocolla, citrine, dioptase, garnet, magnetite, moonstone, moss agate, opal, peridot, purple obsidian, rubellite, rutilated quartz, sapphire, sardonyx, smithsonite, sodalite, sugilite, okenite
Libra	Copper	Dove, all small animals, swan, lizards and small reptiles	Sapphire, opal	Ametrine, apophyllite, aquamarine, aventurine, bloodstone, chiastolite, chrysolite, green spinel, green tourmaline, jade, kunzite, lapis lazuli, lepidolite, mahogany obsidian, moonstone, peridot, prehnite, sapphire, sunstone, topaz
Scorpio	Iron, plutonium	Scorpion, eagle, snake, lizard	Topaz, turquoise	Apache tear, aquamarine, beryl, boji stone, charoite, dioptase, emerald, garnet, green tourmaline, herkimer diamond, hiddenite, kunzite, malachite, moonstone, obsidian, red spinel, rhodochrosite, ruby, variscite
Sagittarius	Tin	Horse, stag, all hooved or hunted animals	Topaz, amethyst	Azurite, blue lace agate, chalcedony, charoite, dark blue spinel, dioptase, garnet, gold sheen obsidian, labradorite, lapis lazuli, malachite, snowflake obsidian, okenite, pink tourmaline, ruby, smoky quartz, sodalite, spinel, sugilite, turquoise, wulfenite
Capricorn	Lead, platinum	Goat and all cloven-footed creatures, bear, bat	Jet, garnet	Amber, annabergite, aragonite, azurite, carnelian, fluorite, galena, green and black tourmaline, jet, labradorite, magnetite, malachite, onyx, peridot, quartz, ruby, smoky quartz, turquoisc
Aquarius	Lead, uranium, aluminium, platinum	Peacock, large, far-flying birds	Aquamarine, amethyst	Amber, amethyst, angelite, antacamite, aquamarine, blue celestite, blue obsidian, boji stone, chrysoprase, fluorite, labradorite, magnetite, moonstone
Pisces	Tin	Fish, dolphin, all sea mammals	Amethyst, moonstone	Aquamarine, beryl, bloodstone, blue lace agate, calcite, chrysoprase, fluorite, labradorite, moonstone, smithsonite, sunstone, turquoise

Hall's Place, Herb and Food Correspondences

SIGN	PLACES	HERBS	FOODS
Aries	England, Germany, Israel; Burgundy, France; Florence, Naples and Padua, Italy; Krakow, Poland; Las Vegas and Brunswick, USA; all capital cities; places with sporting facilities; places formerly occupied by sheep, cattle, deer, thieves, limekilns or brickworks; newly cultivated land; sandy or hilly ground; ceilings, plasterwork, wall coverings, stables	Milk thistle, hops, nettles, burdock root, gentian, cayenne, broom, honeysuckle, red clover, gotu kola, fo-ti, sassafras, yellow dock, St John's wort, yarrow, garlic	Hot, spicy and strong-tasting foods; anything red; garlic, onions, capers, mustard, cayenne
Taurus	Cyprus, Iran, Greek islands, Switzerland, Turkey; Dublin, Ireland; Leipzig, Germany; Mantua, Parma and Palermo, Italy; St Louis, USA; luxury hotels; anywhere warm, comfortable and luxurious with excellent food; gently rolling countryside, stables or pastureland, arable or scrubland, newly cleared and sown land; cellars and low rooms, furniture repositories	Sage, thyme, plantain, tansy, silverweed, licorice, slippery elm, goldenrod, bearberry, fenugreek	Apple, spinach, beet, wheat and other cereals, grapes, pears, asparagus, artichokes
Gemini	Armenia, Sardinia, Belgium; New York and San Francisco, USA; London, England; Lombardy, Italy; Cordoba, Spain; Nuremberg, Germany; city centres; hills, mountains and barren places; barns and close to a storehouse; wainscot, plaster and walls, coffers, trunks and chests, playhouses, dining rooms, educational establishments	Coltsfoot, lobelia, mullein, horehound, yerba santa, hyssop, elecampane, lemon balm, skullcap, lily-of-the-valley, flax, parsley, meadowsweet, caraway, lavender, marjoram, aniseed	Nuts, seeds, vegetables grown above ground, except cabbage
Cancer	Canada, Scotland, Mauritius; Amsterdam, Netherlands; Venice, Italy; Istanbul, Turkey; New York, USA; anywhere peaceful near or on water; all navigable waters, especially large rivers and the sea; houses near water catchments; lakes, wells, springs or marshy ground; cellars, laundries, ditches and sinks	Water lily, chickweed, honeysuckle, peppermint, spearmint, papaya, dogtooth violet, lettuce, verbena, tarragon	Shellfish, lettuce, mushrooms, cucumber, squashes, melon, fig, cabbage; milk, foods with a high water content
Leo	Rome, Italy; Riviera, France; Prague, Czech Republic; Turkey, southern Iraq, Lebanon, Bohemia; Mumbai, India; Chicago and Philadelphia, USA; exclusive resorts; jungles, woods, forests, hot deserts, inaccessible places, anywhere near a fire or furnace; castles, fireplaces, chimneys, ovens and stoves	Eyebright, borage, St John's wort, marigold (calendula), wake robin, hawthorn, mistletoe, motherwort	Parsley, rich foods, meat, walnuts, honey, spinach, kale, watercress
Virgo	Switzerland, the eastern Mediterranean; Paris and Lyon, France; Greece, Turkey, Crete; Heidelburg, Germany; Boston, USA; health farms, dairies, cornfields, granaries, malthouses, hayricks, libraries, bookcases, closets, barns; anywhere ploughed or cultivated	Skullcap, blackberry, dill, fennel, flax, plantain	Nuts, endive, millet, corn, wheat, barley, oats, rye, rice, potatoes, carrots, turnips, swedes; all vegetables that grow under the earth

SIGN	PLACES	HERBS	FOODS
Libra	Argentina, Burma, Austria, alpine regions, China; Lisbon, Portugal; Vienna, Austria; Arles, France; large cruise liners; barns, windmills, outhouses, sawpits; the side of hills, top of mountains, anywhere with pure, clear air; barren, sandy or gravely fields where hawking was formerly practised; inner chambers, attics	Cleavers, pennyroyal, violet, thyme, feverfew, catmint, silverweed, archangel, bearberry, burdock, corn silk, juniper, parsley, prince's pine, uva ursi, buchu leaves	Watercress, strawberry, milk, honey, fruit, wheat, artichoke, asparagus, spices
Scorpio	Norway, South Africa; Fez, Morocco; Uruguay, Syria; Cincinnati and Washington, DC, USA; desert islands; anywhere near water, stinking pools, muddy swamps, quagmires, marshes; caves, ruins near water, moors, gardens, orchards, vineyards, kitchens, larders, washhouses, battlefields; places where vermin and reptiles breed or rubbish is stored	Horehound, blackberry leaves, milk thistle, horseradish, toadflax, wormwood, sarsaparilla, black cohosh, blue cohosh, aloe vera, milk thistle, cascara sagrada, cramp bark, dong quai, ginseng, pennyroyal, raspberry leaf, senna, saw palmetto, squaw vine, false unicorn	Beans, onions, leeks, heather, charlock, horehound, wormwood, meat; spicy, pungent and strong-tasting foods
Sagittarius	China, India, Spain, South Africa, Arabia, Madagascar; Sydney, Australia; Stuttgart, Germany; Tuscany, Italy; Toronto, Canada; anywhere foreign; stables, great houses, fields, hills and high places; fireplaces in upper rooms	Dandelion, horsetail, mandrake, wild yam, agrimony, red clover, burdock, oak	Asparagus, mulberry, tomato, currants, sultanas, bilberries, grapefruit, chicory; vegetables with bulbs
Capricorn	India, Afghanistan, Mexico, Macedonia; Orkney, Shetland; Greece and the former Yugoslavia; Brussels, Belgium; Oxford, England; mountains, hills and high, barren and rocky places; low and dark places, quarries, storehouses, sheep and cow pens, dunghills, thresholds, toolhouses, old lumber piles, fallow fields, thorny places	Comfrey, sarsaparilla, white oak, wintergreen, rue, horsetail, slipper elm, thuja, shepherd's purse, fumitory, thyme	Onions, meat, salted nuts, potatoes, beets, barley, malt, starchy foods, quinces, spinach
Aquarius	Poland, Croatia, Scandinavia, Russia, Siberia; Los Angeles, USA; Ethiopia; the hippie trail; hilly and uneven places; places for machinery, quarries where minerals are extracted, vineyards, wells, recently cultivated ground, springs and conduits; windows, roofs and eves; surgeries and lecture rooms	Snakeroot, southernwood, prickly ash, chamomile, catnip, passion flower, skullcap, lady's slipper, valerian, hops	Peppers, chillies; foods with sharp, distinctive flavours; health foods
Pisces	Portugal, Sahara, Scandinavia; Normandy, France; Lisbon and Seville, Spain; Vermont and Hollywood, USA; Alexandria, Egypt; Warsaw, Poland; Jerusalem; watery places of all kinds, especially marshes, the sea or where springs flow; fishponds and places where waterfowl breed, watermills, houses near water, cisterns, well or pump houses, dams, moats, old hermitages	Goldenseal, myrrh, chaparral, echinacea, eyebright, mugwort, kava kava, Irish moss (sea lettuce)	Figs, fruit; vegetables with a high water content

ALCHEMY

There are various origins ascribed to the word 'alchemy': from the Arabic ***al-kimiya*** or ***al-khimiy***, meaning 'gold'; or from the Coptic ***al-khemt***, referring to the Black Arts of Egypt – in this case the transmutation of gold and silver. Up to the 18th century alchemy was mainstream science. Isaac Newton, for example, devoted more time to writing about alchemy than he did to either optics or physics. Other eminent alchemists of the Western world were John Dee, Roger Bacon, St Thomas Aquinas, Tycho Brahe, Thomas Browne and Carl Jung. Jung felt that there was an inner meaning to alchemical symbolism, and from it he devised a spiritual path using techniques that came directly from the magickal traditions.[24]

In medieval times one could be an astrologer without having any interest in alchemy, but the reverse was never true. Astrology was a fundamental aspect of all alchemical studies. The following table from a modern school of alchemy shows how the two disciplines can be married, and how we might create something from the union.

Correspondences of Astrology and Numerology[25]

OPERATION	PLANET	DAY OF THE WEEK	PLANETARY INFLUENCE	ZODIAC SIGN	NUMEROLOGY	NOTE
Calcination	Saturn	Saturday	Limitation, suppression of emotions	Aries, Sagittarius	Monad	Do
Dissolution	Jupiter	Thursday	Expansion, creation of sociality, humility	Cancer	Dyad	Re
Separation	Mars	Tuesday	Assertiveness, driving energy	Scorpio	Triad	Mi
Conjunction	Venus (Earth, Sun)	Friday	Pleasure, love, freeing of emotions, confidence	Taurus	Tetrad	Fa
Fermentation	Mercury (Venus)	Wednesday	Increased consciousness, inspiration	Leo, Capricorn	Pentad	So
Distillation	Moon (Mercury)	Monday	Purification of instincts, wisdom	Virgo, Libra	Hexad	La
Coagulation	Sun (Moon)	Sunday	Vitality, true individuality	Gemini, Pisces, Aquarius	Heptad	Ti

HINDU ASTROLOGY

Astrology was never a purely Western preoccupation. In Hindu mythology the nine planets are referred to as the ***Navagraha*** and are believed to have a profound impact on the individual. ***Nava*** means 'nine' and ***graha*** means 'planet', but also literally 'to grab'. The study of these planets along with ***Rahu*** (ascending mode) and ***Ketu*** (descending mode) is the essence of Vedic astrology. In addition to the nine planets there are 27 ***nakshatras***, through which the Moon passes, plus the 12 zodiacal signs – all of which are regarded as deities. There is also the Hindu concept of Seven Rays, which had great prominence within the Theosophical and magickal schemes of the early 20th century and is still used extensively today.

The Navagraha

PLANET	RULING DEITY	OVER-RULER	STONE
Surya – Sun	Agni – god of fire	Shiva	Red ruby
Soma – Moon	Apas – water goddess	Parvati	Moonstone
Mangal – Mars	Bhumi – earth goddess	Skanda	Red coral
Buddha – Mercury	Vishnu – the preserver	Vishnu	Emerald
Brihaspati – Jupiter	Indra – king of the gods	Brahma	Yellow topaz
Sukra – Venus	Indrani – queen of the gods	Indra	Diamond
Shani – Saturn	Yama – god of death	Prajapati	Black stones
Rahu – Dragon's Head	Durga – goddess of power	Sarpa	Hessonite
Ketu – Dragon's Tail	Chitragupta – god of karma	Brahma	Cat's eye

The Seven Rays

NUMBER	RAY	PURPOSE
1	Sun (Sushumna)	Determines the status of an individual
2	Moon (Hariesh)	Determines the level of wisdom that an individual will have
3	Mercury (Visvakaran)	Determines the level of intellect
4	Mars (Visvatyarchas)	Determines the physical and scientific tendencies
5	Jupiter (Sannaddha)	Determines the religious observance
6	Saturn (Sarvavasu)	Determines the implementation of ideas and plans
7	Venus (Svaraj)	Determines the level of harmony and comfort in life

CHINESE ASTROLOGY

If Western astrologers were drawn to the ecliptic (the path of the Sun across the sky), the earliest Chinese astrologers were drawn to the circumpolar stars. Indeed, because the circumpolar stars are seen all year round, the Chinese empire saw itself as the counterpart on Earth of the Middle Kingdom of Heaven, the region of the stars that never set. The Emperor, necessarily representing the Pole Star, sat facing south to give audiences; and his astrologers used a system of four 'palaces'. It was only in the 1st century CE that the ecliptic was given a name in Chinese: 'The Yellow Road', as opposed to the equator, which was known as 'The Red Road'.

Calculated to be almost 5,000 years old, the Chinese zodiac is widely known for the animal names attached to each year. These were later additions, however, and the original system was based on the theory of the 12 Earth Branches, governed by the 12-year lunar cycle.[26] The correspondences with Western astrological signs are shown in the table below.

Just as the 12 signs of the Western zodiac can be grouped according to their elements, so the cycle of 12 Earth Branches can be divided into four Triangles of Affinity. The 24 hours of the day are divided into 12 segments of ascendant hours, each of which is governed by one of the Earth Branches. From this, the personality types most likely to be incompatible can be worked out (see the Circle of Conflict opposite).

THE 12 EARTH BRANCHES AND WESTERN CORRESPONDENCES

BRANCH NUMBER	BRANCH NAME	ANIMAL NAME	PERSONALITY TYPE	SAYING	WESTERN SIGN
1	Zi	Rat	Initiator	'I do'	Sagittarius
2	Chou	Ox	Enforcer	'I will'	Capricorn
3	Yin	Tiger	Idealist	'I feel'	Aquarius
4	Mao	Rabbit	Conformist	'I comply'	Pisces
5	Chen	Dragon	Visionary	'I see'	Aries
6	Si	Snake	Strategist	'I plan'	Taurus
7	Wu	Horse	Adventurer	'I act'	Gemini
8	Wei	Sheep	Peacemaker	'I love'	Cancer
9	Shen	Monkey	Innovator	'I think'	Leo
10	You	Rooster	Administrator	'I count'	Virgo
11	Xu	Dog	Guardian	'I watch'	Libra
12	Hai	Boar	Unifier	'I join'	Scorpio

The Triangles of Affinity

Affinity	Animal Signs
Triangle of Doers	Rat, Dragon, Monkey
Triangle of Thinkers	Ox, Snake, Rooster
Triangle of Protectors	Tiger, Horse, Dog
Triangle of Compatibility	Rabbit, Sheep, Boar

The Ascendant Hours

Branch Number	Branch Number	Animal	Ascendant Hours
1	Zi	Rat	11 pm–1 am
2	Chou	Ox	1 am–3 am
3	Yin	Tiger	3 am–5 am
4	Mao	Rabbit	5 am–7 am
5	Chen	Dragon	7 am–9 am
6	Si	Snake	9 am–11 am
7	Wu	Horse	11 am–1 pm
8	Wei	Sheep	1 pm–3 pm
9	Shen	Monkey	3 pm–5 pm
10	You	Rooster	5 pm–7 pm
11	Xu	Dog	7 pm–9 pm
12	Hai	Boar	9 pm–11 pm

The Circle of Conflict

Animal	Opposes	Animal
1: Rat	opposes	7: Horse
2: Ox	opposes	8: Sheep
3: Tiger	opposes	9: Monkey
4: Rabbit	opposes	10: Rooster
5: Dragon	opposes	11: Dog
6: Snake	opposes	12: Boar
7: Horse	opposes	1: Rat
8: Sheep	opposes	2: Ox
9: Monkey	opposes	3: Tiger
10: Rooster	opposes	4: Rabbit
11: Dog	opposes	5: Dragon
12: Boar	opposes	6: Snake

LUNAR ASTROLOGY

It is a sad fact that today many astrologers study their art from the safety and comfort of their living rooms and have rarely gone out at night to look at the constellations and heavenly bodies. The one thing no one can avoid, however, is the Moon.

Important though planetary astrology was to all of the foregoing, there is almost a sub-branch of correspondences that show special reverence for the Moon. In fact, there are aspects of our consciousness that resonate to the primeval energies of Moon Magick, which dominated the awareness of our remotest ancestors. And there are certain dates that are crucial for invoking such energies, thus enabling the magician to align with the circuit of cosmic forces.

The table below shows the recognized modern pagan festivals that form what might be termed the 'Wheel of the Year'. This is followed by a thumbnail sketch of preliminary considerations for magical work during these particular festivals. Use these as points of reference to stimulate your own ideas and start relating to the seasons in your own terms.

Samhain

Samhain marked the end of harvest and the beginning of the Celtic and Wiccan New Year. Pronounced *sow-in*, the word is Gaelic for 'summer's end'. It heralds the beginning of winter and the long nights. The eve of *Samhain*, known universally as Hallowe'en, is regarded as the time when the veil between the worlds is at its thinnest. During *Samhain* celebrations the Celts acknowledged the beginning and end of all things. The principal goddess figure is that of the Crone, known in the Scottish Highlands as the *Cailleach Bheur* – the blue-faced hag, the queen of winter and the keeper of wisdom and mysteries. This is the time to plant the seed of new projects and let them germinate in the darkness. It is also the time to let go of old issues and bad compulsions.

Druidic Festivals and the Eight Sabbats of Modern Witches

FESTIVAL	DATE[27]
Yule, Winter Solstice	c.19–22 December
Imbolc, Oimelc, Candlemas	c.31 January/1 February
Ostara, Alban Eiler, Mean Earraigh, Spring Equinox	c.19–22 March
Beltaine, May Day	c.31 April/1 May
Litha, Alban Heruin, Mean Samradh, Summer Solstice	c.19–22 June
Lughnasadh, Lammas	c.31 July/1 August
Mabon, Alban Elved, Mean Foghamar, Autumnal Equinox	c.19–22 September
Samhain, Hallowe'en, Hallowstide	c.31 October/1 November

Beltaine

The name originates from the Celtic sun god, Bel – the 'bright one' – and *beal-tainn*, meaning 'bright fire'. This is the beginning of the warm, expansive months of the year when the days grow longer and the hawthorn blossoms. The goddess figure is that of the Maiden – the May queen, May bride, goddess of spring, flower bride, queen of the faeries: a symbol of purity, growth and renewal.

The modern Wiccan tradition of 'hand-fasting', when a couple's hands are ritually bound together to symbolize their union, generally takes place under the full moon nearest this date.

Imbolc

Imbolc, or *Oimelc*, referred to the lactation of ewes – the flow of milk heralding the return of the life-giving forces of spring. It was also a reference to the goddess Brigid, who in Gaelic mythology was seen as wet-nurse to Jesus, as well as goddess of the hearth fire. The Catholic Church later replaced this festival with Candlemas Day, which is dedicated to the Virgin Mary and features candlelight processions. Brigid the light-bringer can be invoked equally well by pagans and Christians.

Lughnasadh

Sacred to the sun god Lugh, *Lughnasadh* marked the beginning of the harvest season and was therefore a festival of celebrating Mother Earth and the abundance of nature. *Lughnasadh* translates as 'funeral feast of Lugh'. This was the time when the corn king was symbolically sacrificed to ensure that by his felling (as the corn and produce of the fields was being cut) the people would be fed in the coming months of darkness. The festivals lasted for one month, and aside from three days of religious rituals, the celebrations were a time for contests of strength and skill. The alternative name is *Lammas*, from the Saxon 'loaf mass'.

It marks the time when the fruits of the earth are cut and stored for the forthcoming winter months, a time of thanksgiving when we should reap the rewards of what we have sown and look to consolidate our position before the coming dark half of the year.

Festival Associations

EVENT	INCENSE	COLOURS	GEMSTONES
Yule	Rosemary, pine, cedar	Green, red, gold, white	Ruby, rose quartz
Imbolc	Basil	Pink, red, brown	Amethyst, onyx, garnet
Spring Equinox	Jasmine, rose, sage	Pale green, yellow	Jasper, bloodstone
Beltaine	Lilac, frankincense	Dark green hues	All dark green stones
Midsummer	Lemon, myrrh	Blue, green, gold, red	Yellow citrine, topaz
Lughnasadh	Sandalwood	Orange, dark red	Citrine, peridot, garnet
Autumn Equinox	Sage, myrrh	Autumnal colours	Lapis lazuli, sapphire
Samhain	Apple, mint, nutmeg	Black, crimson, silver	Onyx, jet

Phases of the Moon

Successful magic depends on timing the spells and rituals with the phases of the Moon. Obviously the waxing moon is the best time to do a spell for growth or begin new projects, while a waning moon is the time to do spells to banish evil influences, lessen or remove obstacles and illness, neutralize enemies and remove harm. From full moon to new moon is the waning phase when the Moon seems to disappear; it is sometimes called the 'dark of the moon' or black moon. Then the Moon starts to grow once again towards fullness.

The three days after the new moon are the most powerful times to work spells for growth and beginnings, which should manifest at the full moon. The days just before the full moon are the most powerful times for fruition and completion. The black moon is the most auspicious time for banishing and neutralizing spells. Remember that even though the Moon looks full in the sky for two or three nights, it is only full at the exact time posted on any lunar calendar; anything after that time is a waning influence. Do your full-moon ritual just before the exact time listed. (The first quarter is the point between the new moon and the full moon; the last quarter is the midpoint between the full moon and new moon.)

This can all be fine-tuned by consideration of the daylight hours and hours of darkness. The planet that rules the day also rules the first hour after sunrise, and the succeeding hours of daylight are controlled by the other planets in the following order: Sun, Venus, Mercury, Moon, Saturn, Jupiter, Mars.

The Phases of the Moon

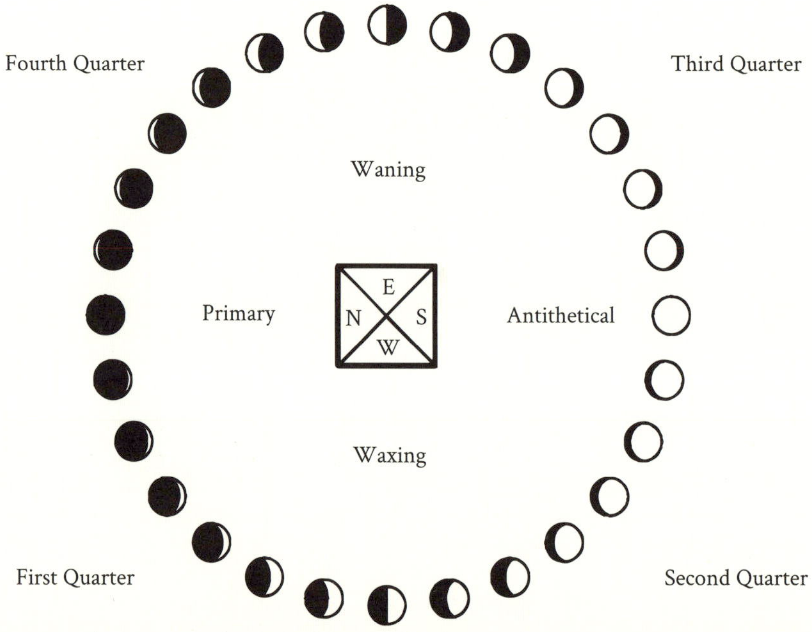

At sunset a different order applies. The first hour after sunset is ruled by the planet fifth in line from the day's own planet:

- The first hour after sunset on a Sunday is ruled by Jupiter
- The first hour after sunset on a Monday is ruled by Venus
- The first hour after sunset on a Tuesday is ruled by Saturn
- The first hour after sunset on a Wednesday is ruled by Sun
- The first hour after sunset on a Thursday is ruled by Moon
- The first hour after sunset on a Friday is ruled by Mars
- The first hour after sunset on a Saturday is ruled by Mercury

The next sunrise marks the start of the new day.

One person who went into rather more detail about the individual phases of the Moon and their potential for influencing the world was Francis Barrett, (c.1770–1830), who delved into the *Three Books of Occult Philosophy* by Cornelius Agrippa and, in 1801, offered the following interpretations in Book Two of his own classic work *The Magus*. Although he was using language and concerns from the heyday of a turbulent maritime empire, with its references to sailors and captives, it can be easily tailored and adapted to modern usage (see pages 124–125); the term 'mansion' simply refers to one of the Moon's four quarters.

Anyone wanting to increase their harvests – in any sense – would choose the 28th phase of the Moon, *Albotham*; they would devise their own system of correspondences involving angels and/or deities, create sigils that were appropriate to the endeavour and planet, involve the elemental forces and launch their pleas towards the inner worlds, using the words of power that they had devised or researched.

Arabic and Hindu Associations

Another lunar table – which is derived from the work of Abenragel (c.1000 CE) and Dorotheus Sidonius (c.100 CE), drawing on Arabic scholars and balancing it with comments from the Indian *nakshatras* (see page 117) – can be used for additional insights (see pages 126–131).

Mathers's and Agrippa's Correspondences

It was Samuel Mathers's translation of the legendary tome *The Greater Key of Solomon* that kick-started a whole new era of correspondences. Subtitled 'A Clear and Precise Exposition of King Solomon's Secret Procedure, Its Mysteries and Magic Rites, Original Plates, Seals, Charms and Talismans', the book gives a table of the magical names of the hours, and of the angels who rule them, commencing at the first hour after midnight of each day and ending at the ensuing midnight; the 24 rows therefore relate to the 24 hours of the day and to the 24 opportunities to access its energies (see page 132).

However, in practical terms the best authority, from whom most later magicians derived their material (and who is still clear and accessible today), was Cornelius Agrippa, whose *Occult Philosophy*, written in 1533, proved something of a benchmark. His table of the phases of the Moon appears on pages 133–137.

How and when you start your magickal work, and what authority you use, is a matter of individual choice. There is no 'wrong' way or time. But by aligning yourself with the ideas of one of the authorities cited, you are telling your unconscious that this is a serious business, and not simply haphazard. You are giving it every chance to make it work. Have confidence in your own choices. The very act of making them ensures that they will be right for you.

MANSIONS IN THE FIRST QUARTER OF HEAVEN

MANSION NUMBER	MANSION NAME	INTERPRETATION
1	Alnath	Discord and journeys
2	Allothaim	Finding of treasures
3	Achaomazon	Profitable to sailors, huntsmen and alchemists
4	Aldebaram	Causes the destruction and hindrances of buildings, fountains, wells, gold mines; the flight of creeping things; begets discord
5	Alchatay	Helps to return from a journey; assists the instruction of scholars; confirms edifices; gives health and goodwill
6	Alhanna	Conducive to hunting, the besieging of towns and the revenge of princes; destroys harvests and fruits, and hinders the operation of the physician
7	Aldimiach	Confers gain and friendship; profitable to lovers; scares flies, destroys magistracies

MANSIONS IN THE SECOND QUARTER OF HEAVEN

MANSION NUMBER	MANSION NAME	INTERPRETATION
8	Alnaza	Love, friendship and the society of fellow travellers; drives away and afflicts captives
9	Archaam	Hinders harvests and travellers, and puts discord between men
10	Algelioche	Strengthens buildings; yields love, benevolence and help against enemies
11	Azobra	Good for voyages and gain by merchandise; also for the redemption of captives
12	Alzarpha	Gives prosperity to harvests, but hinders seamen; good for the bettering of servants, captives and companions
13	Alhaire	Benevolence, gain, voyages, harvests and the freedom of captives
14	Achureth	Causes the love of married folks; cures the sick; profitable to sailors, but hinders journeys by land

MANSIONS IN THE THIRD QUARTER OF HEAVEN

MANSION NUMBER	MANSION NAME	INTERPRETATION
15	Agrapha	Profitable for the extracting of treasures and the digging of pits; assists divorce, discord and the destruction of houses and enemies; hinders travellers
16	Azubene	Hinders journeys and wedlock, harvests and merchandise; prevails for the redemption of captives
17	Alchil	Betters a bad fortune; makes love durable; strengthens buildings; helps seamen
18	Alchas	Causes discord, sedition, conspiracy against princes and mighty ones and revenge from enemies; frees captives; helps edifices
19	Allatha	Assists in the besieging of cities and taking of towns, and in the driving of men from their places, the destruction of seamen and the perdition of captives
20	Abnahaya	Helps in the taming of wild beasts and the strengthening of prisons; destroys the wealth of societies; compels a man to come to a certain place
21	Abeda	Good for harvests, gain, buildings and travellers; causes divorce

MANSIONS IN THE FOURTH QUARTER OF HEAVEN

MANSION NUMBER	MANSION NAME	INTERPRETATION
22	Sadahacha	Promotes the flight of servants and captives, that they may escape; helps the curing of diseases
23	Zabadola	Good for divorce, the liberty of captives and the health of the sick
24	Sadabath	Prevalent for the benevolence of married people and the victory of soldiers; harms the execution of government and prevents it being exercised
25	Sadalabra	Favours besieging and revenge; destroys enemies; causes divorce; confirms prisons and buildings; hastens messengers; conducive to spells against copulation, and so binds every member of the human race, that it cannot perform its duty
26	Alpharg	Causes union; good for the health of captives; destroys buildings and prisons
27	Alcharya	Increases harvests, revenues and gain; heals infirmities, but hinders buildings; prolongs prisons; causes danger to seamen; helps to confer mischief on those whom you shall please
28	Albotham	Increases harvests and merchandise; secures travellers through dangerous places; makes for the joy of married couples; strengthens prisons; causes the loss of treasures

Sidonius's Correspondences

DAY OF THE MOON	ARABIC NAME	STARTING DEGREE	HINDU ANALYSES	DOROTHEUS SIDONIUS
1	Al Sharatain	0° 0' 0" Aries	Good for taking medicines, pasturing livestock, making journeys, except the second hour	Good for buying tame animals, for journeys, especially voyages, for making arms, planting trees, cutting hair or nails, putting on new clothes; bad for contracting marriage (holds for the Moon in Aries), making partnerships or buying slaves, who will be bad, disobedient or run away; if captured, prison will be bad and strong
2	Al Butain	12° 11' 26" Aries	Good for sowing and making journeys	Bad for marriage, buying slaves and for boats and prisoners similar to Alnath
3	Al Thurayya	25° 22' 52" Aries	Good for trading and revenge on enemies; indifferent for travel	Good for buying tame animals and hunting, for all matters involving fire and for doing good; bad for marriage and making partnerships, especially with those who are more powerful; bad for buying cattle or flocks, for planting trees, sowing or putting on new clothes; if captured, prison will be strong and long; water journeys will bring fear and danger
4	Al Dabaran	8° 34' 18" Taurus	Good for sowing, putting on new clothes, receiving women and feminine things, demolishing a building or starting a new one, and for making a journey, except for the third part of the day	Good for building a house, which will be solid, and building in general, for digging a ditch, buying slaves, who will be loyal and honest, and buying livestock; also good for being with kings and lords, and for receiving power or honours; bad for contracting marriage, since woman will prefer another, or for entering partnerships, especially with those more powerful; voyages will involve big waves; if captured, the captivity will be long but, if captured for skills, will involve release through goodwill
5	Al Hak'ah	21° 45' 44" Taurus	Good for contracting marriage, for putting boys to study laws, scriptures or writing, for making medicines or making a journey	Good for buying slaves, who will be good and loyal, for building, travel by water, washing the head (indeed, general washing) and cutting hair; bad for partnerships; if captured, imprisonment will be long, unless captured for skills, when escape will occur

DAY OF THE MOON	ARABIC NAME	STARTING DEGREE	HINDU ANALYSES	DOROTHEUS SIDONIUS
6	Al Han'ah	4° 17' 10" Gemini	Good for kings to declare war, the enrolment of armies and cavalry, for knights seeking better pay, the successful siege of a city, smiting enemies and evil-doers; bad for sowing, seeking a loan or burial	Good for partnerships and ventures; associates will agree and be honest and loyal; good for hunting and journeys by water, though delays will occur; bad for taking medicine and treating wounds; new clothes put on will soon tear; if captured, release within three days or very long imprisonment
7	Al Dhira	17° 36' 36" Gemini	Good for ploughing and sowing, for putting on new clothes, for women's jewellery, for cavalry; bad for journeys, except in the last third of the night	Good for partnerships, which will be beneficial and useful, with loyal and agreeable associates; good for washing the head, cutting hair and new clothes, for buying slaves and livestock, smiting or making peace with enemies, voyages towards a destination, but delays on return; bad for buying land and for giving up medicine; if captured, unless escape occurs in three days, will die in prison; likewise, if escaping something feared, it will be encountered again
8	Al Nathra	0° 0' 0" Cancer	Good for taking medicine, for cutting new clothes, for women's jewellery and putting it on; rain will bring benefit, not damage; bad for travel, except for the last third of the night	Good for voyages, swift on the outward and return journeys; marriages contracted will be harmonious for a while, then discordant; a slave bought will be deceitful, will accuse his master and run away; a partnership started will involve fraud on either side; if captured, long imprisonment
9	Al Tarf	12° 11' 26" Cancer	Bad for sowing, journeys, entrusting anything to anyone or seeking to harm anyone	Good for voyages, both outward and return, for reinforcing doors and making locks, making beds and putting up bed-curtains, and transplanting wheat; bad for partnerships, which will involve fraud on either side; bad for cutting hair or new clothes; putting on new clothes may lead to drowning in them; if captured, long imprisonment
10	Al Jabhah	25° 22' 52" Cancer	Good for contracting marriage, for sugar and what is made with it; bad for journeys and entrusting anything, for putting on new clothes or for women's jewellery	Good for buildings, which will last, and for partnerships, benefiting all parties; if captured, at the command of a leader or because of great deed, a long, hard imprisonment

DAY OF THE MOON	ARABIC NAME	STARTING DEGREE	HINDU ANALYSES	DOROTHEUS SIDONIUS
11	Al Zubrah	8° 34' 18" Leo	Good for sowing and planting, for besieging; indifferent for trade and journeys; bad for freeing captives	Good for buildings and foundations, which will last, and for partnerships, from which associates will gain; good for cutting hair; bad for new clothes; if captured, at the command of a leader, long imprisonment
12	Al Sarfah	21° 45' 44" Leo	Good for starting all building, for arranging lands, sowing and planting, marriage, putting on new clothes, women's jewellery and for making a journey in the first third of the day	Good for buying slaves and livestock, once the Moon is out of Leo, since the Lion is a great devourer (if he eats a lot, it leads to stomach pains, power, boldness and obstinacy); what is lent will not be returned, or only with great effort and delay; voyages will be long, hard and dangerous, but not fatal
13	Al Awwa	4° 17' 10" Virgo	Good for ploughing, sowing, making a journey, marrying, freeing captives	Good for buying a slave, who will be loyal and honest, for starting building, giving oneself to pleasures and jokes, coming before a king or famous man, taking medicines, cutting new clothes, washing or cutting hair; not bad for marrying a corrupted woman and, if marrying a virgin, the marriage will last a while; a voyage undertaken will involve delay in the return; if captured, will be injured in prison, but captivity will end well
14	Al Simak	17° 36' 36" Virgo	Good for marrying a woman who is not a virgin, for medicines, sowing and planting; bad for journeys or entrusting something to someone	Good for starting a voyage and a partnership, which will be profitable and harmonious, for buying a slave, who will be good, honest and respectful; marriage with a virgin will not last long, and it is not bad to marry a corrupted woman; if captured, will soon escape or be released
15	Al Ghafr	0° 0' 0" Libra	Good for digging wells and ditches, curing illnesses to do with wind, but not others; bad for journeys	Good for moving house, for adapting or preparing a house, its owner and site; good for seeking to do a good deed, buying and selling, but selling slaves not livestock, because Libra is a human sign; bad for both land and sea journeys; marriage will not last in harmony, or only for a while; partnerships entered into will lead to fraud and discord; money lent will not be returned; bad for cutting hair

DAY OF THE MOON	ARABIC NAME	STARTING DEGREE	HINDU ANALYSES	DOROTHEUS SIDONIUS
16	Al Jubana	12° 11' 26" Libra	Bad for journeys, trade, medicines, sowing, women's jewellery, cutting or putting on new clothes	A slave bought will be good, loyal and honest; bad for marriage, which will only last in harmony for a while; bad for partnerships, which will lead to dishonesty and mutual suspicion; if captured, will soon be out of prison, if God wills
17	Iklil al Jabhah	25° 22' 52" Libra	Good for buying flocks and livestock, changing their pasture, putting on new jewellery and besieging towns	Good for starting building, which will be solid and durable, for settling a dispute between two people, fostering love, and love begun will be absolutely solid and last for ever; good for all medicine; voyages started will bring anxiety and sorrows, but survival; partnerships started will bring discord, and he who marries will find his wife impure; bad for selling slaves or cutting hair
18	Al Kalb	8° 34' 18" Scorpio	Good for building, arranging lands and buying them, receiving honours and power; if it begins to rain, it will be wholesome, useful and good; eastward journeys are favoured	Building undertaken will be solid; good for planting and taking medicines; if a man gets married and Mars is with the Moon here, he will find her not to be a virgin; if he enters a ship he will come out again; bad for selling slaves, new clothes and cutting hair; partnerships will result in discord
19	Al Shaula	21° 45' 44" Scorpio	Good for besieging towns and encampments, disputing against enemies, making a journey, sowing and for planting trees; bad for entrusting something to somebody	If a man gets married, he will find her not to be a virgin; bad for voyages, which will end in shipwreck, and for partnerships, which will be discordant; bad for selling slaves, and very bad for a captive
20	Al Na'am	4° 17' 10" Sagittarius	Good for buying animals; rain will be good and do no harm; indifferent for journeys	Good for buying small animals; bad for partnerships and captivity

DAY OF THE MOON	ARABIC NAME	STARTING DEGREE	HINDU ANALYSES	DOROTHEUS SIDONIUS
21	Al Baldah	17° 36' 36" Sagittarius	Good for starting any building, sowing, buying lands or livestock, buying and making women's jewellery and clothes; indifferent for journeys	A woman who is divorced or widowed will not marry again; indifferent for slaves bought, since they will think much of themselves and will not humble themselves to their masters
22	Al Sa'd al Dhabih	0° 0' 0" Capricorn	Good for medicine and journeys, except for the last third of the day; good for putting on new clothes	Good for entering a partnership, which will bring profit and usefulness, and for entering a ship, though there will be great anxieties from a strong desire to return and the like; a man who becomes engaged will break the engagement before the wedding and die within six months, or the couple will be in conflict and live badly, with the wife mistreating the husband; bad for buying slaves, who will do ill to their master, or run away, or be irksome or bad; if captured, will soon gain freedom
23	Al Sa'd al Bula	12° 11' 26" Capricorn	Good for medicine, for putting on new jewellery and clothes, for a journey in the middle third of the day; bad for entrusting something to someone	Good for partnerships; bad for marriage, since the wife will mistreat her husband and they will not be together much; bad for entering a ship, if a short voyage is wanted, and for buying slaves; if captured, will soon regain liberty
24	Al Sa'd al Su'ud	25° 22' 52" Capricorn	Good for medicine, sending out armies and soldiers; indifferent for journeys; bad for merchandise, jewellery, putting on new clothes, marrying	A slave bought will be strong, loyal and good; bad for partnerships, which will end in great harm and conflict, and for entering a ship; marriage will only last a while; if captured, will soon be free
25	Al Sa'd al Ahbiyah	8° 34' 18" Aquarius	Good for besieging towns and encampments, for going into a quarrel, pursuing enemies and doing them harm, sending messengers; favours journeys southwards; bad for marriage, for sowing, merchandise, buying livestock	Good for buying slaves, who will be strong, loyal and good; for building, which will be solid and durable; and for voyages, though there will be delays; marriage will only last for a while; bad for partnerships, which will end harmfully, and a slave will escape

DAY OF THE MOON	ARABIC NAME	STARTING DEGREE	HINDU ANALYSES	DOROTHEUS SIDONIUS
26	Al Fargh al Mukdim	21° 45' 44" Aquarius	Good for making a journey in the first third of the day, but the rest is good for neither journeys nor any other beginning	Good for building, which will be solid and durable; for buying a slave, who will be loyal and good; for entering a ship, though there will be delays; bad for partnerships; marriage will not last; if captured, will be in prison for a long time
27	Al Fargh al Thani	4° 17' 10" Pisces	Good for sowing, and useful for trading; good for marriage; indifferent for journeys, except for the middle third of the night, when very bad; bad for entrusting something to someone, or lending anything	If starting a partnership, it will begin well, but end in harm and conflict; entering a ship will bring damage, dangers and travails; a slave bought will be bad; if captured, will not leave prison
28	Al Batn al Hut	17° 36' 36" Pisces	Good for trade, sowing and medicines; good for marriage; indifferent for journeys, except for the middle third of the night, when bad; bad for entrusting something to someone or lending anything	A partnership started will begin well, but end badly; a slave bought will be bad, irascible and very proud; if captured, will not leave prison

Magical Names of the Hours

HOURS	SUNDAY	MONDAY	TUESDAY	WEDNESDAY	THURSDAY	FRIDAY	SATURDAY
1 Yayn	Raphael	Sachiel	Anael	Cassiel	Michael	Gabriel	Zamael
2 Yanor	Gabriel	Zamael	Raphael	Sachiel	Anael	Cassiel	Michael
3 Nasnia	Cassiel	Michael	Gabriel	Zamael	Raphael	Sachiel	Anael
4 Salla	Sachiel	Anael	Cassiel	Michael	Gabriel	Zamael	Raphael
5 Sadedali	Raphael	Sachiel	Anael	Cassiel	Michael	Gabriel	Zamael
6 Thamur	Michael	Gabriel	Zamael	Raphael	Sachiel	Anael	Cassiel
7 Ourer	Anael	Cassiel	Michael	Gabriel	Zamael	Raphael	Sachiel
8 Thainé	Raphael	Sachiel	Anael	Cassiel	Michael	Gabriel	Zamael
9 Neron	Gabriel	Zamael	Raphael	Sachiel	Anael	Cassiel	Michael
10 Yayon	Cassiel	Michael	Gabriel	Zamael	Raphael	Sachiel	Anael
11 Abai	Sachiel	Anael	Cassiel	Michael	Gabriel	Zamael	Raphael
12 Nathalon	Raphael	Sachiel	Anael	Cassiel	Michael	Gabriel	Zamael
1 Beron	Michael	Gabriel	Zamael	Raphael	Sachiel	Anael	Cassiel
2 Barol	Anael	Cassiel	Michael	Gabriel	Zamael	Raphael	Sachiel
3 Thanu	Raphael	Sachiel	Anael	Cassiel	Michael	Gabriel	Zamael
4 Athor	Gabriel	Zamael	Raphael	Sachiel	Anael	Cassiel	Michael
5 Mathon	Cassiel	Michael	Gabriel	Zamael	Raphael	Sachiel	Anael
6 Rana	Sachiel	Anael	Cassiel	Michael	Gabriel	Zamael	Raphael
7 Netos	Zamael	Raphael	Sachiel	Anael	Cassiel	Michael	Gabriel
8 Tafrac	Michael	Gabriel	Zamael	Raphael	Sachiel	Anael	Cassiel
9 Sassur	Anael	Cassiel	Michael	Gabriel	Zamael	Raphael	Sachiel
10 Agla	Raphael	Sachiel	Anael	Cassiel	Michael	Gabriel	Zamael
11 Caerra	Gabriel	Zamael	Raphael	Sachiel	Anael	Cassiel	Michael
12 Salam	Cassiel	Michael	Gabriel	Zamael	Raphael	Sachiel	Anael

Agrippa's Phases of the Moon

Day of the Moon	Name	Meaning of Name	Starting Degree	Significance	Talisman For	With Image Of
1	Alnath	Horns of Aries	0° Aries	Journeys and discord	The destruction of someone	A black man in a garment made of hair and girdled round, casting a small lance with his right hand
2	Albothaim	Belly of Aries	12° 51' 22" Aries	Finding treasure and retaining captives	Reconciliation with a prince	A king crowned
3	Achaomazone Athoraye	Rainy ones or Pleiades	25° 42' 51" Aries	Profits sailors, huntsmen, alchemists	Happy fortune and every good thing	A woman well clothed, sitting in a chair, her right hand being lifted up on her head
4	Aldebram Aldelamen	Eye or head of Taurus	8° 34' 17" Taurus	Destruction and hindrances of buildings, fountains, wells and gold mines; the flight of reptiles; creates discord	Revenge, separation, enmity and ill will	A soldier on a horse, holding a serpent in his right hand
5	Alchataya Albachaya	–	21° 25' 40" Taurus	Helps safe return from a journey, the instruction of pupils; confirms buildings; gives health and goodwill	The favour of kings and officers	The head of a man
6	Alhanna Alchaya	Little star of great light	4° 17' 09" Gemini	Favours hunting, besieging towns, the revenge of princes; destroys harvests and fruits, hinders medicine	Procuring love betwixt two	Two images embracing one another

DAY OF THE MOON	NAME	MEANING OF NAME	STARTING DEGREE	SIGNIFICANCE	TALISMAN FOR	WITH IMAGE OF
7	Aldimiach Alarzach	Arm of Gemini	17° 08' 34" Gemini	Brings money and friendship; profits lovers; disperses flies; destroys teaching authorities	Obtaining every good thing	A man well clothed, holding his hands up to heaven as if praying and supplicating
8	Alnaza Anatrachya	Misty or cloudy	0° Cancer	Creates love, friendship, travellers' fellowship; drives away mice; confirms captivity	Victory in war	An eagle with the face of a man
9	Achaam Alcharph	Eye of Leo	12° 51' 22" Cancer	Hinders harvests and travellers; creates discord between men	Causing infirmities	The image of a man wanting his privy parts, shutting his eyes with his hands
10	Algeliache Aglebh	Neck or forehead of Leo	25° 42' 51" Cancer	Strengthens buildings; extends love, goodwill and help against enemies	Facilitating child-bearing	The head of a lion
11	Azobra Ardaf	Leo's mane	8° 34' 17" Leo	Assists journeys and money from commerce, and redeeming captives	Fear, reverence and worship	A man riding a lion, holding the ear thereof in his left hand and, in his right, holding forth a bracelet of gold
12	Alzarpha	Tail of Leo	21° 25' 40" Leo	Prospers harvests and plantations; betters servants, captives and allies, but hinders sailors	The separation of lovers	A dragon fighting with a man

DAY OF THE MOON	NAME	MEANING OF NAME	STARTING DEGREE	SIGNIFICANCE	TALISMAN FOR	WITH IMAGE OF
13	Alhayre	Dogs or winged ones of Virgo	4° 17’ 09” Virgo	Favours benevolence, money, voyages, harvests, freedom of captives	The agreement of married couples and dissolving charms against copulation	A man in red wax and woman in white wax embracing
14	Achureth, Arimes, Azimeth, Albumech, Alcheymech	Virgo’s ear of corn	17° 08’ 34” Virgo	Favours marital love, healing of the sick; good for journeys by sea, but bad for land	Divorce and separation of the man from the woman	A dog biting his tail
15	Agrapha Algarpha	Covered or flying covered	0° Libra	Good for extracting treasures, digging pits; helps divorce, discord, destruction of houses and enemies; hinders travel	Friendship and goodwill	A man sitting and indicting letters
16	Azubene Ahubene	Horns of Scorpio	12° 51’ 22” Libra	Hinders journeys and marriage, harvests and commerce, but helps redemption of captives	Much merchandising	A man sitting on a chair, holding a balance in his hands
17	Alchil	Crown of Scorpio	25° 42’ 51” Libra	Improves bad fortune; helps love to last; strengthens buildings; helps sailors	Opposing thieves and robbers	An ape
18	Alchas Altoh	Heart of Scorpio	8° 34’ 17” Scorpio	Causes discord, sedition, conspiracy against the powerful, revenge from enemies; frees captives and helps buildings	Opposing fevers and pains of the belly	A snake holding his tail above his head

DAY OF THE MOON	NAME	MEANING OF NAME	STARTING DEGREE	SIGNIFICANCE	TALISMAN FOR	WITH IMAGE OF
19	Allatha, Achala, Hycula, Axala	Tail of Scorpio	21° 25’ 40” Scorpio	Helps the besieging and taking of cities, driving people from positions; destroys sailors and captives	Facilitating birth and provoking the menses	A woman holding her hands upon her face
20	Abnahaya	The beam, transom	4° 17’ 09” Sagittarius	Helps to tame beasts; strengthens prisons; destroys allies’ wealth; compels a man to come to a certain place	Hunting	Sagittary, half-man and half-horse
21	Abeda Albeldach	The desert	17° 08’ 34” Sagittarius	Favours harvests, money, buildings, travellers; causes divorce	The destruction of somebody	A man with a double countenance, before and behind
22	Sadabacha, Zodeboluch, Zandeldena	The shepherd	0° Capricorn	Incites the flight of slaves and captives, helping escape; helps the curing of diseases	The security of (that is, catching) runaways	A man with wings on his feet, bearing a helmet on his head
23	Sabadola Zobrach	Swallowing	12° 51’ 22” Capricorn	Causes divorce, the freedom of captives, healing of the sick	Destruction and wasting	A cat with a dog’s head
24	Sadabath Chadezoath	Star of fortune	25° 42’ 51” Capricorn	Helps marital understanding, the victory of soldiers; causes disobedience, hindering the execution of authority	The multiplying of herds of cattle	A woman giving suck to her son

DAY OF THE MOON	NAME	MEANING OF NAME	STARTING DEGREE	SIGNIFICANCE	TALISMAN FOR	WITH IMAGE OF
25	Sadalabra Sadalachia	The butterfly, unfolding	8° 34' 17" Aquarius	Helps siege and revenge, divorce, prisons and buildings; speeds messengers; destroys enemies; helps spells against sex or to cause impotence	The preservation of trees and harvests	A man planting
26	Alpharg Phtagal Mocaden	The first drawing, draining	21° 25' 40" Aquarius	Helps union, the love of men, health of captives; destroys prisons and buildings	Love and favour	A woman washing and combing her hair
27	Alcharya Ahhalgalmoad	The second drawing, draining	4° 17' 09" Pisces	Increases harvests, revenue and money; heals illnesses; weakens buildings; prolongs imprisonment; endangers sailors; helps to bring evil against anyone	Destroying fountains, pits, medicinal waters and baths	A winged man, holding in his hand an empty vessel, perforated
28	Albotham Alchalh	The fishes, Pisces	17° 08' 34" Pisces	Increases harvests and commerce; helps the safety of travellers in dangerous places; causes marital harmony; strengthens prisons and causes loss of treasures	Gathering fish together	A fish

Wiccan Correspondences

Modern Wiccans use evocative names for what might be termed the 'moonths' of the year: a simple list is given in the table below.

A more detailed chart has been provided by a modern Wiccan, explaining that as the full moon occurs once every 28 days, we normally have 13 full moons a year: generally one a month, plus one extra; when there is a month that contains a second full moon, that moon is called a 'blue moon'. Listed in the Expanded Celtic Correspondences table opposite are the 12 months of the year (plus a variable month) and their specific full moons, their common and tree names, along with the correspondences associated with each.

Wiccan Moon Names

MONTH	MOON	QUALITY
January	Wolf Moon	Protection, strength
February	Chaste Moon	Fertility
March	Seed Moon	Spirituality, success
April	Hare Moon	Growth, wisdom
May	Faery Moon	Love, good health
June	Mead Moon	Marriage, abundance
July	Herb Moon	Magick, strength
August	Barley Moon	Harvest, bounty
September	Wine Moon	Protection, confidence
October	Blood Moon	Stability, remembrance
November	Snow Moon	Hope, healing
December	Oak Moon	Peace, love

Expanded Celtic Correspondences

MONTH	COMMON NAMES	CELTIC TREE NAME	TYPE OF MOON	CELTIC TREE CORRESPONDENCES
January	Wolf, Cold Moon	Birch	Moon of Inception, Moon of Beginning	Protection of children, purification
February	Storm, Quickening Moon	Rowan	Moon of Vision, Astral Travel Moon	Healing, empowerment
March	Chaste Moon	Ash	Moon of Waters	Prosperity, protection, healing
April	Seed, Wind Moon	Alder	Moon of Utility, Moon of Efficacy, Moon of Self-guidance	Completeness, spirituality
May	Hare, Flower Moon	Willow	The Witches' Moon, Moon of Balance	Love, healing, protection, fertility
June	Dyad (pair), Strong Sun Moon	Hawthorn	Moon of Restraint, Moon of Hindrance	Fertility, prosperity
July	Mead, Blessing Moon	Oak	Moon of Strength, Moon of Security	All positive purposes
August	Wyrt (green plant), Corn Moon	Holly	Moon of Encirclement, Moon of Polarity	Protection, prophecy, magic for animals
September	Barley, Harvest Moon	Hazel	Moon of the Wise, Crone Moon	Manifestation, protection, fertility
October	Blood Moon	Vine	Moon of Celebration	Courage, protection, prosperity, healing, inspiration, spirituality
November	Snow, Mourning Moon	Ivy	Moon of Buoyancy, Moon of Resilience	Healing, protection, cooperation, exorcism
December	Oak, Long Night Moon	Elder	Moon of Completeness	Exorcism, prosperity, banishing, healing
(variable)	Blue Moon	Reed	Moon of the Home, Hearth Moon, Moon that Manifests Truth	Fertility, protection, love
Harvest	Nearest Mabon	–	–	–

8

MEDICAL ASTROLOGY & ITS CORRESPONDENCES

MEDIEVAL MEDICINE

In medieval times all medicine was folk medicine, combining prayer, astrology, spells, magic and what might now be termed 'faith healing'. Spells and incantations were used in conjunction with herbs and gems. The basic principle of medieval medicine was Hippocrates' theory of the humours (see page 143), which dominated all Western medicine until the 19th century. A balance of the humours could be achieved through diet, herbs and by blood-letting with leeches.

Naturally, astrology became an integral part of this system, being regarded as a profound science, in a way that the rest of medical practice was not (see page 144).

The Use of Herbs

The success of herbal remedies was ascribed to their action upon the humours within the body. The use of herbs also drew upon the Doctrine of Signatures (see page 15), which stated that God had provided some form of alleviation for every ill, and that these things – be they animal, vegetable or mineral – carried a mark or 'signature' upon them that gave an indication of their usefulness. With the expansion of the monasteries came highly developed herb gardens for use in the production of herbal cures. The Benedictine order stated that care of the sick was to be placed above and before every other duty.

One noticeable aspect of medieval medicine was the influence of female physicians. Abbess Hildegard of Bingen (1098–1179) wrote the ***Liber Simplicis Medicinae*** (Simple Book of Medicine) around 1160. Another famous woman physician was the Italian Trotula of Salerno (born c.1090), whose works on women's ailments spread across Europe, her name being anglicized in England to 'Dame Trot'.

However, the professionalization of medicine in the later medieval period, and the development of university faculties of medicine, came to exclude women from the profession almost entirely, and they tended to continue as midwives or nurses.

Culpeper's Astrological Influences and Effects

One of the true giants of the era, whose name still resonates today, was Nicholas Culpeper (1616–1654). Born in London, Culpeper wrote several books on astrology, which was then a fundamental part of the medical and scientific tradition. These included ***Opus Astrologicum*** (1654) and ***Astrological Judgement of Diseases*** (1655). But it was through his classic ***Complete Herbal*** and ***The English Physician*** that he achieved a kind of immortality, bringing a holistic viewpoint to the principles of Graeco-Arabic medicine that were extant in his time.

Equally important, he also integrated astrological knowledge with herbalism in a way that meant that every person of his time – rich or poor – would have been able to make medicinal use of plants in a simple and logical way. Culpeper used the English common names of plants rather than Latin names, and preferred to prescribe single local herbs rather than the exotic and costly imported plant materials and drugs favoured by the medical establishment of his day. In this way his poorer clients could collect their required remedies free of charge in the nearby countryside.

In medical astrology each of the seven planets provides its own unique influence towards the outcome of an illness, depending on the location of the planet in the zodiac. The 12 zodiac signs represent certain aspects of the physical body, which include specific regions and one or more organs and their functions. The 12 'houses' represent environmental or 'mundane' influences or effects. Culpeper's table of correspondences can be seen on page 145. Again, in an age of information technology and its overload, there is ample scope for someone to create a new system for the 21st century and beyond.

The Humours and Their Correspondences

HUMOUR	TEMPER	ORGAN	NATURE	ELEMENT
Black bile	Melancholic	Spleen	Cold dry	Earth
Phlegm	Phlegmatic	Lungs	Cold wet	Water
Blood	Sanguine	Heart	Warm wet	Air
Yellow bile	Choleric	Gall bladder	Warm dry	Fire

Astrological Influences

PLANET	ATTRIBUTIONS
Sun	Heart, spine, general vitality
Moon	Stomach, digestive system, female organs, lymphatic system
Mercury	Brain, central nervous system, thyroid gland, five senses, hands
Venus	Throat, kidneys, thymus gland, sense of touch, ovaries
Mars	Muscles, head, adrenal glands, sense of smell and taste
Jupiter	Liver, thighs, feet, growth, pituitary gland
Saturn	Skin, hair, teeth, bones, the body's defences, spleen
Uranus	Parathyroid gland, neural activity, aura
Neptune	Pineal gland, psychic healing
Pluto	Pancreas, metabolism, elimination

Table of Planetary Influences

PLANETS	INFLUENCES
Sun	Vital, tonic, warming and drying; relates to heart function and to vital energy
Moon	Collecting, diluting, cleansing, cold and moist, phlegmatic; relates to the emotions, fluid balance and the hormones
Mercury	Cold and dry; relates to the nervous system and to nervous activity
Venus	Relaxing, warm and moist; relates to nutrient assimilation, sugar metabolism, tissue tone and lymphatic function
Mars	Inflammatory, aggressive, eruptive, warm and dry, choleric; relates to sex drive and to oxygen metabolism
Jupiter	Expansive, nourishing, warm and moist, sanguine; relates to the blood circulation, liver and fat metabolism, and cellular nutrition
Saturn	Contracting, slowing, binding, restricting, hardening, devitalizing, cold and dry, melancholic

Culpeper's Zodiac Sign/ Body Correspondences

ZODIAC SIGN	AREAS RULED
Aries	Head, cerebrum, eyes, face, upper jaw, carotid arteries, front of the body
Taurus	Neck, ears, lower jaw, throat, cerebellum, thyroid gland
Gemini	Lungs, bronchi, trachea, shoulders, arms, hands, fingers, sympathetic nervous system
Cancer	Breast, diaphragm, stomach, oesophagus, taste, left side of the body
Leo	Heart, vena cava, back, spine, spinal cord, thymus gland
Virgo	Intestines, duodenum, Peyer's patches, solar plexus, abdomen, parasympathetic nervous system
Libra	Kidneys, ureter, adrenal glands, skin, loins, lumbar region, back of the body
Scorpio	Bladder, urethra, genitals, ovaries/testes, prostate, sigmoid colon, pubic bone, nose, haeme
Sagittarius	Hips, thighs, ilium, femur, sacrum, coccyx, ischium, blood vessels, sciatic nerves, pituitary
Capricorn	Knees, bones, teeth, skin, joints, hair, parathyroids, right side of the body
Aquarius	Lower legs, ankles, circulation, pineal body
Pisces	Feet, toes, thalamus, blood fibrin

Table of Significance of the Houses in Astrology

HOUSE	AREAS OF SIGNIFICANCE
First house	Physical body, physical appearance; personality; attitudes to health
Second house	Material circumstances; matters relating to the diet
Third house	Communication; close relatives; education; ability to adapt to and learn from situations
Fourth house	Home and immediate family; genetic influence from a parent, usually the mother
Fifth house	Romantic issues and offspring; tendency towards risk-taking; entertainment
Sixth house	Most important house for determining health; doctors, nurses and dentists; health and lifestyle
Seventh house	Partnerships; the type of people one tends to attract; compliance with treatment procedures
Eighth house	Shared resources; legacies from past illnesses and lifestyles; life expectancy
Ninth house	Philosophy, spirituality, higher education and travel; professionals sought out for advice
Tenth house	Status and reputation; career; genetic influence from a parent, usually the father
Eleventh house	Hopes and wishes; friends; sources of assistance in overcoming obstacles and illness
Twelfth house	Misfortune, worries; adversity due to ill-considered decisions; hospitals, hospices, retreats

OTHER MEDICAL/ ASTROLOGICAL CORRESPONDENCES

In the tables below, Judy Hall links individual planets with musical notes, which, when used with imagination, can have healing effects upon individual organs. The body systems can also be related to the different paths on the Tree of Life. And the neglected art and science of alchemy has its own role within the medical system, since it looks at the whole scheme of human beings from a different perspective, which modern alchemists find both valid and workable.

Hall's Musical Correspondences

PLANET	NOTE MUSICAL	PHYSIOLOGY
Sun	C	Cardiovascular system, including the heart and pericardium; back, spine, thymus, life force; hot feverish complaints
Saturn	D	Skeleton, gall bladder, spleen, skin, teeth, nails, vagus nerve, joints; secretion of bile
Mercury	E	Brain, nervous system, eyes, bronchial tubes, respiration, thyroid, thymus; organs of speech and hearing
Moon	F	Breasts, nipples; alimentary canal, digestive juices and lymphatic system; glands, regulation of fluids; sympathetic nervous system, emotional disturbances
Mars	G	Muscular and urinogenital systems, ovaries and testes, adrenals and suprarenals, red blood corpuscles, kidneys; resistance to disease, elimination of toxins
Venus	A	Throat, kidneys, lumbar region, parathyroids; venereal disorders, glandular swellings of the neck
Jupiter	B	Liver, pancreas, pituitary gland, sciatic nerve, tumours; disposition of fats, obesity and excess

Body Systems and the Tree of Life

PATH	HUMAN BODY
11	Respiratory organs
12	Cerebral and nervous system
13	Lymphatic system
14	Genital system
15	Head and face
16	Shoulders and arms
17	Lungs
18	Stomach
19	Heart
20	Back
21	Digestive system
22	Liver
23	Organs of nutrition
24	Intestines
25	Hips and thighs
26	Genital system
27	Muscular system
28	Kidneys, bladder
29	Legs and feet
30	Circulatory system
31	Organs of circulation
32	Excretory system

Correspondences of Physiological Alchemy[28]

Operation	Chakra	Physiological Action	Spectral Position	Gemstones	Healing Effects
Calcination	Muladhara (physical, instinctual, Lead Chakra)	Sacrum, anus, gonads, thick mucus	Infrared, dark red	Garnet, red jasper, haematite, obsidian	Courage, strength, grounding
Dissolution	Svadhisthana (sexuality, sociality, Tin Chakra)	Genitals, spleen, lungs, black bile	Orange	Carnelian, fire opal	Warm energy, fertility
Separation	Manipura (will, intellect, Iron Chakra)	Solar plexus, gall bladder, navel, adrenals, red bile	Bright yellow	Yellow citrine, tiger's eye, ruby	Detoxification, self-esteem, uplifting, cheerful, balancing
Conjunction	Anahata (emotions, feelings, Copper Chakra)	Heart, blood	Green	Malachite, emerald, jade, aventurine, kunzite, quartz	Strengthens the heart and blood, releases fear, enhances dreams
Fermentation	Vishuddha (concepts, communication, Mercury Chakra)	Throat, thymus, thyroid, sound, vibration	Turquoise, light blue	Turquoise, blue topaz, aquamarine, iolite	Balance of nerves, aligning chakras, creativity, channelling, revitalizing energy
Distillation	Ajna (intuition, second sight, Silver Chakra)	Brow, pituitary, liver, life force	Indigo, deep blue	Lapis lazuli, sodalite, sapphire, moldavite, opal, moonstone	Lymphatic, mental clarity, psychic powers
Coagulation	Sahasrara (imagination, Gold Chakra)	Brain, pineal gland, crown of head, elixir, ambrosia	Violet, ultraviolet	Amethyst, fluorite, yellow topaz, pearl, diamond	General whole-body healing, regeneration

THE CHAKRAS

In esoteric terms, a crucial addition to what might be termed the 'occult constitution of man' is that of the chakras. These are now so well known that the term is almost common knowledge. The word *chakra* is Sanskrit for 'wheel'. Each chakra, or energy centre, spins in relation to the degree of energy within the body's system. The chakras serve as a linking mechanism between physical matter and subtle matter. Much of the information about them was found in Hindu canonical literature in the Upanishads, but teachings concerning the chakras can also be found in many other major spiritual traditions.

Within Buddhism, knowledge of the chakras is thoroughly integrated into medical practice. The centres are known as channel wheels and are used extensively in certain significant visualizations by the practitioner. Taoist yoga is a complex discipline, based on the control and circulation of vital energies. The Western alchemical tradition also had a deep understanding of the chakras. Metals and planets were assigned to the chakras in an elaborate system of correspondences that formed the basis of the alchemists' approach to the quest for spiritual transformation. However, with the decline of the alchemical arts, codified knowledge about the chakras faded for a time in the West.[29]

In the main Eastern traditions there are seven chakras. They are very easy to visualize, and by directing consciousness towards them, it is possible to energize them. This is rather like rubbing a hurt part of your body to send blood flowing to it. Whether the chakras are psychic/spiritual expressions of functions within the body, or the physical organs and their functions are a material expression of the chakras depends upon your approach to matter and spirit.

The basic table relating to the chakras describes their associated endocrine gland and colour, and these are illustrated on diagrams of the human body (see opposite).

The chakras are also allocated geometric shapes (known as *yantras*), elements, deities, Sanskrit letters, animal symbols and sounds (known as mantras). Moreover, each chakra is described as having a particular number of petals (in a particular colour), which some people feel represents the vibratory rate of each chakra and/or refers to the spinal nerves related to each plexus. The chakras' ruling deity, or pair of deities, (see page 150) acts as a guide into the essential experience of the chakra in question and can be used in the same way as the magical images on the Tree of Life (see page 151).

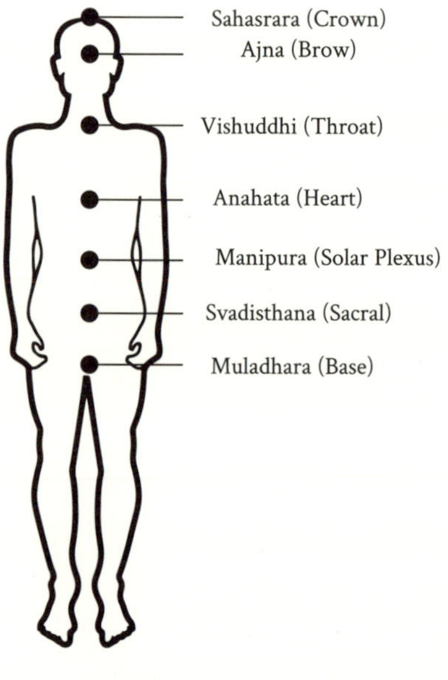

The seven main chakras

Basic Chakra Associations

CHAKRA	ENDOCRINE GLAND	COLOUR
Sahasrara	Pituitary gland	Violet
Ajna	Pineal gland	Indigo
Vishuddhi	Thyroid and parathyroid glands	Blue
Anahata	Thymus	Green
Manipura	Adrenal glands	Yellow
Svadisthana	Pancreas	Orange
Muladhara	Testes or ovaries	Red

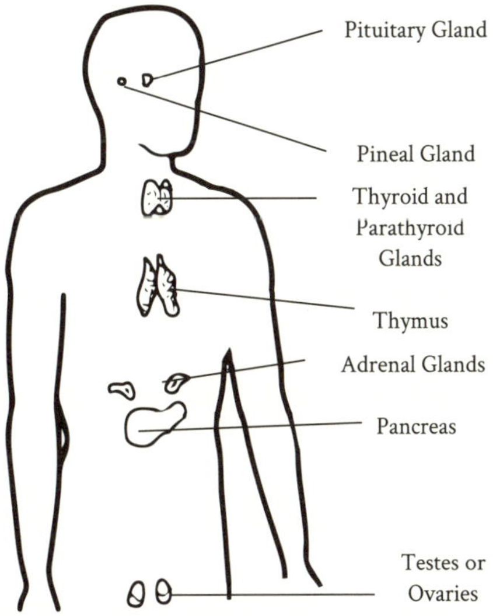

The endocrine glands

Petals, Colours, Yantras and Elements

CHAKRA	PETALS	COLOUR	YANTRA	ELEMENT
Sahasrara	1,000	–	–	–
Ajna	2	White	White (no yantra)	–
Vishuddhi	16	Red	White circle	Akasha
Anahata	12	Vermilion	Smoky-green hexagon	Air
Manipura	10	Blue	Red triangle	Fire
Svadisthana	6	Lightning	White crescent moon	Water
Muladhara	4	Gold	Yellow square	Earth

Wider-Ranging Chakra Correspondences

Naomi Ozaniec, a practitioner of high magic in the Western tradition, but equally at home with all things Eastern, gives more details in her book *Chakras*, published in 2000, and some examples are given in the first table below. According to the researchers at the Polaris Fellowship, the chakra energy centres are associated with the seven elder planets and the seven associated alchemical metals. This combination of planet and metal has given rise to the concept of 'seven interior alchemical stars' (as depicted on Tarot card 17, The Star). These 'interior stars' and their associations are given in the subsequent table (see below).

Chakra and Deity Correspondences

CHAKRA	DEITIES
Sahasrara Crown	Shiva
Ajna Brow	Sakti Hakini holding a book, drum or staff with a skull or rosary
Vishuddhi Throat	Sadasiva holding a noose, goad, serpent, trident, fire weapon, *vajra* (thunderbolt), sword, battle axe or bell; Gauri holding a noose, goad, arrow or bow
Anahata Heart	Isa holding nothing; Kakini holding a noose or skull
Manipura Solar Plexus	Rudra holding a rosary or fire weapon; Lakini holding a thunderbolt or fire weapon
Svadisthana Sacral	Vishnu holding a conch shell, disc, war club or lotus; Rakini holding a trident, lotus, drum or battleaxe
Muladhara Base	Brahma holding a staff, gourd or rosary; Dakini holding a spear, staff with a skull atop, sword or cup

Interior Star Associations[30]

PLANET	ELEMENT	CHAKRA
Mercury	Mercury	Crown
Moon	Silver	Brow
Venus	Copper	Throat
Sun	Gold	Heart
Jupiter	Tin	Solar Plexus
Mars	Iron	Sacral
Saturn	Lead	Base

Body Systems and the Tree of Life

CHAKRA	BASE	SACRAL	SOLAR PLEXUS	HEART	THROAT	BROW	CROWN
Function	Survival, grounding	Pleasure, sexuality, procreation, creativity	Will, power	Love	Creativity, communication	Direct perception	Union
Element	Earth	Water	Fire	Air	Akasha	–	–
Inner state	Stability	Self-confidence, well-being	Intense emotion, laughter	Compassion, love	Intuition, synthesis	Self-mastery	Bliss
Glands	Adrenals	Ovaries, testicles	Pancreas	Thymus	Thyroid, parathyroid	Pituitary	Pineal
Body parts	Legs, feet, bones, large intestine	Womb, kidneys, reproductive system, circulation system, bladder	Digestive system, liver, spleen, stomach, small intestine	Lungs, heart, arms, hands	Neck, shoulders	Eyes, two hemispheres of the brain	Cerebral cortex, brain, the whole body
Malfunction	Obesity, haemorrhoids, constipation, sciatica	Impotence, frigidity, uterine, bladder or kidney trouble	Ulcers, diabetes, eating disorders such as anorexia and bulimia, hypoglycaemia	Asthma, blood pressure, heart disease, lung disease	Sore throat, swollen glands, colds, thyroid problems	Headaches, nightmares, defects of vision	Alienation
Colour	Red	Orange	Yellow	Green	Bright blue	Indigo	Violet
Seed sound	Lam	Vam	Ram	Yam	Ham	Om	–
Sense	Smell	Taste	Sight	Touch	Hearing	–	–
Petals	4	6	10	12	16	2	1,000
Animal symbols	Bull, elephant, ox	Makara, fish, sea creatures	Ram	Antelope, birds, dove	Elephant	–	The risen serpent
Deities	Brahma, Dakini, Gaia, Demeter, Persephone, Erishkagel, Ana, Ceres, Ceridwen, Geb, Hades, Pwyll	Vishnu, Rakini	Rudra, Lakini, Apollo, Agn	Isa, Kakini	Sadasiva, Sakini	Paramasiva, Sakti Hakini	Shiva

9

MINERAL, VEGETABLE & ANIMAL CORRESPONDENCES

THE POWER OF GEMSTONES & PLANTS

There is an old saying that God sleeps in the stone, dreams in the plant, wakes in the animal and lives in humans.

When Crowley wrote ***Liber 777*** in the early years of the 20th century only a handful of people had any interest in the spiritual possibilities of crystals, minerals, gems or plants. Today, in the early years of the 21st century, almost everyone has some notion of their importance. Pan-animism (the belief that ***everything*** contains life and consciousness, however inanimate it may appear to us) has become almost mainstream again, instead of being regarded as a tiny side-branch of long-dead tribal systems. The magician can pick up a piece of jet and know that it is linked, via Saturn, to the dark gods and goddesses of Binah. Meditating while holding the stone could give access to any of the realms behind the Tarot cards that link with Binah, such as the Hermit, Judgement, the Hanged Man and Death – and to all levels of understanding contained therein. Relax your mind. Ask to be shown.

TREE OF LIFE AND GEMSTONE CORRESPONDENCES

SPHERE	GEM
1	Diamond
2	Pearl
3	Jet
4	Amethyst, sapphire
5	Ruby
6	Topaz, yellow diamond
7	Emerald
8	Citrine
9	Quartz
10	Rock crystal
11	Chalcedony
12	Agate
13	Opal
14	Jacinth
15	Garnet
16	Lapis Lazuli
17	Tourmaline
18	Amber
19	Onyx
20	Cornelian
21	Jade
22	Chrysolite
23	Aquamarine
24	Beryl
25	Topaz
26	Turquoise
27	Garnet
28	Bloodstone
29	Moonstone
30	Sunstone
31	Tiger's eye
32	Pearl

TREE OF LIFE AND PLANT ASSOCIATIONS (REAL OR IMAGINARY)[31]

SPHERE	PLANT
1	Almond in flower
2	Amaranth
3	Cypress, opium poppy
4	Olive, shamrock
5	Oak, Nux vomica, nettle
6	Acacia, bay, laurel, vine
7	Rose
8	Peyote
9	Mandrake
10	Willow, ivy, lily
11	Aspen
12	Vervain
13	Mugwort
14	Myrtle
15	Tiger lily, geranium
16	Mallow
17	Hybrid, orchid
18	Lotus
19	Sunflower
20	Snowdrop, lily, narcissus
21	Hyssop, oak, poplar
22	Aloe
23	Lotus, all water plants
24	Cactus
25	Rush
26	Marijuana, orchis root
27	Absinthe, rue
28	Coconut
29	Opium
30	Sunflower, laurel, heliotrope
31	Red poppy
32	Ash, cypress, hellebore, yew, nightshade

Culpeper's and Modern Wiccan Correspondences

Culpeper[32]			Modern Wiccan
Medicinal plant	Ruling planet or sign	Element	Qualities
Adder's tongue	Moon, Cancer	Water	Healing
Amaranthus	Saturn	Earth	Protection
Barley	Saturn	Earth	Love, healing
Basil (garden)	Venus	Water	Exorcism, wealth, flying
Briony	Mars	Fire	Image magic, money
Burdock	Venus	Water	Protection, healing
Coltsfoot	Venus	Water	Love, visions
Dandelion	Jupiter	Fire	Divination, wishes, calling spirits
Dill	Mercury	Air	Protection, money, lust, luck
Fennel	Mercury, Virgo	Air/Earth	Protection, healing, purification
Garlic	Mars	Fire	Protection, healing, exorcism, lust, anti-theft
Hemlock	Saturn	Earth	Destroy sexual drives, poison*
Hemp	Saturn	Earth	Healing, love, vision, meditation
Hyssop	Jupiter	Fire	Purification, protection
Lily-of-the-valley	Mercury	Air	Mental powers, happiness
Mistletoe	Sun	Fire	Protection, love, hunting, fertility, health, exorcism
Mustard	Mars	Fire	Fertility, protection, mental powers
Pennyroyal	Venus	Earth	Strength, protection, peace
Ragwort	Venus	Earth	Protection
Saffron	Sun	Fire	Love, healing, happiness, wind-raising, lust
Vervain	Venus	Water	Love, protection, purification, peace, money
Willow tree	Moon	Water	Love, divination, protection, healing

*NB Hemlock is a deadly poison.

Culpeper's Correspondences

Nowadays we talk to our plants and even play them music; there is no longer anything unusual about that. We can add another level of perception by linking them with cosmic patterns and associations. Culpeper, writing two centuries before Crowley, produced a near-exhaustive list of plants and their astrological possibilities, which is given in the Appendix (see pages 244–255). However, we can look at a concise version overleaf and add some correspondences from the Wiccan tradition in order to compare, balance and extend our understanding. The final column depends entirely upon personal intuition as to what qualities a plant might have for the individual concerned; this is a completely valid – and some might say essential – method of approach.

Perfumes, Incenses and Essential Oils

The sense of smell can, of course, evoke powerful responses from the mind: for example, the smell of babies, new-mown hay, lovers, ozone – there is an infinite range of possibility here. In more artificial terms, perfumes have always been used in connection with Magick.

Crowley's and Modern Wiccan Correspondences

Crowley[33]		Modern Wiccan	
Sphere	Perfume	Incense or essential oil	Qualities
1	Ambergris	Ambergris	Psychic ventures, dreams
2	Musk	Musk	Aphrodisiac, courage, purification
3	Myrrh, civet	Myrrh, civet	Healing, protection, peace
4	Cedar	Cedar	Protection, spirituality, money
5	Tobacco	Balsam fir	Strength, breaking negativity
6	Olibanum	Frankincense	Exorcism, love, consecration
7	Benzoin, rose	Myrtle	Love, lust
8	Storax	Peppermint	Energy, mental stimulant
9	Jasmine, ginseng	Jasmine	Love, money, dreams
Path			
10	Dittany of Crete	Narcissus	Earth, grounding, sleep
11	Galbanum	Patchouli	Mastery, growth
12	Mastic, mace	Geranium	Power in rituals
13	Camphor, aloe	Ylang ylang	Euphoria, harmony, love
14	Sandalwood	Cherry	Spells, divination, destiny
15	Dragon's blood	Dragon's blood	Potency, protection, love, healing

ANIMAL POWER

Until the modern era, animals were a natural part of everyday augury or divination. Some were good omens, others not. The idea that a black cat crossing your path is lucky is a tiny fragment of this lore.

Many of the animals mentioned in the correspondences are dream creatures; they can actually help to analyse dreams and give you some indication of which path your consciousness has been following while you were asleep. If you dreamed about a scorpion, for example, it might be that your mind was wandering along the 23rd path between Hod and Geburah, which could betoken imminent changes at work and warn you that you are stinging yourself in the realm of office politics.

Table of Animals (Real or Imaginary)

SPHERE	ANIMALS[34]
1	God
2	Man
3	Woman
4	Unicorn
5	Basilisk
6	Phoenix, lion, child
7	Lynx
8	Hermaphrodite, jackal
9	Elephant
10	Sphinx
11	Eagle
12	Swallow, ibis, ape
13	Dog
14	Sparrow, dove, swan
15	Ram, owl
16	Bull
17	Magpie, hybrids
18	Crab, turtle
19	Lion
20	Virgin, anchorite
21	Eagle
22	Elephant
23	Eagle, snake, scorpion
24	Beetle, lobster or crayfish, wolf
25	Centaur, horse, hippogriff
26	Goat, ass
27	Horse, bear, wolf
28	Man, eagle
29	Fish, dolphin
30	Lion, sparrowhawk
31	Lion
32	Crocodile

10

ASSORTED ANGELS & DEMONS

THE ANGELIC REALM

There are orders of beings that coexist with us, the inhabitants of other dimensions. Some of them are aware of us; some have a vested interest in working with us; others are supremely indifferent to our existence. In the Judaeo-Christian tradition of the West, magicians and mystics have long been concerned with the nature of the angels and with developing techniques that may summon their assistance and protection.

The word 'angel' simply means, according to one etymology, messenger – derived as it is from the Greek word ***angelos***. Others believe it comes from the Sanskrit ***Angiras***, meaning a divine spirit; or from the Persian ***Angaros***, meaning courier; or even from the Hebrew ***Malakh***, meaning angel. Esoteric lore insists that angels were created before the Earth: they are not our dearly departed loved ones in transfigured states. Belief and faith in angels was never a part of Christianity until the Council of Nicaea in 325 CE.

If we can take away the cloying religiosity that has evolved in connection with angels and instead regard them as denizens of another realm, they can be invoked with relative ease. Whether they will come or not is another matter. Those individuals who made direct, conscious contact with such beings were explorers of inner space. They brought names back with them, or struggled to give names that they deemed fit to these energies and otherworldly consciousnesses. Go to any reference library and there are ancient tomes giving huge lists of names that are, by and large, meaningless to anyone except the person who made the initial contact. This is comparable to someone going to a foreign country where they don't speak the language, have no guide or interpreter, and then coming back to try to explain the people, customs and social structure.

Angels are living beings of a particular kind. They do not want our worship. Tap the word 'angel' into any internet search engine and be prepared for the huge range of angel names, endless hierarchies and countless examples of modern experience. The traditional angel hierarchies are shown below:

FIRST HIERARCHY	Seraphim, Cherubim, Thrones or ***Ophanim***
SECOND HIERARCHY	Dominions or ***Kyriotetes***, Virtues or ***Dynameis***, Powers or ***Exousiai***
THIRD HIERARCHY	Principalities or ***Archai***, Archangels, Angels

Names have been recorded for some of these beings, but the lists are not regarded as definitive or complete. Remember that the medieval magicians who produced exhaustive and (to the modern ear) bizarre lists were probably boasting. To be able to name a 'new' angel was as much an act of making a statement as it was a piece of mystical observation.

Angels of the Planets, Days and Hours

Johannes Trithemius (1462–1516) was abbot of Sponheim until 1506, when he left to become abbot of the Monastery of St Jacob in Wurzburg. Under the auspices of the Church, he also wrote some influential works that later magicians developed, especially ***Steganographia***, written around 1499; ***Polygraphiae***, a cryptographic work; and ***De Septum Secundeis***, a history of the world based on astrology. His writings combined Christianity, Hermetic philosophy and its attendant sciences of magic, astrology, alchemy and the Kabbalah.

Steganographia is primarily concerned with the sending of secret messages by angels, though it also touches on cryptography and a system of rapid learning. Trithemius set forth a hierarchy of angels and spirits ruling over regions of the Earth as well as days and hours. Ultimately these angels are subject to the seven planetary angels, which were also set forth in Trithemius's ***De Septum Secundeis***.

The tables on pages 164–167, taken from ***The Art of Drawing Spirits into Crystals***,[35] have an obvious and immediate use in any ritual involving both angels and planets, and should be used in conjunction with those given for the Mansions of the Moon in Francis Barrett's ***The Magus***. Barrett adds helpfully:

> The day is divided into 12 equal parts, called Planetary Hours, reckoning from sunrise to sunset, and, again, from the setting to the rising; and to find the planetary hour, you need but to divide the natural hours by 12, and the quotient gives the length of the planetary hours and odd minutes, which shews you how long a spirit bears rule in that day; as Michael governs the first and the eighth hour on Sunday, as does the o. After you have the length of the first hour, you have only to look in the Table, as if it be the fourth hour, on Sunday, you see in the Table that the Y and Gabriel rules; and so for the rest it being so plain and easy you cannot err.

To complete the time scheme there are also angels and zodiac signs associated with the different months of the year (see page 167).

First Hierarchy

SERAPHIM	Seraphiel, Metatron, Michael, Uriel, Nathanael, Jehoel, Chamuel, Lucifer, Abaddon, Asmodeus, Astaroth, Leviathan, Samael, Semyazza
CHERUBIM	Cherubiel, Gabriel, Ophaniel, Raphael, Uriel, Zophie, Azazel, Beelzebub, Berith, Lauviah, Lucifer, Marou, Salikotal, Shamsiel
OPHANIM (THRONES)	Bodiel, Jophiel, Zaphkiel, Oriphiel, Raziel, Astaroth, Gressil, Focalor, Forneus, Murmur, Nelchael, Phenex, Purson, Raum, Samael, Sonneillon, Verrine

ANGELS OF THE HOURS: SUNDAY

HOURS OF DAY	ANGEL	PLANET	HOURS OF NIGHT	ANGEL	PLANET
1	Michael	Sun	1	Sachiel	Jupiter
2	Anael	Venus	2	Samiel	Mars
3	Raphael	Mercury	3	Michael	Sun
4	Gabriel	Moon	4	Anael	Venus
5	Cassiel	Saturn	5	Raphael	Mercury
6	Sachiel	Jupiter	6	Gabriel	Moon
7	Samael	Mars	7	Cassiel	Saturn
8	Michael	Sun	8	Sachiel	Jupiter
9	Anael	Venus	9	Samael	Mars
10	Raphael	Mercury	10	Michael	Sun
11	Gabriel	Moon	11	Anael	Venus
12	Cassiel	Saturn	12	Raphael	Mercury

ANGELS OF THE HOURS: MONDAY

HOURS OF DAY	ANGEL	PLANET	HOURS OF NIGHT	ANGEL	PLANET
1	Michael	Sun	1	Sachiel	Jupiter
2	Anael	Venus	2	Samiel	Mars
3	Raphael	Mercury	3	Michael	Sun
4	Gabriel	Moon	4	Anael	Venus
5	Cassiel	Saturn	5	Raphael	Mercury
6	Sachiel	Jupiter	6	Gabriel	Moon
7	Samael	Mars	7	Cassiel	Saturn
8	Michael	Sun	8	Sachiel	Jupiter
9	Anael	Venus	9	Samael	Mars
10	Raphael	Mercury	10	Michael	Sun
11	Gabriel	Moon	11	Anael	Venus
12	Cassiel	Saturn	12	Raphael	Mercury

ANGELS OF THE HOURS: TUESDAY

HOURS OF DAY	ANGEL	PLANET	HOURS OF NIGHT	ANGEL	PLANET
1	Samael	Mars	1	Cassiel	Saturn
2	Michael	Sun	2	Sachiel	Jupiter
3	Anael	Venus	3	Samael	Mars
4	Raphael	Mercury	4	Michael	Sun
5	Gabriel	Moon	5	Anael	Venus
6	Cassiel	Saturn	6	Raphael	Mercury
7	Sachiel	Jupiter	7	Gabriel	Moon
8	Samael	Mars	8	Cassiel	Saturn
9	Michael	Sun	9	Sachiel	Jupiter
10	Anael	Venus	10	Samael	Mars
11	Raphael	Mercury	11	Michael	Sun
12	Gabriel	Moon	12	Anael	Venus

ANGELS OF THE HOURS: WEDNESDAY

HOURS OF DAY	ANGEL	PLANET	HOURS OF NIGHT	ANGEL	PLANET
1	Raphael	Mercury	1	Michael	Sun
2	Gabriel	Moon	2	Anael	Venus
3	Cassiel	Saturn	3	Raphael	Mercury
4	Sachiel	Jupiter	4	Gabriel	Moon
5	Samael	Mars	5	Cassiel	Saturn
6	Michael	Sun	6	Sachiel	Jupiter
7	Anael	Venus	7	Samael	Mars
8	Raphael	Mercury	8	Michael	Sun
9	Gabriel	Moon	9	Anael	Venus
10	Cassiel	Saturn	10	Raphael	Mercury
11	Sachiel	Jupiter	11	Gabriel	Moon
12	Samael	Mars	12	Cassiel	Saturn

ANGELS OF THE HOURS: THURSDAY

HOURS OF DAY	ANGEL	PLANET	HOURS OF NIGHT	ANGEL	PLANET
1	Sachiel	Jupiter	1	Gabriel	Moon
2	Samael	Mars	2	Cassiel	Saturn
3	Michael	Sun	3	Sachiel	Jupiter
4	Anael	Venus	4	Samael	Mars
5	Raphael	Mercury	5	Michael	Sun
6	Gabriel	Moon	6	Anael	Venus
7	Cassiel	Saturn	7	Raphael	Mercury
8	Sachiel	Jupiter	8	Gabriel	Moon
9	Samael	Mars	9	Cassiel	Saturn
10	Michael	Sun	10	Sachiel	Jupiter
11	Anael	Venus	11	Samael	Mars
12	Raphael	Mercury	12	Michael	Sun

ANGELS OF THE HOURS: FRIDAY

HOURS OF DAY	ANGEL	PLANET	HOURS OF NIGHT	ANGEL	PLANET
1	Anael	Venus	1	Samael	Mars
2	Raphael	Mercury	2	Michael	Sun
3	Gabriel	Moon	3	Anael	Venus
4	Cassiel	Saturn	4	Raphael	Mercury
5	Sachiel	Jupiter	5	Gabriel	Moon
6	Samael	Mars	6	Cassiel	Saturn
7	Michael	Sun	7	Sachiel	Jupiter
8	Anael	Venus	8	Samael	Mars
9	Raphael	Mercury	9	Michael	Sun
10	Gabriel	Moon	10	Anael	Venus
11	Cassiel	Saturn	11	Raphael	Mercury
12	Sachiel	Jupiter	12	Gabriel	Moon

Angels of the Hours: Saturday

HOURS OF DAY	ANGEL	PLANET	HOURS OF NIGHT	ANGEL	PLANET
1	Cassiel	Saturn	1	Raphael	Mercury
2	Sachiel	Jupiter	2	Gabriel	Moon
3	Samael	Mars	3	Cassiel	Saturn
4	Michael	Sun	4	Sachiel	Jupiter
5	Anael	Venus	5	Samael	Mars
6	Raphael	Mercury	6	Michael	Sun
7	Gabriel	Moon	7	Anael	Venus
8	Cassiel	Saturn	8	Raphael	Mercury
9	Sachiel	Jupiter	9	Gabriel	Moon
10	Samael	Mars	10	Cassiel	Saturn
11	Michael	Sun	11	Sachiel	Jupiter
12	Anael	Venus	12	Samael	Mars

Monthly Correspondences

MONTH	ANGEL	ZODIAC
January	Gabriel	Aquarius
February	Barchiel	Pisces
March	Machidiel	Aries
April	Asmodel	Taurus
May	Ambriel	Gemini
June	Muriel	Cancer
July	Verchiel	Leo
August	Hamaliel	Virgo
September	Uriel	Libra
October	Barbiel	Scorpio
November	Adnachiel	Sagittarius
December	Anael	Capricorn

Olympic Spirits

There are also Olympic planetary spirits to be considered, from the *Arbatel de magia veterum*, a treatise on ceremonial Magick first published anonymously in 1575, but translated and published by Robert Turner in London in 1655 as the *Arbatel of Magick*. It gives the sigils by which each spirit can be invoked (see opposite).

According to the *Arbatel*, the Olympic spirits rule for 490 years each. Bethor ruled from 60 BCE to 430 CE; Phaleg ruled until 920 CE; then Och until 1410 and Hagith until 1900. The current ruler of the world is Ophiel. The Elizabethan occultist John Dee (1527–1608) made several references in his diaries to the *Arbatel* and especially to the spirit Och. Along with grimoires such as the *Sworn Book of Honorius* and the mysterious *Soyga* (*The Book of Soyga* or *Aldaraia*), the *Arbatel* may have inspired some of Dee's 'Enochian' system of angelic language (see page 171).

To invoke the Olympic spirits, draw the appropriate sigil on a new sheet of paper on the day and at the planetary hour of the spirit with which you seek to work. After using a banishing and opening ritual, such as the 'lesser banishing ritual of the pentagram' (see pages 40–41), read aloud the first prayer to summon the spirit:

Omnipotent and eternal God, who hast ordained the whole creation for thy praise and thy glory, as also for the salvation of man, I beseech Thee to send Thy Spirit [*name*], of the [*solar/lunar*, etc.] order, that he may instruct me concerning those things about which I design to ask him. Nevertheless, not my will be done, but thine, through Jesus Christ, thy only begotten Son, Who is our Lord. Amen.

Watch for any signs in the outer world that the spirit may have manifested. That is to say, look out for omens involving animals, birds, plants or weather. Ask for the help required – whether this is teaching, healing or insight – but make sure that something is offered to the world in return. The *Arbatel* warns that you should not keep the spirit for more than one hour.

The second prayer is then read to discharge the spirit, and the paper with the sigil and prayers can then be stored in a safe place or turned into a talismanic object, for your own eyes only. The second prayer is equally simple:

Forasmuch as thou camest in peace and quietly, having also answered unto my petitions, I give thanks unto God, in Whose Name thou camest. Now thou mayst depart in peace unto thy orders; but return unto me again, when I shall call thee by thy name, or by thy order, or by thy office, which is granted from the Creator. Amen.

A E Waite (1857–1942), another senior figure within the Golden Dawn, who approached his high Magick from an inherently Christian perspective, analysed the planetary spirits in his *Book of Black Magic and Ceremonial Magic* (see page 170).

The Seven Olympic Planetary Spirits

SPIRIT	PLANET	SIGIL	CONCERNS
Arathron	Saturn	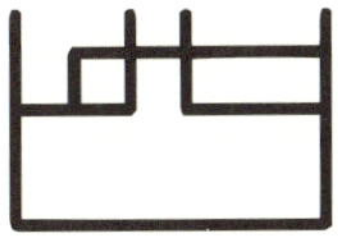	Change, transmutation
Bethor	Jupiter	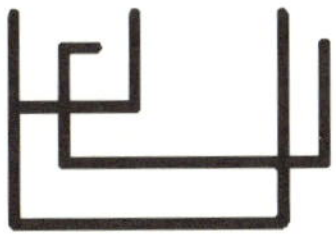	Truth, reconciliation
Phalegh	Mars	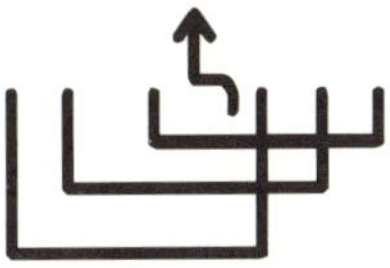	Courage
Och	Sun	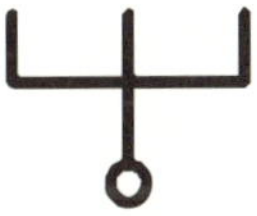	Health, balance
Hagith	Venus		Beauty, love
Ophiel	Mercury	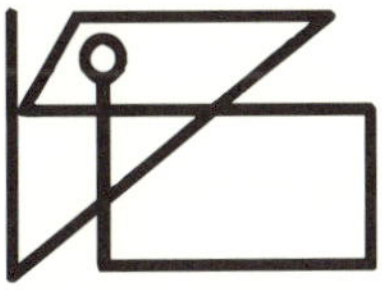	Magick, knowledge
Phul	Artemis	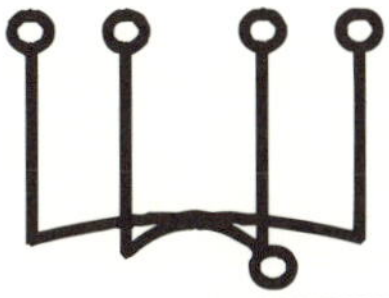	Dreams, spirits

WAITE'S ANALYSES OF THE PLANETARY SPIRITS

PLANETARY SPIRIT	DESCRIPTION
Arathron or Aratron	Governs those things which are ascribed astrologically to Saturn. He can convert any living organism, plant or animal into stone, and that in a moment of time; he can also change coals into treasure and treasure into coals; he gives familiars and reconciles subterranean spirits to men; he teaches Alchemy, Magic and Medicine, imparts the secret of invisibility, makes the barren fruitful and, lastly, confers long life.
Bethor or Bether	Responds quickly when called. The person dignified by his character may be exalted to illustrious positions and may obtain large treasures. He reconciles the Spirits of the Air to man, so that they will give true answers, transport precious stones and compose medicines having miraculous effects. Bethor also grants familiars of the firmament, and can prolong life to seven hundred years, subject to the will of God, which qualification imparts an air of caution.
Phalegh or Phalec	Governs the things that are attributed to Mars. The person who possesses his character is raised by him to great honour in military affairs.
Och	Prolongs life to six hundred years, with perfect health therein. He imparts great wisdom, gives excellent (familiar) spirits, composes perfect medicines, converts any substance into the purest of metals, or into precious stones; he also bestows gold and a purse, quaintly described by the English translator of the *Arbatel* as 'springing with gold'. He causes the possessor of his character to be worshipped as a god by the kings of the whole world.
Hagith	The government of Venereal concerns is entrusted to Hagith, and the person possessing his character is adorned with all beauty. He converts copper into gold in a moment and gold instantaneously into copper; he also gives faithful serving spirits.
Ophiel	Is the ruler of those things which are attributed to Mercury; he gives familiar spirits, teaches all arts, and enables the possessor of his character to change quicksilver immediately into the Philosopher's Stone.
Phul	Lunary concerns are under the government of Phul, who truly transmutes all metals into silver, heals dropsy and provides Spirits of the Water, who serve men in a corporal and visible form; he also prolongs life to three hundred years.

JOHN DEE

There is, of course, a natural human tendency to explore the Dark Side. Or, if not to explore it as such, at least be aware of what it holds and how to avoid it. Crowley evoked beings that were demons by any standard. He also evoked beings of light, which were branded by some as denizens of pure evil. Some of the beings that he summoned and communed with were first discovered by Dr John Dee.

John Dee, born by his own reckoning on 13 July 1527 in London, was an alchemist, astrologer, magician and mathematician who contributed greatly to the revival of interest in mathematics in England. He was also instrumental in the foundation of a secret service, used his astrological knowledge to name a propitious day for his patron and protector Elizabeth I's coronation, and gave useful information to those pilots and navigators who were exploring the New World.

With the aid of spirit medium Edward Kelley (1555–1597) and a mystic 'shew-stone', Dee also stumbled upon angels. Together Dee and Kelley recorded hundreds of spirit conversations, which were conducted in an angelic language that Dee called 'Enochian', composed of non-English letters, but which computer analysis has recently shown to have a curious grammatical relationship to English. The visions and experiences were intense and dense. Centuries later Aleister Crowley, with the help of Victor Neuburg, set about exploring the whole range of Dee's 'Aires' or 'Aethyrs' (the spiritual levels of existence that block the Earth from the stars) and made sure that Dee's work was not forgotten.

This is such a dense and potentially dangerous system that attempts to give a workable summary of it would achieve nothing worthwhile. But we can at least list the 30 Aethyrs or Aires, and give some sense of the infinite and astonishing variety of otherworldly existence that can be explored when the magician is ready (see pages 172–173).

As always, if in doubt then leave well alone until you get an inner impulse to look again.

Dee's Synopsis of the 30 Aires or Aethyrs

NUMBER	AIRE OR AETHYR	MAGICKAL VISION
30	TEX Aethyr that is in 4 parts	'The Vision of the Dawn of the Aeon of Horns (Atu XVII)'
29	RII Aethyr of the mercy of heaven	'The Vision of the Initiation of Hecate (Atu XIV), The Redemption of the Woman of Witchcraft by Love'
28	BAG Aethyr of doubt	'The Slave-Gods superseded (The Vision of Atu XX, the Stl), The Vision of the Stl of Revealing, abolishing the Aeon of the Slave-Gods'
27	ZAA Aethyr of solitude	'The Path of Teth (Atu XI. The Fire-Kerub in the Initiation), The Vision of the Fruit of the Great Work of the Beast – 666. The Lion'
26	DES Aethyr that accepts that which is	'The Rose (The Woman of Atu XIV. Minister of Babalon; The Water-Kerub in the Initiation)'
25	VTI Aethyr of change	'The First Kiss of the Lady of Initiation'
24	NIA Aethyr of travelling	'The Kerubim of Earth and Air (Minor officers in the Initiation to Sx = 3 [square x]), The Vision of the Interplay and Identity of Earth and Air'
23	TOR Aethyr that sustains	'The 49-fold Table (First Appearance of the Crowned and Conquering Child to the Exempt Adept as in the Pastos), The Vision of the Rose, the Heart of BABALON and of the Birth of the Universe'
22	LIN Aethyr of the void	'Kether (The Hierophant prepares the Candidate), The Vision of the Ineluctable Destiny'
21	ASP Aethyr of causation	'The Path of Kaph (Atu X), The Hiereus prepares the Candidate), The Vision of the Wheel of Fortune, The Three Energies of the Universe'
20	CHR Aethyr of the wheel	'The Path of Gimel (The Hegemone between the Pillars. Preliminary: The Vision of the Unguided Universe)'
19	POP Aethyr of division	'Tiphereth. (The King's Chamber. The Vision of the holy Guardian Angel), The Instruction Concerning the Obtaining of the Vision and the Voice of the Thirty Aethyrs'
18	ZEN Aethyr of sacrifice	'The Preparation of the Candidate'

NUMBER	AIRE OR AETHYR	MAGICKAL VISION
17	TAN Aethyr of one's equilibrium	'The Path of Lamed (The combination Gimel, Lamed, Samech. The Vision of the Justice or Balance of the Universe')
16	LEA The first aethyr of the (higher) self	'Keter (Path of Pe), The Overthrow of the Slave-Gods by The Beast 666'
15	OXO Aethyr of dancing	'The Vision of the Rose of 49 Petals, and of the Holy 12-fold Table, Examination of the Candidate for M.T.'
14	VTA Aethyr of semblances	'The Vision of the City of the Pyramids, The Reception Of the Master of the Temple'
13	ZIM Aethyr of application	'The Garden of Nemo, The Work of the Magister Templi'
12	LOE The first aethyr of glory	'The Path of Cheth, The Bearer of the Sangraal, The Black Brothers'
11	ICH Aethyr of tension	'Yesod, The Frontier of the Abyss'
10	ZAX Aethyr of the One with a Great Name	'The Abyss. Choronzon, his Nature'
9	ZIP Aethyr for those who are not	'Malkuth (The Pure Virgin), The reward of the Magister Templi'
8	ZID Aethyr of one's God	'The Holy Guardian Angel, His instruction'
7	DEO Aethyr of selfishness	'The Path of Daleth, The Black Brothers'
6	MAZ Aethyr of appearances	'The Vision of the Urn, The Magus 9x = 2 [square x], The Three Schools of Magick'
5	LIT Aethyr that is without a supreme being	'The Vision of the Middle Pillar (Arrow), The Mystery of Atheism'
4	PAZ Aethyr of impending expression	'The Marriage of Yod and He, The Seer identifies himself with it'
3	ZOM Aethyr of self-knowledge	'The Magus of the Tarot (Atu 1), Mayan, the Maker of Illusion'
2	ARN Aethyr of fulfilment	'The Seer in Illusion (Lilith)'
1	LIL The First Aethyr	'The Vision of The Crowned and Conquering Child, the Lord of the Aeon'

TIMOTHY LEARY

There are modern explorers of inner space who are just as noteworthy as John Dee, and who have come back to describe realms that are just as valid. Of these, Dr Timothy Leary (1920–1996) had his own take on such levels of consciousness (see the first table below). His analyses are every bit as valid as the work of John Dee – if not more so. Leary added a magickal gloss with his interpretations in ***The Game of Life*** (see opposite), which shows that in his own way he was exploring realms in the 20th century that would have intrigued Dee four centuries earlier. The Chapel Perilous is an initiatory phase marking the transition between the first four intelligences and the latter four. It relates to post-Factor X activities in that both refer to 'out-of-body' states. However, the Chapel Perilous is where souls go when they are lost, and Factor X communications refer to how souls are found. The Chapel Perilous is the place 'souls' go to after leaving their robot bodies, while these bodies are still alive and walking the planet's surface. It is also known as 'The Dark Night of the Soul' and can be seen as a negative activation of the 'neurosomatic circuit', which is endured for as long as it takes the neophyte to effect a positive activation, or permanent body rapture.

Leary's Eight Circuits of the Nervous System[36]

NUMBER	TERRESTRIAL CIRCUIT	INTELLIGENCE
1	The Biosurvival Circuit: Imprinted in infancy; concerned with sucking, nourishment, cuddling, biosecurity	Physical
2	The Emotional-Territorial Circuit: Imprinted in the toddling stage; concerned with territorial demands, emotional power tactics, political domination-and-submission strategies	Emotional
3	The Semantic Circuit: Imprinted by human artefacts and symbol systems; concerned with handling the environment, invention, calculation, prediction, building a 'map' of the universe	Conceptual
4	The Socio-Sexual Circuit: Imprinted by the first orgasm-mating experiences and tribal 'morals'; concerned with sexual pleasure, local definitions of 'moral' and 'immoral', reproduction, nurture of the young	Social
	EXTRATERRESTRIAL CIRCUIT	INTELLIGENCE
5	The Neurosomatic Circuit: Imprinted by ecstatic experience via physiological or chemical yogas; concerned with neurological-somatic (body-brain) feedbacks, feeling high, somatic reprogramming	Sensory
6	The Neuroelectric Circuit: Imprinted by advanced yogas; concerned with re-imprinting and reprogramming all earlier circuits, the relativity of 'realities' perceived, cybernetic consciousness	Psychic
7	The Neurogenetic Circuit: Imprinted by advanced yogas; concerned with evolutionary consciousness (past and future), DNA-RNA-brain feedbacks, Jung's 'Collective Unconscious'	Mythic
8	The Neuroatomic Circuit: Imprinted by shock or near-death experience; concerned with quantum consciousness, non-local awareness (beyond space-time), so-called 'PSI' or 'Magick' powers, illumination	Spiritual

Leary's Observations From *The Game of Life*[37]

LEVEL OF INTELLIGENCE	MEDIUM OF OPERATION	ECOLOGICAL NICHE	REALITY GOAL
Spiritual	Subatomic mysteries	Atomic, gravity fields	Cosmic mind
Mythic	DNA and the planet	DNA structure	DNA mind
Psychic	CNS	One's own brain	Mind control
Sensory	The body's five senses	One's own body	Body control

Chapel Perilous

LEVEL OF INTELLIGENCE	MEDIUM OF OPERATION	ECOLOGICAL NICHE	REALITY GOAL
Social	Code of ethics	Monotheistic Hive: City	Socio/sex role
Conceptual	Conceptual framework	Man-made symbol, artefact	Hive sanity
Emotional	Belief systems	Land	Herd security
Physical	The organism	Water	Safety

ASSORTED DEMONS

The most dramatic and malign aspect of the forces on the Tree of Life can be found in the realms of the *Klippoth* (or *Qlipoth*, as Crowley and others preferred to spell it). The word is said to mean 'shells, cortices, or even harlots' in Hebrew.

William G Gray goes into more detail:[38]

- QLL means to vilify, curse or bring a curse on oneself
- QLQL means mean and vile
- PVTh means to be apart or separated
- PTh means interstice, or a space between things
- PThVTh is a euphemism for the female pudenda

Gray gives an entirely modern and accessible take on the qualities of the *Qlipoth* in the tables on the opposite page, which should be absorbed by anyone bold enough (or crass enough) to want to evoke demons.

Devil Rankings

One of history's most famous exorcists, Father Sebastien Michaelis,[39] described the ranking of devils below Lucifer himself in his *Admirable History* written in 1612 (see page 178). He also noted the sins of which each devil was in charge. And a modern researcher, Tony Caldwell, has identified the information contained in the tables on pages 178–180.

Gray's Tree of Life

SPHERE	TREE OF LIFE
10	The kingdom (of God)
9	Foundation (of life)
8	Glory
7	Achievement
6	Beauty (harmony)
5	Discipline
4	Compassion
HERE THE ABYSS IS CROSSED BY EXPERIENCE	
3	Understanding
2	Wisdom
1	The apex of spirit
0	Light

Gray's Tree of Evil

SPHERE	TREE OF EVIL
10	Materialism
9	Instability
8	Greed
7	Lust
6	Ugliness, disharmony
5	Cruelty
4	Apathy
HERE THE ABYSS IS IMPOSED BY IGNORANCE	
3	Antipathy
2	Stupidity
1	Atheism
0	Darkness

Crowley's Qliphotic Correspondences[40]

SPHERE	ORDERS OF QLIPOTH
1	Thaumiel
2	Ghagiel
3	Satariel
4	Gha'agsheblah
5	Golachab
6	Thagirion
7	A'arab Zaraq
8	Samael
9	Gamaliel
10	Lilith

PATH	ORDERS OF QLIPOTH
11	Oriens
12	Samael
13	Gamaliel
14	A'arab Zaraq
15	Bahimoron
16	Adimiron
17	Tzalalimiron
18	Schichiriron
19	Schalenbiron
20	Tzaphiriron
21	Gha'agsheblah
22	A'abiriron
23	Ariton
24	Necheshthiron
25	Necheshiron
26	Dagdagiron
27	Golachab
28	Ba'airiron
29	Nashimiron
30	Thagirion
31	Paimon
32	Satariel

Michaelis's Devil Rankings[41]

FIRST HIERARCHY	SECOND HIERARCHY	THIRD HIERARCHY
Beelzebub (pride)	Carreau (hard-heartedness)	Belisa (arrogance)
Leviathan (sins 'directly repugnant unto faith')	Carnivean (obscenity)	Oliver (mercilessness towards the poor)
Asmodeus (luxuriousness and wantonness)	Oeillet (temptations to 'break the vow of poverty')	Iuvart (various)
Balberith (homicides, quarrels, blasphemy)	Rosier (causes people to fall hopelessly in love, turning them from God or spouse)	
Astaroth (idleness and sloth)	Verrier (disobedience)	
Verrine (impatience)		
Gressil (impurity and uncleanliness)		
Sonneilon (hatred)		

De Plancy's Devil Rankings[42]

DEVIL	RANK
Asmodeus	The destroyer
Astaroth	Obtains friendship of great lords
Behemoth	Demon of indulgence
Ronwe	Demon of lingual knowledge
Urobach	Of the lower order of demons
Andras	Grand Marquis of Hell, causes discord and quarrels
Beelzebub	Lord of the flies

Barrett's Devil Rankings[43]

DEVIL	RANK
Mammon	Prince of temptors
Asmodeus	Prince of vengeance
Satan	Prince of deluders
Beelzebuth	Chief of false god
Pytho	Prince of the spirits of deceit
Beliel	Prince of iniquity
Merihim	Prince of the spirits of pestilence
Abaddon	Prince of war
Astaroth	Prince of accusers and inquisitors

Honorius's Devil Rankings[44]

PRINCIPAL INFERNAL SPIRITS	Lucifer – Emperor, Beelzebub - Prince, Astarot – Grand Duke
SUPERIOR SPIRITS	Lucifage Rofocale – Prime Minister, Satanchia – Grand General, Agaliarept – Aussi General, Feurety – Lieutenant Commander, Sargantanas – Major Nebiros – Field Marshal
SUBORDINATE SPIRITS	Bael, Bathim, Agares, Pursan, Marbas, Abigar, Pruslas, Loray, Aamon, Valefar, Barbatos, Forau, Buer, Ayperos, Gusoyn, Nuberus, Botis, Glasyabolis

Weyer's Devil Rankings[45]

DEVIL	RANK
Beelzebuth	Supreme Chieftain
Satan	Occupies second place as prince of darkness
Eurynomous	Prince of death
Moloch	Prince of the land of tears
Pluto	Prince of fire
Baal	Commander of the armies of hell
Lucifer	Dispenses justice
Asmodeus	Gambling
Baalberith	Minister of pacts and treaties
Proserpine	Prince of demonic spirits
Astaroth	Prince and treasurer of hell
Nergal	Chief of secret police

Dukante's Devil Rankings[46]

DEVIL	RANK
Satan	King
Unsere (f.)	Fertility and sorcery
Delepitore (f.)	Demoness of sorcery enlightenment
Satanchia	Grand General (war)
Agaliarept	Assistant Grand General (war)
Lucifage	High Command (control)
Flereous	Fire elemental
Lucifer	Air elemental
Leviathan	Water elemental
Belial	Earth elemental
Beelzebuth	Lord of insects
Belphegore	Master of armament and weaponry
Mesphito	Keeper of the book of death
Amducious	The destroyer
Asmodeus	Demon of lust
Sonnielion (f.)	Demoness of hate
Abaddon	Adviser
Ammon	Demon of domination
Mammon	Demon of avarice
Rosier	Demon of love
Ashtaroth (f.)	Priestess of friendship
Eurynomous	Demon of death
Verrine	Demon of health
Verrier (f.)	Demoness of plants
Ronwe	Demon of knowledge
Babeal	Keeper of graves

The Seven Princes of Hell[47]

DEVIL	RANK
Baal-beryth	Master of rituals and pacts
Dumah	Commander of the demons of Gehenna
Meririm	Prince of air
Rahab	Prince of oceans
Sariel	Prince of the Moon
Mephistopholes	The destroyer
Lucifer Rofocale	Prime Minister and controls wealth

Arch She-Demons[48]

DEVIL	RANK
Leviathan	The Chaos Dragon
Barbelo	Unknown
Proserpine	Destroyer
Astarte	Queen of spirits of the dead
Agrat-bat-mahlaht	One of Satan's wives and demoness of whores
Eisheth Zenunim	Same as above
Lilith	Satan's favourite wife
Naamah	Demoness of seduction

Arch Demons of Hell[49]

DEVIL	RANK
Adramaleck	Prince of fire
Carniveau	Demon of possession
Python	Prince of lying spirits
Mammon	Prince of temptors
Rimmon	Prince of lightning

Demons Listed by Purpose and Rulership

LIFE HEALING	Unsere, Verrine, Verrier, Belial, Death, Eurynomous, Baalberith, Babael, Nature, Belial, Lucifer, Satan, Flereous, Leviathan, Rimmon, Dagon, Rahab Seriel
HATE, VENGEANCE, ANGER, WAR	Amducious, Andras, Merihim, Abaddon, Satanchia, Lucifuge, Rofocale, Agaliarept, Feurety, Sargatanas, Nebiros, Baal, Sonnilion, Tezrian, Olivier, Mephestophiles, Dumah, Proserpine, Belphegore, Svengali
LOVE, COMPASSION, RELATIONSHIPS, LUST	Rosier, Astarte, Ashtaroth, Astaroth, Asmodeous, Agrat-bat-mahlaht, Eisheth Zenunim, Lilith, Naamah, Asafoetida, Rashoone, Taroone
MONEY, PROSPERITY, LUCK	Behemoth, Belphegore, Asmodeous, Astaroth, Oeillet, Olivier, Beelzebub, Mammon
KNOWLEDGE, SECRETS, SORCERY	Ronwe, Pytho, Lucifer, Leviathan, Baalberith, Unsere, Delepitorae, Mesphito, Luithian, Abaddon, Verrier

GNOSTIC AEONS

Gnosticism is a general term for a number of philosophies or religions that existed in the few centuries immediately before and after the birth of Christ, and which flourished in Hellenistic culture. Their common features include a belief in two gods: one who created the world of Spirit ('the Logos'), the other who created the world of Matter ('the Demiurge'). Gnosticism emphasized a return to the world of Spirit by a process of mystical knowledge (Gnosis) and a belief in reincarnation.

In many Gnostic systems the various emanations of God are called aeons. According to this system, the First Being, known as Bythos (depth or profundity), contained within itself another inner being known variously as Ennoea (thought), Charis (grace) or Sige (silence). The perfect form of the 'split' being conceived the second male aeon Caen (power) to be within itself, along with the female aeon Akhana (truth, love). These male/female pairs of aeons were called *syzygies*. When combined, these *syzygies* constituted the *pleroma* or 'region of light'. The lowest regions of the *pleroma* were closest to the darkness – that is, the physical world.

When an aeon named Sophia emanated without her partner aeon, the result was the Demiurge, or half-creator (occasionally referred to as Ialdaboth in Gnostic texts), a creature that should never have come into existence. This creature did not belong to the *pleroma*, and the One emanated two saviour aeons, Christ and the Holy Spirit, to save humanity from the Demiurge. Christ then took the form of Jesus, in order to teach humanity how to achieve gnosis – that is, return to the *pleroma*.

The Gnostic Valentinus (c.100–c.153 CE) named 30 different aeons (see right).

Valentinus's Pairs of Aeons

AEON I	AEON II
Bythos (the One)	Sige (silence), Charis (grace), Ennoea (thought)
Caen (power)	Akhana (love)
Nous (mind)	Aletheia (truth)
Sermo (the word)	Vita (life)
Anthropos (humanity)	Ecclesia (church)
Bythios (profound)	Mixis (mixture)
Ageratos (Never old)	Henosis (union)
Autophyes (essential nature)	Hedone (pleasure)
Acinetos (immovable)	Syncrasis (co-mixture)
Monogenes (only-begotten)	Macaria (happiness)
Paracletus (comforter)	Pistis (faith)
Patricas (paternal)	Elpis (hope)
Ainos (praise)	Synesis (intelligence)
Ecclesiasticus (son of Ecclesia)	Macariotes (blessedness)
Theletus (perfect)	Sophia (wisdom)

11

EGYPTIAN MAGIC

EGYPTIAN DEITIES

Ankh-f-n-Khonsu lived in Thebes during the 25th and 26th dynasties (c.725 BCE). He served as a priest of the Egyptian falcon-headed or bull-headed god Mentu and is remembered today because he created a funerary tablet before his death, known as the Stele of Revealing. In the museum in Cairo this is numbered as exhibit 666.

Crowley, who came to believe that in a previous life he had been Ankh-f-n-Khonsu, found the stele in the museum while he and his wife, Rose, were visiting Cairo in 1904. Soon after making his discovery, Crowley received a revelation from his holy guardian angel, Aiwass, which he wrote up as the ***Book of Law***, inaugurating what some occultists believe is the New Aeon of Horus.

It is hardly surprising that ***Liber 777***, written a few years later, brings Egyptian Magick into its correspondences. And it is hardly surprising that the whole Golden Dawn system is suffused with Egyptian undertones, because at the time that Samuel Mathers and his peers were creating the rituals and writing the Knowledge Papers of the Golden Dawn, Egypt was having its antiquities and wonders uncovered on a daily basis. It might be argued that the two impulses were not unconnected.

There is a belief in Magick that when you become aware of a god, that god becomes aware of you. What happens is that you might find yourself drawn towards a particular deity and start working from that point on. Many people's first magickal exercises are with Egyptian deities simply because they are easy to visualize. You might be attracted to the Celtic goddess of the hearth fire, Bride/Bridget, but you have to create her 'telesmatic image' from those impulses that she inspires. With the Egyptian goddess Isis, however, the lines and lineage are precise. The act of visualizing yourself in one of these forms is known as 'assuming the god-form'. It involves not just imagining the basic outlines, but trying to ***feel*** within yourself the qualities of that deity. You are then in a position to channel the energies of that god or goddess. When it is done properly, a good psychic would actually see the god-form around you.

The names of deities also have enormous importance. The Egyptians themselves attached great significance to the concept of the ***ren***, or name, and simply uttering it would invoke the god's essence. As with your own name, correct pronunciation by others is less important than the tone of utterance, and the emotions directed your way.

Major Egyptian Deities

NAME	TITLE	ASSOCIATIONS
Amun	The hidden one	Unseen power
Andjety	Underworld god	Rebirth
Ankt	War goddess	Feminine strength
Anti	The ferryman	Psychopomp
Anubis	Opener of the way	Lord of the dead
Anuket	The embracer	Deity of childbirth
Apep	Serpent god	The challenger

NAME	TITLE	ASSOCIATIONS
Apis	Sacred bull	Animal power
Aset (Isis)	Great mother	Primal goddess
Aten (Aton)	Sun god	Illumination
Atum	Primeval god	Self-creation
Bastet	Cat goddess	Music and dance
Bennu	Phoenix bird	Creation
Bes	Ithyphallic dwarf god	Music, dance, revelry
Chnum (Khnum)	Ram god	Protection of sources
Chons (Khonsu)	Moon god	Dreams and the unconscious
Ernutet (Renenet)	Serpent-headed goddess	Power of names
Geb	Earth god	Earth Magick
Harachte	Horus of the Horizon	Inspiration
Hoor par Kraat	Horus the child	Initiation
Hathor (HetHert)	Lady of the sycamore	Romance, love, lust
Heqet	Frog-headed goddess	Death and childbirth
Horus (Heru)	Hawk god	Supremacy
Khnum	Craftsman god	Creation
Máahes (Mahes)	God of war	Protection of sacred places
Maat	Goddess	The ecosystem of balance
Meret	Goddess of song	Rejoicing
Mut	Vulture goddess	Wisdom and motherhood
Neith	Primordial goddess	Self-creation
Nepthys	Invisible one	Shape-shifting
Nut (Nuit)	Star goddess	Stellar consciousness
Opet	Goddess of pregnancy	Homes and childbirth
Osiris (Asar)	The Green Man	The Underworld
Ptah	Creator god	Crafts of sciences
Ra	Sun god	Renewal
Seker (Sokar)	God of craftsmen	The dead and funerals
Sekhmet	Lion goddess	Fire and revenge
Seshet	Goddess of scribes	Libraries and archives
Seth (Set)	Lord of darkness	Powers of night and knowledge
Sothis (Sopdet)	Goddess of fertility	Sirian Magick
Thoth (Djehuti, Tahuti)	Ibis-headed god	Learning and recording
Wadjet (Uatchet)	Cobra goddess	Enlightenment and royalty

THE EGYPTIAN ALPHABET

The Egyptian alphabet has a curious appeal and power in its own right, and is often used in making talismans. The very act of drawing them while brooding upon your scheme of work will help to 'charge' them.

The Egyptian Alphabet[50]

PHARAONIC HIEROGLYPH	SOUND FOR	PHOENICIAN ALPHABET	HEBREW LETTER NAME	GREEK LETTER NAME	DEVELOPED INTO MODERN LETTER
	A		Alpha	Alpha	A
	B		Beth	Beta	B
	G		Gimel	Gamma	C (G)
	D		Daleth	Delta	D
	H		He	Epsilon	E
	W		Waw	Digamma	F (UVWY)
	Z		Zayin	Zeta	G (Z)
	Ch		Chet	Eta	H
	It		Teth	Theta	I (T)
	J		Yodh	Iota	J (I)
	K		Kaph	Kappa	K
	L		Lamedh	Lambda	L
	M		Mem	Mu	M
	N		Nun	Nu	N
	kS		Samekh	Xi	X (ks)
	rO		Ayin	Omicron	O
	Pr		Pe	Pi	P (Ph)
	sS		Sadhe	San	S
	K		Qoph	Qoppa	Q
	R		Resh	Rho	R
	Sh		Shin	Sigma	Sh
	Dj		Taw	Tau	Th

PRACTICAL EGYPTIAN MAGICK

For the most part, ancient Egyptians worshipped a pantheon consisting of numerous gods and goddesses. But during the time of Amenhotep IV (14th century BCE) only one god was worshipped, and this was the sun god who later evolved into Aten. Amenhotep changed his name to Akhenaten and proceeded to erase all signs of the worship of Amun. Upon his death, however, the Egyptians reverted to worshipping all of their former pantheon.

The Egyptian Book of Rites was called *Hebet En Ba*. The Egyptians were known to make use of the sacred circle within their rites, and four 'deities' or ***neteru*** (***neter*** being the Egyptian word for 'spiritual powers', see page 13) represented the four quarters (see below).

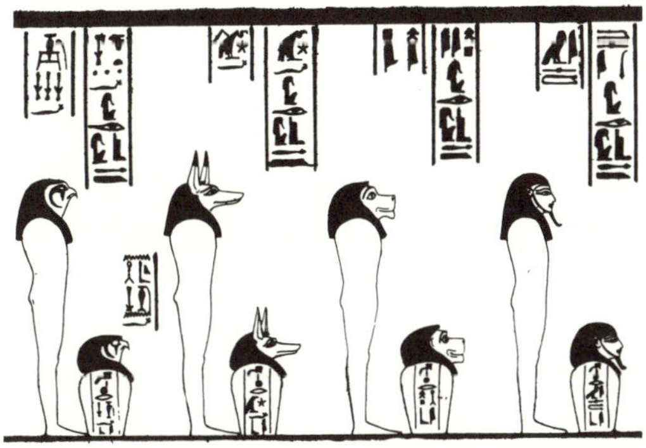

Left to right: Qebsenuv, Duamutef, Hapi, Imsety

The *Neters*

HIEROGLYPHS	*NETER*	QUARTER	BODY ORGAN
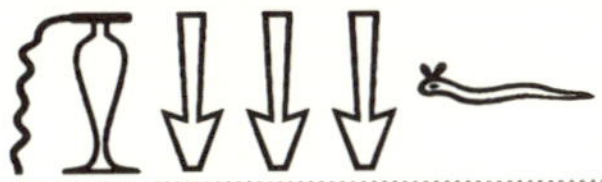	Qebsenuv	West	Intestines
	Imsety	South	Liver
	Duamutef	East	Stomach
	Hapi	North	Lungs

One of the most practical interpretations of the *Hebet En Ba* was given by the late Khiron (1948–1999), founding Master of the Maitreyan Order of Hsien Tao. He felt that reciting spells or utterances in the Egyptian language was conducive to their having a potent effect:

> According to the Egyptians themselves, their language was given them directly from the Spiritual World, by the *neteru* or 'gods'. Certainly ancient Egyptian has similarities and common roots shared with some other ancient languages, though Egypt's claim that the very sounds comprising their language are themselves 'Powers' should not be dismissed lightly (future generations of scientists may yet discover that Sounds are Powers in their own right). But perhaps the best argument in favour of the use of 'reconstructed' Egyptian in these Rites is that Egyptian 'divinity' may very well still 'speak' the Egyptian tongue. Silly as this may sound to you right now, you may change that opinion, should you happen to meet one of the *Neteru* as a result of these Rites. Be that as it may, these are the Egyptian Mystical Rites we have used, and found to be worthy.[51]

One of these rites was the 'invocation of astral flight' and was derived from the ancient Egyptian perception that we live on no fewer than ***nine*** other dimensions, including many that are so non-physical we can only dream of them...yet they remain very important parts of our lives. This rite can stimulate the awakening of the dreamer within what Khiron termed the astral and causal planes or dimensions. Used before sleep at night, it can trigger vivid dream-life recall and the ability to direct your dreams consciously.

Another ritual or evocation concerned the 'invocation of soul memory'. It was designed to bring to the surface all those bits and pieces of karma that might be surviving bits of past lives, and put you in touch with the other self-fragments hidden within your psyche. Khiron wrote:

> The Three Paths spoken of are called by Kabbalists 'the Hermetic, the Orphic and the Mystical Paths'; and the Two Pillars mentioned here are Aima/Anima the Black (feminine) Pillar of Psyche and its White Twin, Abba/Animus, the masculine side of Self. All of these things this Rite gives you entry to as you explore the Akashic Records of *soul memory* within you.

The Invocation of Astral Flight

Pa-na May I fly, *au-a* May I *temt-kua* gather myself together *em* like *bah-k* a hawk

nepver beautiful *en* of *nub;* gold; *an-na* may come to me *ab-a* my heart *em* from *tu* the land

Abtet; of Beginnings *an-na-a* may it come to me *er* *amitu* among the gods *neteru*

The Invocation of Soul Memory

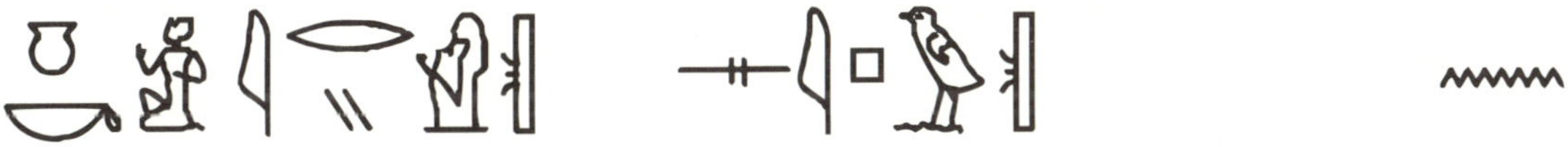

Nuk I am *ari* the keeper of my Akashic Records, of all which is *sapu* *en*

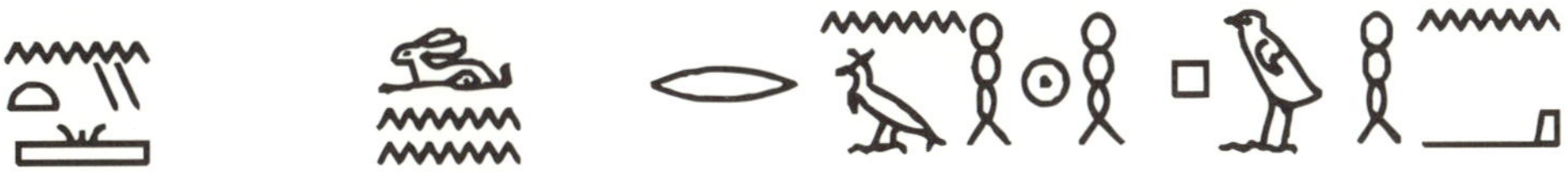

enti and *unen;* which shall be *er* *neheh* Eternity *pu* it is *hen-eh* and

t'etta Everlastingness *ar* *Aukush* Oh, *sep kshemt,* Three paths and

t'eb-eh sen; Two Pillars; *eh-ba-k,* open your *ter-k!* portals!

Van Den Dungen's Ritual Postures[52]

Ritual Posture	Semantics	Extended Semantics
	'wrd' – tire, exhaustion	Non-activity, inertia, funerary rituals and lamentations
	'hnw' – jubilation	Commemoration of the victory of Horus over Seth, the Henu Rite
	'ksi' – bow down	Honouring the deities and divine king, and rites of submission and respect
	'nis' – summon, call, invoke	Formal invocation of the deities and the noble dead
	'sHr' – drive away, execrate	Ritual banishments

Ritual Posture	Semantics	Extended Semantics
	'xbi' – dance, jubilate	Expressions of joy and happiness in the presence of the divine
	'wab' – pure, clean	Preparing for ritual, purifications
	'dWa' – praise, supplicate, adore	Reciting hymns and giving praise to the deities and pharaoh
	'dwA' – supplicate, adore	Paying homage (praise) and acts of supplication
	'Hai' – high, joy, rejoice, laud	Highest expression of celebration and spiritual joy

THE *NOMES*

Under that oft-quoted Hermetic axiom of 'as above, so below' we find within Egypt an example of a whole nation that felt it was a reflection not just of the circuit of heaven above and the Underworld below, but of their own souls as the linking energy.

Thus the 42 *nomes*, or districts of Egypt, equated directly with the 42 *neters* ('gods and goddesses'), which related to the 42 laws in the Chamber of Maat and the 42 portions of the human being.

In a very real sense the land and the people were one; the king and the land were also one. In the light of the foregoing, the *nomes* can be seen as areas of consciousness rather than mere geographical districts. By using the *nome* symbols in the same way as the *tattwas* (see page 51), or as Hebrew letters when exploring the paths on the Tree of Life, you can catch glimpses of the people who inhabited these areas and touch upon the *neters* concerned.

The Nile Showing the 42 *Nomes*

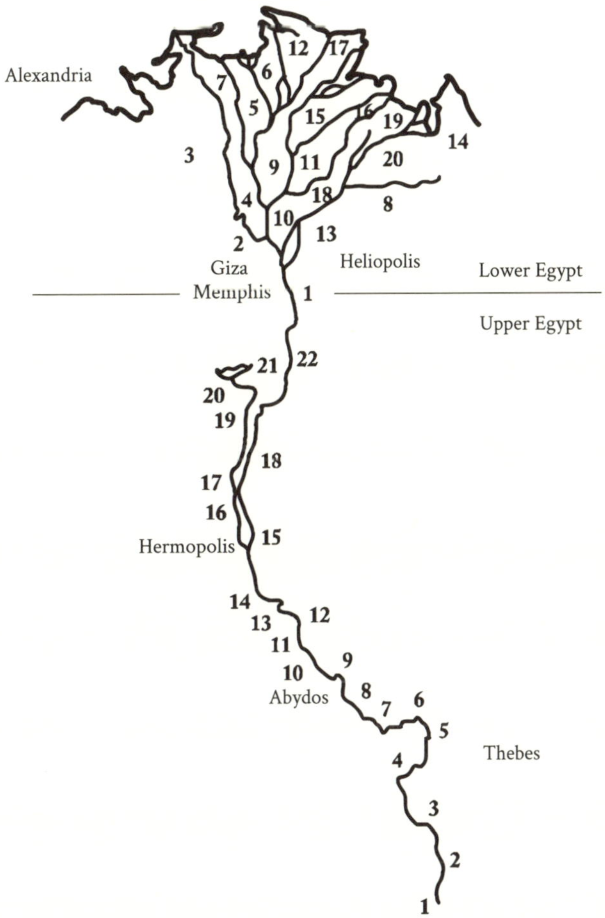

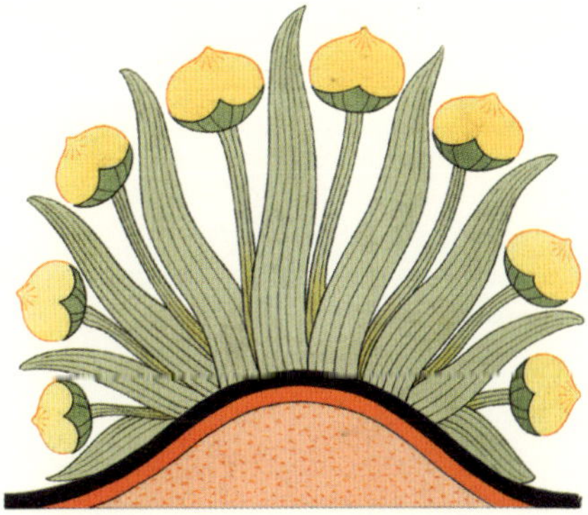

THE *NOMES* OF LOWER EGYPT AND THEIR ASSOCIATIONS[53]

NOME	NAME	SYMBOL	DEITIES	CITY AND TEMPLES
1	White fortress (White wall)	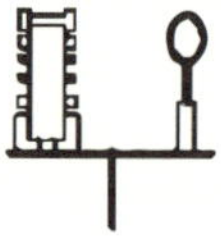	Ptah, Sokar, Apis	Inebhed/Mennefer (Greek Memphis, Arabic Mit Rahina), Ptah, Hathor
2	Cow's thigh (foreleg)		Horus, Kherty	Khem (Greek Letopolis, Arabic Ausim), Horus-foremost-of-Khem
3	West		Hathor	Imu (Arabic Kom el-Hisn), Hathor-Sekhmet
4	Southern shield		Neith	–
5	Northern shield		Neith	Sau (Greek Sais, Arabic Sa al-Hagar), Neit
6	Mountain bull		Re	Khasu (Greek Xois, Arabic Sakha), Ra/Pe and Dep (Greek Buto, Arabic Tell el-Farain), Wadjyt
7	West harpoon		Ha	–
8	East harpoon		Atum	Peratum (biblical Pithom, Arabic Tell al-Maskhuta), Atum
9	Anezti (Andjti, anD.t, Andjety)		Osiris, Andjety	Djedu (Greek Busiris, Arabic Abu Sir Bana), Horus-Khentkhety
10	Black bull		Horus (km-wr, Black Ox)	Hutherib (Greek Athribis, Arabic Tell Atrib), Osiris and Isis

NOME	NAME	SYMBOL	DEITIES	CITY AND TEMPLES
11	Heseb bull (Ox count)		Shu, Tefnut, Mihos	Taremu (Greek Leontopolis, Arabic Tell al-Moqdam), Maihesa
12	Cow with calf (calf and cow)		Onuris	Tjebennetjer (Greek Sebennytus, Arabic Samanud), Inheret-Shu and Mehyt Perhebyt (Arabic Behbeit), Isis of Hebyt
13	Undamaged sceptre (prospering sceptre)		Atum, Iusaas, Mnevis	Iunu (Greek Heliopolis, Arabic Matariya), Ra-Atum, Hathor Kheraha (Greek 'Babylon of Egypt', part of Old Cairo), Atum
14	East or anterior *nome* (foremost of the East)		Seth	Tjaru (Greek Sile, Arabic Qantara), Horus of Mesen
15	Ibis		Thoth	Weprehwy (Greek Hermopolis, Arabic Baqliya), Thoth
16	Dolphin (Fish)		Banebdjedet, Hatmehyt	Djedet (Greek Mendes), Banebdjedet
17	The throne (zmA-bHd.t, Behdet)	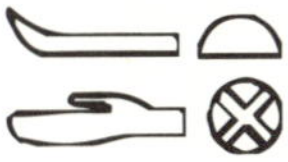	Horus	Semabehdet (Arabic Balamun), Amun
18	Royal child upper *nome* (Prince of the South)		Bast	Bast (Greek Bubastis, on edge of modern Zagazig), Bast
19	Royal child lower *nome* (Prince of the North)		Wadjyt	Imet (Arabic Nebesha), Wadjyt, Djanet (Greek Tanis), Amun, Mut and Khonsu
20	East (plumed falcon)		Sopdu	Per-Sopdu (Arabic Saft al-Henna), Sopdu

The *Nomes* of Upper Egypt and Their Associations[54]

NOME	NAME	SYMBOL	DEITIES	CITY AND TEMPLES
1	Land of the arch or To Khentit: the frontier (Ta-Seti)		Khnum, Satis, Anukis, Isis, Horus the Elder, Sobek	Abu (Greek Elephantine), Khnum, Satet Sunet (Greek Syene, Arabic Aswan), Isis Nubyt (Arabic Kom Ombo), Sobek with Horus
2	Throne of Horus		Horus	Djeba (Greek Apollonopolis, Arabic Edfu), Horus
3	The rural (shrine)		Horus, Nekhbet, Khnum, Neith	Nekhen (Greek Hierakonpolis, Arabic Kom al-Ahmar), Hous Nekheb (Greek Eleithyiaspolis, Arabic Elkab), Nekhbet and Sobek, Nekheb desert valley, Hathor, Shesmetet
4	The sceptre		Amun, Mut, Khons, Montu, Buchis, Sobek	Perhathor (Greek Pathyris, Arabic Gebelein), Hathor Imiotru (Arabic Rizeiqat), Mont Djerty (Arabic Tod), Mont Waset (Greek Thebes, Arabic Qurneh for West Bank, Luxor and Karnak for East Bank), Amun, Mut, Khons and various Madu (Arabic Medamud), Mont
5	The two falcons		Min, Seth	Shenhur (retains name in Arabic), Isis Gis (Greek Apollonopolis Mikra, Arabic Qus), Horus and Heqet, divine child Khons-Thoth, Gebtyu (Greek Coptos, Arabic Qift), Min and Isis, Nubt (Greek Ombos, Arabic Naqada), Seth
6	The crocodile		Hathor	Iunet (Greek Aphroditipolis, Arabic Dendera), Hathor, Ihy
7	Sistrum		Bat	Hut-Sekhem-Senusret (Arabic Hu)
8	Great land		Khentamentiu, Osiris, Onuris	Abdju (Greek Abydos, Arabical-Arabah), Osiris Khentamentiu
9	Minu (Min)		Min	Khentmin (Greek Panopolis, Arabic Akhmim), Min
10	Cobra		Seth, Mihos, Nemty	Tjebu (Greek Antaeopolis, Arabic Qau al-Kabir), Nemty
11	The Set animal (Seth)		Seth (Arabic Shutb)	Shashotep (Greek Apotheke), Arabic Shutb

NOME	NAME	SYMBOL	DEITIES	CITY AND TEMPLES
12	Viper mountain	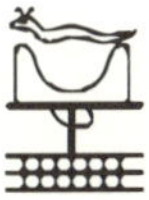	Nemty	Hut-Sekhem-Senusret (Arabic Hu)
13	Upper pomegranate tree (upper sycamore and viper)		Wepwawet, Anubis	Saut (Greek Lycopolis, Arabic Asyut), Wepwawet
14	Lower pomegranate tree (lower sycamore and viper)		Hathor	Qesy (Greek Cusae, Arabic al-Qusiya), Hathor
15	Hare		Thoth, Ogdoad, Aten	Khemenu (Greek Hermopolis, Arabic Ashmunein), Thoth
16	Oryx		Pakhet, Khnum	Hebenu (Arabic Kom al-Ahmar), Horus-Tadehnet (Greek Akoris, Arabic Tehna), Amun and Sobek
17	The black dog (jackal)		Anubis	Saka (Arabic al-Qes), Bata, Hardai, Anubis
18	Falcon with spread wings (Nemty)		Nemty	Hutnesut (Arabic Sharuna), Horus-Dunanwy
19	The pure sceptre (two sceptres)		Seth, Mormyrus fish	Permedjed (Greek Oxyrhynchus, Arabic Bahnasa)
20	Upper laurel (southern sycamore)	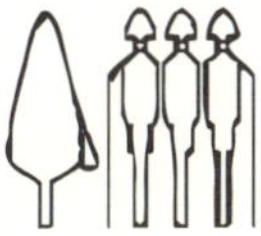	Heryshef	Henennesut (Greek Heracleopolis, Arabic Ihnasya), Heryshef
21	Lower laurel (northern sycamore)		Khnum, Seneferu	Shenakhen, Semenuhor (Greek Akanthon, perhaps near Arabic Kafr Ammar and Kafr Tarkhan)
22	Knife		Hathor	Tepihu (Greek Aphroditopolis, Arabic Atfih), Hathor

12

CELTIC MAGIC

THE CELTIC TRADITION

Until Christine Hartley wrote her seminal book ***The Western Mystery Tradition*** in 1968, no one had openly looked at what might be called the 'Native British' sources of wisdom. Until then all eyes were focused on the East as the source of spirituality. Aleister Crowley was such a classicist that he seemed unaware of the power that lay beneath the Celtic and Arthurian traditions, or of north-western European deities in general. W B Yeats (1865–1939) and Maud Gonne (1866–1953) were privately obsessed with the Celtic Mysteries, but it was Dion Fortune (1890–1946) who developed these within her lodge, the Fraternity of the Light, and it was her pupil Christine Hartley who made some of her own magickal workings public via her book.

Thanks to their work, and the work done by those whom they inspired, the ancient gods and goddesses of the West are being invoked more now in the first decades of the 21st century than they were two thousand years ago.

A modern exponent of such mysteries is Mike Harris (born 1947), magus of the Company of Avalon, who has spent most of his adult life in north Wales in the area where the ***Mabinogi*** (tales from medieval Welsh traditions), Arthurian and related myths originated. He points out in ***Merlin's Chess*** that:

A handful of bards with names like Taliesin and Myrddin (Merlin) stalk the pages of British 'Arthurian' mythology...As *awenyddion* [inspired ones], they claimed to have seen the past and 'remembered' the future. They realized that time, as we know it, has no validity in the general terms of spiritual evolution, but that spiritual evolution must nonetheless fix its roots in the particular world of every 'here and now'.[55]

These are the beings that we can aspire to work with, although their mindset is very different from anything we might find in Egyptian, kabbalistic or Hermetic realms. Harris gives a simple but effective illustration of the Celtic cosmos (see right).

With this kind of pattern and fluidity, the best way to understand the deities and their inner work is to start with the crucial names and their realms. These, in conjunction with some idea concerning their function or status, provide the raw material from which you can build up your own correspondences.

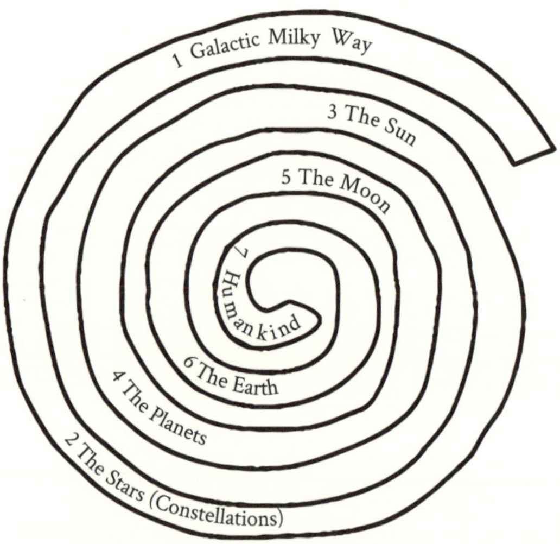

The Celtic cosmos

Harris's Three Worlds and the Three Faces of the Goddess[56]

WORLD	DEITIES	ATTRIBUTES	GODDESS
Heaven worlds	Archetypal gods and goddesses associated with stars; the night sky as the dark base of a cauldron that contains the *awen* (inspiration) of stars; the constellations are islands in the dark waters of space	Destiny and judgement	Arianrhod, goddess of the starry realms; the archetypal heaven worlds
Underworld	*Annwn* means 'the deep', the cauldron womb of the inner earth; an area of quantum potential between heaven and earth; in this *Annwn* is an 'island' or series of seven islands, facilitating the interaction of 'above' and 'below'	Transformation and inspiration	Ceridwen, Cthonic goddess of *Annwn*; the Welsh ancient British Underworld
Material world	From the potential of *Annwn* outcomes materialize in the phenomenal world, yet the phenomenal world is partly embraced by *Annwn*; it is this area, which is simultaneously in the physical world and in *Annwn*, that may, in a sense, be called Avalon	Action and consequences	Blodeuwedd, the goddess made from flowers and thus manifest in the phenomenal, natural human world; therefore displaying human vices, not least duplicity and infidelity

Figures From Celtic Myth [57]

NAME	STATUS	ASSOCIATION	NATIONALITY	LITERATURE	NOTES
Arthur	Hero, sacred king	Hero associated with the Bear (Welsh *Arth*) stars and precession of the equinoxes	Welsh	Mabinogi *Canu Aneirin, Trioedd ynys Prydain* (called Triads); Geoffrey of Monmouth, etc. most Welsh and later British/Arthurian mythological and legendary material	See also Uther Pendraig, who was associated with the Pole star in the Constellation of Draco, hence Pendraig (Pendragon), succeeded by Arthur (bear) when Pole star preceded into Ursa Minor (Little Bear)
Bran	Hero	Association with other-world travel	Irish	*Voyage of Bran*, 7th-century Irish	Irish Bran as distinct from the Welsh god; travels over the sea and enters *Tir na nÓg*, land of the ever young
Cu Chulainn	Hero	–	Irish, Ulster cycle	*Tain bo Cuailnge*	Name means 'Hound of Culann', which he offers to become, having slain the hound of Culann the smith; later made invincible by the supernatural Scathach
Culwch	Hero	Associated with the pig totem	Welsh	*Mabinogion* (Culwch ac Olwen)	Undergoes various trials to gain the hand of the giant's daughter Olwen
Elen	Historically based, subsequently mythologized heroine	Elen of the ways, with (Roman) roads and ancient trackways, particularly in Gwynedd	Welsh	*Mabinogion* (The Dream of Macsen Wledig)	A length of ancient trackway; a Roman road called the Sarn Elen near Trawsfynydd (a Roman outpost) still bears her name
Fionn	Hero	Sovereignty; almost an Irish counterpart of Arthur	Irish, Ulster	*Agallamh na Seanorach* (Colloquy of the Old Men), 12th century	From the noun *fian*, denoting a band of wandering warriors with allegiance only to their leader

NAME	STATUS	ASSOCIATION	NATIONALITY	LITERATURE	NOTES
Goewin	Sacred queen	Sovereignty	Welsh	*Mabinogion* (Math ap Mathonwy)	See also Virgin queen
Virgin queen, empowerer of the high King Math (until she was raped by Gilfaethwy, at Gwydion's instigation)	Sacred queen	Sovereignty	Welsh	*Mabinogi*, Triads and later British Arthurian literature	Name means 'white phantom'; popularised as Arthur's queen, Guinevere, Gwynhyfar
Mab Darogan	Divine child	'The prophesied son'	Welsh	Triads	–
Mabon	See Modron, below		Welsh	*Mabinogion* (Math ap Mathonwy), Triads	Son of Modron
Mac ind Og	Divine son	Son of the Dagdha	Irish	(see also Oenghus on page 206)	Irish equivalent of Welsh Mabon
Macsen Wledig	Hero	Historical Roman general mythologized	Welsh	*Mabinogion* (The Dream of Macsen Wledig)	–
Matholwch	Tanist (heir apparent)	–	Welsh (name for Irish king)	*Mabinogion* (Branwen fech Llyr)	The Irish king who married and then imprisoned Branwen

NAME	STATUS	ASSOCIATION	NATIONALITY	LITERATURE	NOTES
Merlin, Myrddin	Sage, wizard	Based upon a historical bard of the Dark Ages; promoted to superhuman proportions, mainly by Geoffrey of Monmouth	Welsh	*Canu Aneirin, Black Book of Carmarthen*, Triads, Geoffrey of Monmouth, much Welsh and British	Arthurian, mythological and legendary material
Modron	'Divine mother'	–	Welsh	–	Associated with the Matrona cult from Celtic Gaul and the River Marne
Niall	Sacred king	–	Irish	–	Kisses the crone of sovereignty (like the Arthurian Lady Ragnell tale) and the desolate Irish landscape is restored
Olwen	Semi-divine heroine	Daughter of a giant	Welsh	*Mabinogion* (Culhwch ac Olwen)	The hero Culwch has to perform tasks to win her hand; also 'Olwen of the white track' suggests stellar goddess facets
Ossian	–	–	Irish	–	–
Owain	Arthurian hero	–	Welsh	*Mabinogion*	–
Pryderi	–	–	Welsh	–	–
Pwyll	Hero	–	Welsh	*Mabinogion* (Pwyll, prince of Dyfed)	–

NAME	STATUS	ASSOCIATION	NATIONALITY	LITERATURE	NOTES
Taliesin	Bards (*awenyddion*), or those poetically inspired by the *Awen*, the nectar sipped from the cauldron of the Underworld (*Annwn*) goddess Ceridwen	–	Welsh	*Hanes Taliesin*, Triads	The name adopted by historical, magical bards throughout most of the medieval period in Wales, based upon an archetypal bard of that name whose myth is to be found in the *Hanes Taliesin*
Tuatha de Danann	Dynasty of immortals, latterly associated with the faery world	Magic and druidry	Irish	*Book of Invasions* (*Leabhar Gabhala Eireann*), 12th century	'The people of the goddess Danu'; fought for the rule of primordial Ireland with other quasi-divine beings in the two battles of Magh Tuiredh
Twylth Teg	Welsh faery	–	Welsh	–	'The fair folk'
Uther Pendraig	Sacred king	Father of Arthur, 'Uther head of the Dragon' – pendragon	Welsh	Geoffrey of Monmouth, Triads	See Arthur and precession of the equinoxes; associated with the 'Dragon' star(s) Alpha Draconis

Celtic Deities[58]

DEITY	STATUS	ASSOCIATION	NATIONALITY	LITERATURE	NOTES
Anu	(Earth) mother goddess	'Paps of Anu' mountain in Kerry	Irish	*Mabinogi* (Pwyll, prince of Dyfed)	–
Arawn	Underworld god	See also Gwynn ap Nudd	Welsh	*Mabinogi* (Math ap Mathonwy) and Taliesin material	Underworld (*Annwn*) god who enlists the help of the mortal prince Pwyll to overthrow his enemy
Arianrhod	Goddess	Stellar goddess associated with the Corona Borealis	Welsh	*Mabinogi* (Math ap Mathonwy)	Associated with destiny (Geasa); sister-wife of Gwydion and the nemesis of bards
Bloddeuwedd	Goddess	Associated with Earth; made from flowers (by Math and Gwydion)	Welsh	*Mabinogi* (Branwen fech Llyr) Triads	Her name derives from the Welsh word for flowers, *Bloddeu*; later in the myth she is changed into an owl that has a (dished) 'flower face'
Bran	God, sacred king	Associated with a raven totem (Bran means raven in Welsh); reputedly a benevolent giant who was king of Britain	Welsh	*Voyage of Bran*	A god of many facets in Welsh literature; reputed in one instance to have brought Christianity to Britain; invaded Ireland to liberate his sister Branwen, but was mortally wounded and asked his seven companions to take his head back to Britain; they did so and it remained animated for some time and is reputedly buried beneath the Tower of London
Branwen	Goddess, heroine	Name means 'white raven; the 'white' prefix suggests an association with *Annwn*, the Welsh Underworld	Welsh	*Mabinogi* (Branwen fech Llyr)	Sister of (Welsh) Bran who married Matholwch, King of Ireland, who later restrained her until she was liberated by her brother; returned to Britain and died of grief

DEITY	STATUS	ASSOCIATION	NATIONALITY	LITERATURE	NOTES
Brighid	Historical Celtic saint based upon a pagan goddess	Healing, herding, smithcraft, poetry; name means 'The exalted one'	Irish	*Mabinogi*, Triads, *Hanes Taliesin*	Brighid (also Brede, Bride, Brigid, Ffread in Welsh) is a unique goddess (originally the daughter of the Daghda), whose name was taken by a historical Celtic saint whose cult spread throughout Ireland and the British Isles
Ceridwen	Goddess	Underworld, *Annwn*	Irish	*Book of Invasions* (*Leabhar Gabhala Eireann*), 12th century	Cauldron goddess, Taliesin's chief protagonist in the *Hanes Taliesin*
Daghdha	Father God	Underworld, faery	Irish	*Book of Invasions* (*Leabhar Gabhala Eireann*), 12th century	Head of the Tuatha de Danaan, father of the (pagan version of) Brighid
Danu	Mother Godess	(of the) Tuatha de Danann	Irish	*Book of Invasions* (*Leabhar Gabhala Eireann*), 12th century	The mother of the divine people (latterly considered Faery), the Tuatha de Danann; comparable with the Welsh Don, as a source or original deity
Donn	God	God of the dead, also Father God	Irish	–	Associated with Tech Duinn island
Fin, Fintan	God, sage	Salmon	Irish	*Book of Invasions* (*Leabhar Gabhala Eireann*), 12th century	Survivor of the flood, who existed on through time as a salmon of knowledge and as an eagle
Gofannon	God	Divine smith	Welsh	*Mabinogion*	Smith gods (and goddesses like Brighid) were of great importance to Celtic warrior soceity in terms of weapon production
Goibhniu	God	As above	Irish	*Tain bo Cuailnge*	Irish version Gofannon

DEITY	STATUS	ASSOCIATION	NATIONALITY	LITERATURE	NOTES
Gronw	Dark god	Tanist	Welsh	*Mabinogion* (Math ap Mathonwy)	Lover of Blodewedd, who killed her husband Llew; Llew returned to life later to kill Gronw; a standing stone in Gwynedd is called Lech Gronw
Gwydion	Stellar god (associated with the Milky Way)	God of bards	Welsh	*Mabinogion* (Math ap Mathonwy), Triads	Brother and lover of Arianrhod and father to Llew; archetypal bard/sage (god of bards)
Lleu, Llew	God	Sacrificed solar hero	Welsh	*Mabinogion* (Math ap Mathonwy)	Son of Gwydion and Arianrhod; husband of Blodewedd, who betrays him (see Gronw)
Lugh	God	Irish Mercury, god of skills	Irish	*Tain bo Cuailnge*	Associated with the Isle of Man; Welsh Manawydan fab Llyr
Manannan mac Lir	God, sage	Sea god	Irish/Welsh	–	–
Medhbh of Connacht	War goddess	Semi-mythological	Irish	–	–
Medrawd	Malign demigod, Tanist	Mythological bastard child of Arthur	Welsh (English Mordred)	*Mabinogi*, Triads, British Arthurian literature (Mordred)	Son of Arthur from his incestuous relationship with Morgan le Fay
Morrighan	War goddess	–	Irish	–	Associated with the Washer at the Ford who anticipates the death of warriors

DEITY	STATUS	ASSOCIATION	NATIONALITY	LITERATURE	NOTES
Nemhedh	Earth god	Leader of the third (mythological) invasion of Ireland	Irish	*Book of Invasions* (*Leabhar Gabhala Eireann*), 12th century	Associated with the topography of Ireland
Nodens	God	–	Romano-British	See *Mabinogion* (Ludd ac Llefelys)	Nodens, whose temple was at Lydney in the Forest of Dean, would appear to be the same as the Welsh Lludd and the Irish Nuadha
Nuadha	God	Sacred king	Irish	*Book of Invasions* (*Leabhar Gabhala Eireann*), 12th century	Resigned twice from the kingship of Ireland; he is Nuadha Airgedlamh, 'Nuadha silverhand'
Oenghus	God	See Mac ind Og (see page 201)	Welsh	–	–
Oghma	Solar god, divine champion	The Irish 'Hercules'	Irish	–	God of learning and letters; the Irish Ogham marking and writing system is named after him
Rhiannon	Goddess	Welsh Persephone	Welsh	Mabinogion (Pwyll, prince of Dyfed)	Associated with the Epona, white-mare cult
Sulis	Goddess of springs and healing	Welsh/British Minerva, Romano-British Brigid	–	–	Associated with Bath ('Aquae Sulis') and Minerva
Ygraine	Quasi-goddess	Mother of King Arthur	Romano-British	Geoffrey of Monmouth's *History of the Kings of Britain*	Queen of Gorlois of Cornwall or a princess from Lyonesse

THE WORLD OF FAERY

If the Christian tradition has its angels and demons, then the pagan Celtic traditions have more than their share of faeries (denizens of another realm that merges with our own). It was only in Victorian times that the faery races were seen as tiny, cute little beings who lurked in flowers. In truth, the faery races were known in Gaelic as the ***Sidhe*** (pronounced 'Shee') and were originally experienced as otherworldly beings of enormous power (and sometimes enormous danger).

If the ***nomes*** of ancient Egypt (see page 191) had symbols that can enable you to access some of their mysteries, then there is no reason why you should not experiment with the spirits of Celtic Britain. Even today there are areas of Britain that are identified by primal symbols ranging from red roses and dragons, through white horses, to erect giants. There are myths and legends that are only known locally, but which can provide keys to unblocking mysteries. However, be aware that if you tap into ancient tribal consciousness, you will be touching upon atavistic qualities that might seem every bit as worrisome and dangerous as summoning demons.

Faery Correspondences[59]

FAERY BEING	LOCATION	TONE, FUNCTION, ELEMENT	OTHER
Asrais	Scotland	Sea ghosts	Also known as Ashrays
Barguest	England, Scotland	Black dog – death omen	Cu Sith, Cwn Annw, Shuck
Bean-Fionn	Ireland, England	–	Bean-Fionn, Ban-Shoan
Bean Sidhe	Ireland, Scotland	Death omen	Also known as Cointeach, Cyhiraeth, Cyoerraeth, Gwrach y Rhibyn, Eur-Cunnere Noe, Banshee, Bean Chaointe, Kannerez-Noz
Bean Tighe	Ireland	Friendly to humans	Ban-tee or Ban-Teeg
Bendith y Mamau	Wales	Underground spirit, malevolent	Momay or Mother's Blessing
Cailleac Bhuer	Scotland	Crone spirit	The Blue Hag, Black Annis, the Stone Woman
Clurichauns	Ireland	Leprechaun	His Nibs, Himself

FAERY BEING	LOCATION	TONE, FUNCTION, ELEMENT	OTHER
Coblynau	Wales	Mine spirit	Cousin to Cornish Knockers
Drakes	England	Dragon spirit	–
Ellyllons	Wales, Cornwall	Guardians to the Lady of the Lake	–
Fir Darrigs	Ireland, Scotland	Malevolent	Also known as Rat Boys, Fear Durgs
Fireesin	Isle of Man	Harvesters, Farm Faeries	–
Formors	Ireland	Sea creatures	Banished faery race
Geancanach	Ireland, Scotland	Guardians of home hearths	Pixies
Ghillie Dhu	Scotland	Guardian tree spirits	Also known as Gillee Doo or Yoo
Glashtin	Isle of Man, Scotland	Storm spirit	Also known as Hawlaa, Howlies, Howlers
The Glaistig	Scotland	Tutelary guardian of the site to which she is attached	An enchanted woman of human race, and given faery nature
Griffith	Wales, Ireland	Malevolent	Griffin, Gryphon, Geetoe, Phookas, Gitto
Gwyllion	Wales	Mountain faeries	–
Kelpies	Scotland, Ireland, Germany	Steeds of the goddess of the sea and the god of night	Also known as Uisges, Fuath, Shoney, Goborchinu, Afanc, Endrop, Each Uisge
Korrigans	Brittany, Cornwall	Spirits of forests and moors	Also known as Corrigans, Korils, Poulpikans,Teuz, Kornikaned
Leprechauns	Ireland	Treasure-hoarding faeries	Also known as the Gentry, Monaciello, Fir Darrig, Cluricaune, Logherima
Lunantisidhe	Ireland	Guardians of the blackthorn tree	–
Lutins	France, Cornwall	Shape-shifters	Also known as Follet

FAERY BEING	LOCATION	TONE, FUNCTION, ELEMENT	OTHER
Ly Erg	Scotland	Aggressive	–
Merrows	Universal	Sea spirits	Also known as Fish-Folk, Mermaids, Mermen, Water Dancers, Blue Men, Murduchu
Morgan le Fay	England, Scotland, Brittany	Enchantress, shape-shifter	Also known as Lady of Avalon
Murdhuachas	Ireland	Sea spirits	Also known as Walrus People, Sea Cows
Nucklelavees	Scotland	Sea spirits	Also known as Nuchlavis
Phookas	Ireland, Wales, Scandinavia	Air spirits	Also known as Kornbockes, Bookhas, Bwcas, Pouke
Phynnodderees	Isle of Man, Wales	Sea spirits	Also known as Bugganes, Fenoderee
Piskies	Scotland, Cornwall	Air spirits	Also known as Pixies, Pisgies, Pigseys, Pechts
Red Cap	Scotland, Ireland	Fire spirit	Also known as Fir Larrig, Dunters
Robin Goodfellow	Western Europe	Earth spirit	Also known as Puck, Pwca, Phouka, Pooka, Puca, Pan, Green Man
Selkies	Scotland and Orkney Islands	Water spirits	Also known as Roanes
Shellycoats	Scotland	Water spirits	–
Spriggans	England	Guardians of hill treasure	–
Trows	Shetland and Orkney Islands, Scandinavia, Trowbridge in Wiltshire	Air spirits	Also known as Night Stealers, Creepers
Twlwwyth Tegs	Wales	Beautiful humanoids with long golden hair	Also known as the Fair Family, Daoine Sidhe
Urisks	Scotland	Earth	–

CELTIC TREE LORE

Trees were (and are) a fundamental aspect of Celtic Magick. Tree lore has become part of every witch's canon. We all hug trees and try our best to preserve them, knowing that the future of our world is tied up with them. The poet Robert Graves (1895–1985) provided a huge impetus for all of this when he wrote his influential book *The White Goddess*, originally entitled *The Roebuck in the Thicket*. As is now recognized, he was – for the best of bardic reasons – making much of his correspondences up. But he triggered something within the Western psyche that is still reverberating today.

There is nothing written down in concrete when it comes to looking at trees and their influences, so we must make our own connections by looking at what others have intuited, and then by going out to ask – quite literally – individual trees what their associations might be. The answers may come in surprising ways, but they will be just as valid as Graves's apparently learned approach. Michael Viscoli, a dream therapist who lectures on astrology, chiromancy and comparative religion, gives some useful pointers in the following tables. Look to your own dreams for further insights.

Viscoli's Trees of Equinox and Solstice[60]

EQUINOX / SOLSTICE	DATE	TREE
Spring Equinox	21 March	Oak – for its strength and individuality
Summer Solstice	24 June	Birch – tree of the Midnight Sun, tree of light, the hardiest of deciduous trees
Autumn Equinox	23 September	Olive – for its nourishing, oil-rich fruit, and for its long, slow, patient growth
Winter Solstice	22 December	Beech – for its complete leaf canopy, the oil of its nuts, and its sense of when it is necessary to wait and when to grow

Viscoli's Trees of Spring and Autumn

SPRING DATE	TREE	AUTUMN DATE
22–31 March	Hazel – tree of those conceived at an equinox and born nine months later	24 September–3 October
1–10 April	Rowan – red berries popular with birds; tree of brightening and bettering	4–13 October
11–20 April	Maple – tree of relationship and community	14–23 October
21–30 April	Walnut – fruit of high fat and protein, tree of luck and zest	24 October–11 November
1–14 May	Poplar – tree of quick growth, agility and overcoming uncertainty	–
15–24 May	Chestnut – tree of lightness, beauty and truth	12–21 November
25 May–3 June	Ash – tree of aspiration and sacrifice	22 November–1 December
4–13 June	Hornbeam – tree of hard ('iron') wood, of loyalty and peace-making	2–11 December
14–23 June	Fig – tree of diversity and the search for balance, and of sweet fruit	12–21 December

Viscoli's Trees of Summer and Winter

SUMMER DATE	TREE	WINTER DATE
25 June–4 July	Apple – tree of earthly and heavenly love, and of sweet fruit	23 December–1 January
5–14 July	Spruce – tree of independence, privacy and self-nurturing	2–11 January
15–25 July	Elm – tree of good temper, speed and beauty	12–24 January
26 July–4 August	Cypress – tree of resurrection, and of calmness in misfortune	25 January–3 February
5–13 August	Poplar – tree of quick growth, agility and overcoming uncertainty	4–8 February
14–23 August	Cedar – tree of dedication and nobility	9–18 February
24 August–2 September	Pine – tree of healthy moderation, caution and hard work	19–29 February
3–12 September	Willow – tree of flexibility and tolerance	1–10 March
13– 22 September	Lime – tree of perfection and vulnerability	11–20 March

CELTIC TREASURES & ELEMENTS

Each of the four Celtic holy cities of Ireland is associated with a particular treasure and Druid (see below). There are also 13 royal treasures of the Isle of Britain, or *Tri Thlas ar Ddeg Ynys Prydain* (see page 214).

Crowley once did a tongue-in-cheek analysis of nursery rhymes, showing that they were coded references to deep magickal mysteries, with 'Tom, Tom the piper's son' being in reality the mighty being known as Taphtartharath, which he tried to summon up.

In fact it is part of the magician's work to see everything that happens as a secret dealing between himself and the spirit of the gods, and Crowley's essay was thought-provoking as well as fun. In the case of the Celtic myths, and details about such apparent irrelevancies as the 13 treasures of Britain, there is often a tendency to think of them of as 'just stories', when in fact they contain powerful teachings indeed.[61]

Searles O'Dubhain – a Celtic author and lecturer, whose esoteric areas of interest include ogham divination, astral travelling and shamanism – expounded upon the concept of 'dúile' (see page 215), which he felt represented the manifestation of the individual human spirit and its interaction with the surrounding environment. This means that a ***dúile*** can be considered a part of our body that transcends the physical – it can be the effects that physical, mental or spiritual events have upon our 'being'. The deities themselves were thought to be perceptible as ***dúile***. It is a concept that exactly matches that of the Egyptian ***neters*** mentioned earlier (see page 13).

O'Dubhain devised a list of nine elements that he derived from a study of Celtic traditions. The ***neach*** ('living being') or ***duine*** ('person') was composed of nine ***dúile*** ('elements'). Each of these elements had its corresponding cosmic element in the *Bith* (cosmos). It was the interconnection of the ***dúile*** that gave truth to the saying, 'As above, so below'. When the corresponding elements of the self and cosmos were in harmony with one another, that was the time when the greatest Magick could be worked. A Celt's spirit was centred within the house of their body. Their home was focused upon where the hearth fires were 'smoored'. Their life was contained and centred around the clan or ***tuath***. Magick was everywhere and life was only 'real' within the boundaries of the land; everywhere else was considered to be 'other'. The table on page 215 attempts to define how the windows and doors of the body connected to the land, the centre and the cosmos.

Holy Cities of Ireland

HOLY CITY	TREASURE	DRUID
Findias	Claiomh Solais Sword of Nuada	Uscias
Falias	Lia Fal Stone of Destiny	Morfessa
Murias	Coire Anseasc Cauldron of Undry	Semias
Gorias	Spear Luin Spear of Destiny	Esras

Royal Treasures of the Isle of Britain

TREASURE	WELSH NAME	PROPERTY
White-Hilt, the sword of Rhydderch Hael	Dyrnwyn, gleddyf Rhydderch Hael	If anyone but the owner drew it, it would burst into flame from its hilt to its tip
The hamper of Gwyddno Long-Shank	Mwys Gwyddno Garanir	Provided an inexhaustible supply of food
The horn of Bran the Niggard from the North	Korn Bran Galed o'r Gogledd	Whatever drink might be wished for was found in it
The chariot of Arianrod	Kar Arianrod	Would take you where you wished to go
The halter of Clyddno Eiddyn	Kebystr Klyddno Eiddin	Whatever horse he might wish for, he would find in the halter
The knife of Llawfrodedd the Horseman	Kyllell Llawfrodedd Farchog	Would serve for 24 men to eat at table
The cauldron of Dyrnwch the Giant	Pair Dyrnwch Gawr	Would distinguish cowards from brave men
The whetstone of Tudwal Tudglyd	Hogalen Tudwal Tutklyd	If a brave man sharpened his sword on it, and then drew blood from a man, he would die; if a cowardly man did so, then his opponent would be no worse
The coat of Padarn Red-Coat	Pais Badarn Beisrydd	Would only fit well-born men
The crock and the dish of Rhygenydd the Cleric	Gren a desgyl Rhygenydd Ysgolhaig	Whatever food might be wished for in them, it would be found
The chessboard of Gwenddolau, son of Ceidio	Gwyddbwyll Gwenddoleu ap Ceidio	If the pieces were set, they would play by themselves
The mantle of Arthur in Cornwall	Llen Arthyr yng Nghernyw	Whoever was under it could not be seen, but could see everyone

Correspondences of the Dúile[62]

FEIN (THE SELF)	BITH (COSMOS)	DIRECTIONS	MAGICAL TOOLS
Cnaimh (bones)	Cloch (stone)	Thuaidh (north)	Lia Fail (destiny)
Colaind (flesh)	Talamh (earth)	Faoi (under, about)	The nemeton
Gruaigh (hair)	Uaine (plant life)	Amach (outwards)	Ogham and herbs
Fuil (blood)	Muir (sea)	Ior, Siar (west)	Undry (cauldron)
Anal (breath)	Gaeth (wind)	Air, Oithear (east)	The sword of Nuada
Imradud (mind)	Gealach (Moon)	Isteach (inwards)	The well of Segais
Drech (face)	Grian (Sun)	Deas, Deis (south)	The spear of Lugh
Menma (brain)	Nel (cloud)	Thrid (through)	Imbas (inspiration)
Ceann (head)	Neamh (heaven)	Os Cionn (above)	The torque, halo

WORKING WITH CELTIC SYMBOLISM

Feed your consciousness with the richness of mythic symbolism: with fairy tales and local or national legends – anything that can make your heart beat faster.

1. Find a place that is special to you, and private to you, preferably one with potent folkloric associations, or even from your childhood. Go there at a time best calculated to draw upon planetary influences, wearing appropriate colours, perfumes or scents. If you cannot go physically, do so in your imagination.
2. Summon up a protecting deity and visualize yourself becoming that being. Then visualize a tendril of light going down from your solar plexus, into the earth beneath your feet. Finally, visualize yourself drawing up the earth energies through that, into yourself, while asking the land to teach you.

13

OGHAM

OGHAM CORRESPONDENCES

The ogham alphabet was exhumed, in a sense, and popularized by Robert Graves in *The White Goddess* and if we must be cautious about authoritative statements, at least he gave the generations that followed something of an inner history and direction. Drawing upon his work and matching the ogham symbols with parts of the ancient 'Song of Amergin', Deanne Quarrie, a modern exponent of women's mysteries, has partially completed the following table (which has also been altered by me); there are some blanks that you might want to fill in personally.

Combining all of the above, and using the structure of the circle cross and elemental attributions provided in Chapter 2, the reader has now gathered more than enough information to create a complete system of Celtic magic. This will be a beginning, a true initiation.

Ogham Associations[63]

GAELIC LETTER		NAME	TREE	BIRD	STONE OR METAL	COLOUR	SONG LINE
B	ᚁ	Beth	Birch	Pheasant	Carnelian	White	I am a stag of seven tines
L	ᚂ	Luis	Rowan	Duck	Yellow topaz	Grey	I am a lake upon a plain
N	ᚅ	Nion	Ash	Snipe	Sea-green beryl	Clear	I am a wind over the sea
F	ᚃ	Fearn	Alder	Gull	Fire garnet	Crimson	I am a tear of the sun
S	ᚄ	Saille	Willow	Hawk	Ruby	Fine-coloured	I am a hawk upon a cliff
H	ᚆ	Huath	Hawthorn	Night crow	Lapis lazuli	Terrible-coloured	I am a beautiful flower
D	ᚇ	Duir	Oak	Wren	White carnelian	Black	I am a god that sets the head on fire
T	ᚈ	Tinne	Holly	Starling	Smoky quartz	Dark grey	I am a keen spear that pours forth battle
C	ᚉ	Coll	Hazel	Crane	Red agate	Brown	I am a salmon in a pool
Q	ᚊ	Ceirt	Apple	–	–	–	–

GAELIC LETTER	NAME	TREE	BIRD	STONE OR METAL	COLOUR	SONG LINE
M	Muin	Vine	Titmouse	Amethyst	Variegated	I am a hill of skilled ones
G	Gort	Ivy	Mute swan	Yellow serpentine	Blue	I am a boar in battle frenzy
P	Ngetal	Reed	Goose	Green jasper	Glass-green	I am a noise of the sea
Z	Straif	Blackthorn	–	–	–	–
R	Ruis	Elder	Rook	Malachite	Blood red	I am an ocean wave
A	Ailm	Silver fir	Lapwing	Silver	Piebald	I am the womb of every holt
O	Onn	Gorse	Cormorant	Gold	Dun	I am a blaze on every hill
U	Ura	Heather	Lark	Copper	Resin-coloured	I am the queen of every hive
E	Eadha	Poplar, aspen	Whistling swan	Tin	Rufus red	I am the shield for every head
I	Idho	Yew	Eaglet	Lead	Very white	I am the tomb of every hope
EA	Eabhadh	–	–	–	–	–
OI	Oir	Spindle	–	–	–	–
UI	Uilleann	Honeysuckle	–	–	–	–
IA	Ifin	Gooseberry	–	–	–	–
	Eamhancholl	Beech	–	–	–	–
	Eite (Feather)	–	–	–	–	–
	Spas (space)	–	–	–	–	–

14

THE RUNES

THE RUNIC ALPHABET

The runes are another example of a Western magical alphabet – magickal in the sense that the letters are divinatory as well as phonetic. Karl Hans Welz, an Austrian who describes himself as the inventor of the 'orgone generator', goes further and shows how runes can be viewed as shape-vibrations: 'In other words, specific shapes can trigger their energies.' [64]

In Old Norse, the word ***rune*** means 'letter', 'text' or 'inscription'. It also means 'mystery' or 'secret' in Old Germanic languages, and runes became central to the rituals and Magick of those peoples. The alphabet known as the Elder Futhark is probably the oldest version of the runic alphabet, and was used in the parts of Europe that were home to Germanic peoples, including Scandinavia. The names of the letters are shown in Common Germanic, the reconstructed ancestor of all Germanic languages.

However, three slightly different versions of the alphabet developed in Denmark, Sweden and Norway.[65] A number of extra letters were then added to the runic alphabet to write Anglo-Saxon/Old English. Runes were probably brought to Britain in the 5th century CE by the Angles, Saxons, Jutes and Frisians (collectively known as the Anglo-Saxons) and were used until about the 11th century. Their alphabet was known as the *Futhorc* (see opposite).

It is the correspondences of the Elder Futhark that we shall look at in a little more detail. The runes can be divided for convenience into three sets or *Aetts*.

Danish Futhark

ᚠ	ᚢ	ᚦ	ᚬ	ᚱ	ᚴ	ᚼ	ᚾ	ᛁ	ᛅ	ᛋ	ᛏ	ᛒ	ᛘ	ᛚ	ᛦ
f	u	th	a	r	k	h	n	l	a	s	t	b	m	l	R

Swedish-Norwegian Futhark / Short-Twig / Rök Runes

ᚠ	ᚢ	ᚦ	ᚭ	ᚱ	ᚴ	ᚽ	ᚿ	ᛁ	ᛆ	ᛌ	ᛐ	ᛓ	ᛙ	ᛚ	ᛧ
f	u	th	a	r	k	h	n	l	a	s	t	b	m	l	R

Norwegian Futhark

ᚠ	ᚢ	ᚦ	ᚯ	ᚱ	ᚴ	ᚼ	ᚽ	ᛁ	ᛅ	ᛊ	ᛏ	ᛒ	ᛉ	ᛚ	ᛦ
f	u	th	a	r	k	h	n	l	a	s	t	b	m	l	R

The Futhorc

RUNE	NAME	MEANING	MODERN LETTER
ᚠ	feoh	cattle, wealth	f
ᚢ	ur	aurochs	u
ᚦ	horn	thorn	p
ᚩ	os	god	o
ᚱ	rad	journey/ riding	r
ᚳ	cen	torch	c
ᚷ	giefu	gift	gi
ᚹ	vvyn	joy	p
ᚻ	haeg	hail	h
ᚾ	nied	necessity/ trouble	n
ᛁ	is	ice	i
ᛄ	gear	year	j
ᛇ	eoh	yew	eo
ᛈ	peor	–	p
ᛉ	eolh	sledge	x
ᛋ	sigel	sun	s
ᛏ	tiwitir	a god	t
ᛒ	beorc	birch	b
ᛖ	eoh	horse	e
ᛗ	man	man	m
ᛚ	lagu	water/sea	l
ᛝ	lng	a god	ng
ᛟ	ebel	land/estate	oe
ᛞ	deeg	day	d

First Aett of the Elder Futhark

RUNE	NAME MEANING	DEITY	TREE	POSITIVE MEANING	NEGATIVE MEANING
ᚠ	Fehu – cattle, wealth	Frey, Freya, Nord	Elder	Foresight, luck, abundance	Greed, atrophy
ᚢ	Uruz – auroch	Audhumla, Urd	Birch	Strength, energy	Weakness, inconsistency
ᚦ	Thurisaz – thorn or giant	Thor	Oak	Change, will-power	Danger, betrayal
ᚨ	Ansuz – ancestral gods	Odin (Woden)	Ash	Messages, blessings	Delusion, treachery
ᚱ	Raidho – wagon or chariot	Forseti	Oak	Travel, expansion	Stasis, disruption
ᚲ	Kenaz – beacon or torch	Freya, dwarves	Pine	Vision, illumination	Disease, false hope
ᚷ	Gebo – gift	Odin, Freya	Elm	Gifts, balance	Greed, loneliness
ᚹ	Wunjo – joy	Freya, elves	Ash	Reward, fellowship	Sorrow, alienation

Second Aett of the Elder Futhark

RUNE	NAME MEANING	DEITY	TREE	POSITIVE MEANING	NEGATIVE MEANING
ᚺ	Hagalaz – hail	Ymir	Yew	Mastery, inner harmony	Stagnation, crisis
ᚾ	Naudhiz need	Norns (Nornir)	Beech	Endurance, innovation	Constraint, deprivation
ᛁ	Isa – ice	Frost giants	Alder	Challenge, introspection	Illusion, deceit
ᛃ	Jera – a year, good harvest	Frey	Oak	Peace, prosperity	Setback, conflict
ᛇ	Eihwaz – yew tree	Odin, Ullr	Yew	Strength, reliability	Destruction, weakness
ᛈ	Perthro – cup, vagina	Norns (Nornir)	Hornbeam	Mystery, gnosis	Addiction, malaise
ᛉ	Algiz – elk, protection	Valkyries	Rowan	Protection, purity	Hidden danger, rejection
ᛊ	Sowilo – sun	Balder	Juniper	Success, wholeness	Bad counsel, gullibility

Third Aett of the Elder Futhark

RUNE	NAME MEANING	DEITY	TREE	POSITIVE MEANING	NEGATIVE MEANING
ᛏ	Tiwaz – sky god	Tyr	Oak	Honour, self-sacrifice	Separation, psycho-babble
ᛒ	Berkano – birch goddess	Frigg, Nerthus, Hel	Birch	Birth, fertility, growth	Family problems, anxiety
ᛖ	Ehwaz – horse, two horses	Frey	Oak, ash	Movement, improvement	Restlessness
ᛗ	Mannaz – man, humankind	Heimdall	Holly	Intelligence, creativity	Depression, self-delusion
ᛚ	Laguz – water or a leak	Njord	Willow	Fertility, creativity renewal	Avoidance, perversity
ᛜ	Ingwaz – the earth god	Ing, Frey	Apple	Family love, self-awareness	Impotence
ᛞ	Dagaz – day or dawn	Odin	Spruce	Breakthrough, transformation	Blindness, hopelessness
ᛟ	Othala – ancestral property	Odin	Hawthorn	Inheritance, revelation	Bad luck, narrow-mindedness

RUNE & TAROT CORRESPONDENCES

Although the Tarot and runes are two quite different systems, a number of students have managed to create working comparisons; Edred Thorsson's associations are given below. There are tremendous possibilities for new research and new magical systems here.

Thorsson's Futhark Correspondences[66]

RUNE	TAROT	ASTROLOGY	GOD, WIGHT (SPIRIT)	TREE	HERB
Fehu	Tower	Aries	Aesir	Elder	Nettle
Uruz	Priestess	Taurus	Vanir	Birch	Sphagnum moss
Thurisaz	Emperor	Mars	Thor	Oak	House leek
Ansuz	Death	Venus	Odin	Ash	Fly agaric
Raidho	Hierophant	Sagittarius	Forseti	Oak	Mugwort
Kenaz	Chariot	Venus	Freya, dwarves	Pine	Cowslip
Gebo	Lovers	Pisces	Odin, Freya	Ash/Elm	Heartsease
Wunjo	Strength	Leo	Freyr, elves	Ash	Flax
Hagalaz	World	Aquarius	Ymir	Yew/Ash	Lily-of-the-valley
Nauthiz	Devil	Capricorn	Nornir, Etins	Beech	Bistort
Isa	Hermit	Moon	Rime Thurses	Alder	Henbane
Jera	Fool	Sun	Freyr	Oak	Rosemary
Eihwaz	Hanged Man	Scorpio	Idhunna, Ullr	Yew	Mandrake
Perthro	Wheel of Fortune	Saturn	Nornir	Beech	Aconite
Algiz	Moon	Cancer	Valkyrjur	Yew	Angelica
Sowilo	Sun	Sun	Sol	Juniper	Mistletoe
Tiwaz	Justice	Libra	Tyr, Mani	Oak	Sage
Berkano	Empress	Virgo	Frigg, Nerthus, Hel	Birch	Lady's Mantle
Ehwaz	Lovers	Gemini	Freya, Freyr, Aclis	Oak /Ash	Ragwort
Mannaz	Magician	Jupiter	Heimdall, Odin	Holly	Madder
Laguz	Star	Moon	Njord, Balder	Willow	Leek
Ingwaz	Judgement	New Moon	Ing, Freyr	Apple	Selfheal
Dagaz	Temperance	Half Moon	Odin, Ostara	Spruce	Clary
Othala	Moon	Full Moon	Odin, Thor	Hawthorn	Goldthread

RUNES & THE MAGICKAL DIRECTIONS

Working within the runic tradition, 'Odindis' (a variation of the name Odin) makes a case for the sigils being ascribed to the magickal directions:

In the Edda there are mentioned the four Dwarfs who hold up Ymir's skull (the sky). Their names are Northri, Austri, Sudhri, and Vestri: North, South, East and West. We are told Niflheim is to the north, and Hel also is in that direction, but lies ever downward. We are told also that Jötunheim lies to the East, and Muspelheim to the South, from whence the fire Giant Surtr someday will come in flame. Vanaheim then must lie in the West...The worlds of the vertical axis of the cosmos have to do with the spirit realm, as the Worlds of the four directions have to do with the elemental forces that make up the Earth plane.

'Odindis' provides a practical and important diagram of this below, giving the usual tabulated correspondences an extra dimension. Within this you can determine the magic circle, the underworld, overworld and innerworld, and see how the runes can be allocated in ways that make them useful keys.

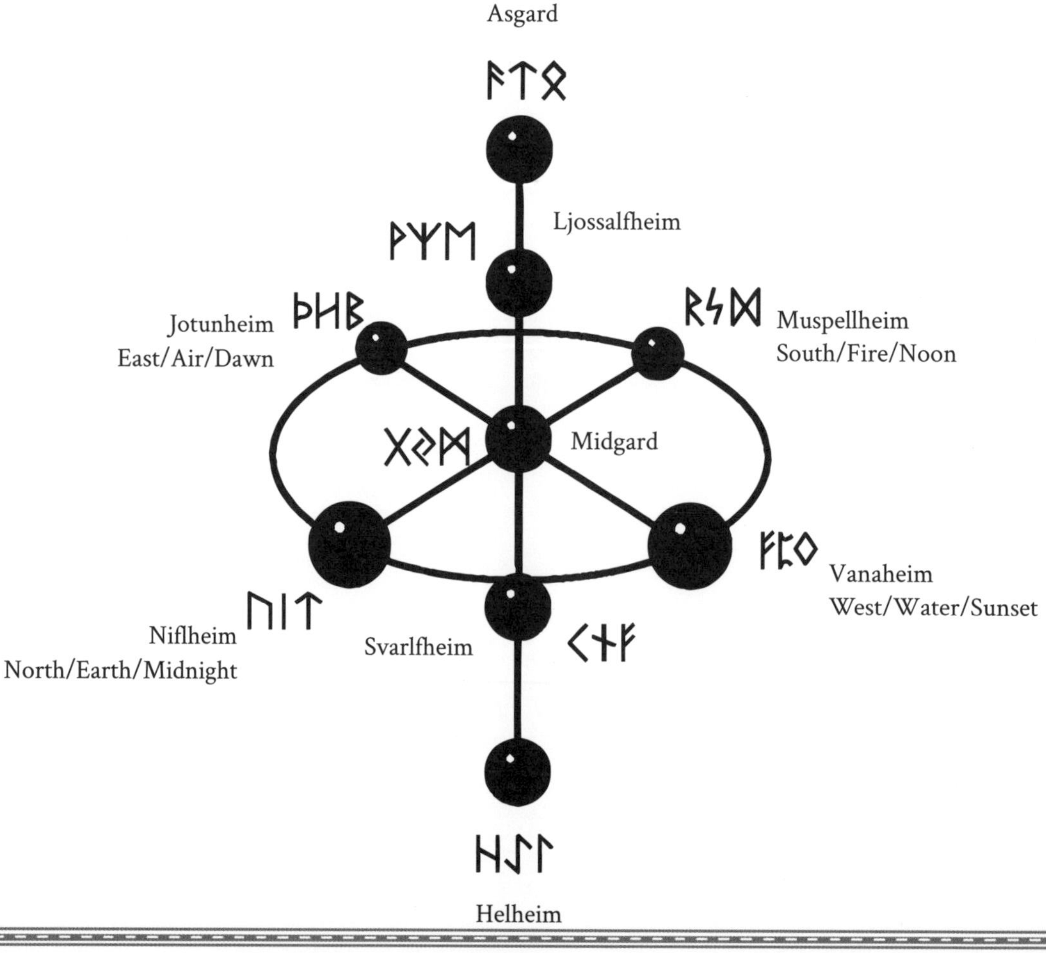

RUNES & THE DEITIES

An insight into the correspondences relating to the ancient northern gods can be seen in Donald Tyson's chart below, with further details of the Norse deities following.

Tyson's Deity Associations[67]

DEITIES	COLOUR	METAL	OBJECT	FIREWOOD	JEWEL
Balder	Yellow	Gold	Bow	Mistletoe	Topaz
Heimdall	Blue	Steel	Horn	Yew	Sapphire
Loki	Mist-grey	Arsenic	Shoes	Thorn	Opal
Thor	Orange	Tin	Hammer	Oak	Jasper
Tiw	Red	Iron	Sword	Fir	Ruby
Odin	White	Mercury	Spear	Ash	Diamond
Frija	Green	Copper	Necklace	Apple	Emerald
Hel	Black	Lead	Veil	Willow	Jet
Freyja	Purple	Silver	Cloak	Birch	Amethyst
Frey	Red-brown	Bronze	Chariot	Pine	Tree agate

Norse Deities

DEITY	CONSORT OR RELATION	FUNCTION
Ægir	Rán	Ruler of the sea
Baldr-balder (Phol)	Nanna	Represents beauty, innocence, peace and rebirth
Borr	Bestla	Father god, ancestors
Bragi (Brego)	Iðunn	God of poetry
Dagr	Son of Delling and Nótt	God of the daytime
Delling	Father of Dagr by Nótt	God of dawn
Eir	Companion of Frigg	Goddess of healing
Forseti (Forasizo)	Son of Baldr and Nanna	God of justice and truth
Freyja (Frowa)	Óðr	Goddess of sexuality and war
Freyr (Fro Ing)	Gerð	God of fertility
Frigg (Frick)	Óðinn	Goddess of marriage and motherhood
Gefjun	Skjold	Goddess of the plough and soil
Hel (Hellia)	Daughter of Loki	Queen of Hel, the Norse Underworld
Heimdall (Iring, Rigr)	One of the Aesir	Guardian of Ásgarð
Hermóðr (Hermut)	Son of Óðinn	Represents courage in battle
Hlín	Handmaid of Frigg	Goddess of consolation
Hœnir	One of the Aesir	The silent god
Hoðr	Brother of Baldr	God of winter
Iðunn	Bragi	Goddess of youth
Jorð (Erda)	Mother of ðórr by Óðinn	Goddess of the earth
Kvasir	Created from the saliva of all the gods	God of inspiration

DEITY	CONSORT OR RELATION	FUNCTION
Loki	Sigyn (also called Saeter)	Trickster god
Máni	Son of Mundilfari and Glaur	Moon god
Mímir (Mime)	Uncle of Óðinn	God of knowledge and wisdom
Nanna	Married to Baldr and mother of Forseti	One of the Aesir
Nerthus	Sister of Njord	Earth goddess
Njerðr	Father of Frey and Freya	God of sea, wind, fish and wealth
Nótt	Daughter of Narvi	Goddess of night
Óðinn (Wodan)	Frigg	Lord of the Aesir, god of wisdom and war
Rán	Ægir	Keeper of the drowned
Sif	Wife of Thor	Goddess of the home
Skaði	Wife of Njerrð	Goddess of vengeance
Sol (Sunna)	Wife of Glen	Goddess of the Sun
Thórr (Donar)	Sif	God of thunder and battle
Tðr (Ziu, Saxnot)	Son of Oðinn	God of war and justice
Ullr (Wulder)	Son of Sif	God of ski, hunt and duel
Váli	Son of Oðinn	God of revenge
Var	One of the Asynja	Goddess of contracts
Vé	Brother of Óðinn and Vili	One of the three gods of creation
Verr	One of the Asynja	Goddess of wisdom

RUNES & RITUAL POSTURES

Finally, tying it together in ways that can offer magical effectiveness, Karl Hans Welz's work involves runes and ritual postures. The very act of trying these out can have a marked effect on your mind, and posture has been shown to influence the actual direction of shamanic visions. Welz writes:

Hand and body positions add extremely valuable dimensions to your runic practice. Especially when those positions are practised in a ceremonial set-up, by several persons, each person perhaps representing one specific Rune, or several persons forming one single Rune.[68]

Ritual Body Postures

RUNE	SYMBOL	BODY POSTURE	HAND POSITION
Fa		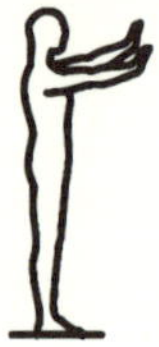	
Ur			
Thorn			
Os			

RUNE	SYMBOL	BODY POSTURE	HAND POSITION
Othil			
Rit			
Ka			
Hagal			

RUNE	SYMBOL	BODY POSTURE	HAND POSITION
Not			
Is			
Ar			
Sig			
Tyr		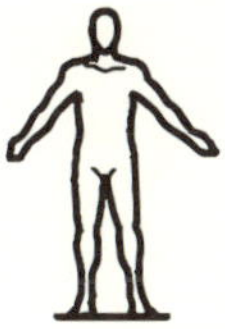	
Bar			

RUNE	SYMBOL	BODY POSTURE	HAND POSITION
Laf			
Man			
Yr			
Eh			
Gibor			

15

THE I CHING

THE BOOK OF CHANGES

The *I Ching* or *Book of Changes* (often spelled *Yi Ching*, *I Jing*, *Yi King* or *Yi Jing*) is the oldest of the classic Chinese texts. It describes an ancient system of cosmology and philosophy that lies at the heart of Chinese cultural beliefs. This philosophy centres on the ideas of the dynamic balance of opposites, the evolution of events as a process, and acceptance of the inevitability of change. In Western cultures, the *I Ching* is regarded by many as simply a system of divination; however, there are those who believe that it expresses a complete philosophy.

The earliest records of simple divination in China date back to the early Shang dynasty (c.1766 BCE–c.1050 BCE). Their practices involved heating animal bones in a fire and studying the resulting cracks in order to answer certain questions: was it right to make a sacrifice, or to communicate with the spirits and ancestors? Legend tells us that the *I Ching* was originally devised by Fu Hsi, a sage who was China's first emperor. According to the tale, Fu Hsi found eight trigrams (a trigram being a stack of three lines, each with specific attributes relative to the Earth, humankind and heaven) on the shell of a tortoise, and from these eight trigrams he derived the 64 line-figures (or hexagrams) that the Chinese call ***kua***.

Whatever the *Book of Changes'* true origins, there is enough symbolism within four of its oldest ideograms (graphic characters) – Yuan, Heng, Li and Zhen – to show that at the deepest levels the *I Ching* is as much to do with contacting the spiritual world, and understanding the quality of the moment, as it is to do with predicting the future.

元
亨
利
贞

Crowley used the *I Ching* during an era when only a handful of westerners had even heard of it. At one stage he appears to have consulted the *Yi* daily for a period of several years, and took a number of crucial decisions based on his interpretation of its advice, including the siting of his infamous Abbey of Thelema at Cefalu in Sicily. His diaries reveal numerous references to the *Yi*, which are all usefully collated under the various hexagrams. Carl Jung insisted that the *I Ching* was ***never*** wrong.

GENERATING HEXAGRAMS

To generate a hexagram and immediately start using the *I Ching* you will need three coins. The head side of the coin is yang, while the tail side is yin. You toss the coins and, by assigning values to yin (two points) and yang (three points), generate each of the six lines in the hexagram.

1. First of all, meditate on a question, holding the question in your mind. Then throw the three coins into the air together, while thinking of your question. Each head counts three points; each tail counts two. Add up the result: it will be six, seven, eight or nine. For example, head (3) plus head (3) plus tail (2) makes 8. You can use the following table to translate this number into the first line of your hexagram:
2. Write down the lines you received, working *from the bottom up* to the sixth and last line. This is your 'primary hexagram' and forms the basis of your whole answer. There is no need to do any more casting: this primary hexagram is the key. However, you can also take into account the changing (or moving) lines – that is, any lines with a value of six or nine. These add new possibilities and depth, and highlight moments of change (present or future). They may point to important choices, opportunities or dangers, and provide useful advice on the best way to deal with them.
3. It is traditional to read the bottom line of your hexagram as referring to the present or near future, and the higher lines as referring to a more distant future. But the different lines can also refer to alternative approaches to the basic situation described by the primary hexagram, or even to different people.

Hexagram Lines

NUMBER	LINE TYPE	COINS	YIN / YANG	WRITTEN
6	Changing broken line	Three tails	Old yin	
7	Unchanging solid line	Two tails, one head	Young yang	
8	Unchanging broken line	Two heads, one tail	Young yin	
9	Changing solid line	Three heads	Old yang	

Crowley's Trigrams of the *I Ching*

QUARTER	PLANETARY ATTRIBUTION	HINDU ATTRIBUTION	FIGURE	NAME	BODY PART
South	Sun	Lingam	☰	Khien	Head
South-east	Venus	Apas	☱	Tui	Mouth
East	Jupiter	Mano (prana)	☲	Li	Eyes
North-east	Mars	Tejas	☳	Kan	Feet
South-west	Mercury	Vayu	☴	Sun	Thighs
West	Saturn	Akasa	☵	Khan	Ears
North-west	Earth	Prithivi	☶	Kan	Hands
North	Moon	Yoni	☷	Khwan	Belly

Crowley's and Wilhelm's[69] Hexagrams of the *I Ching*

HEXAGRAM	NUMBER	NAME	NATURE	CROWLEY	WILHELM
䷀	1	Khien	Yang/yang	Heaven	The creative
䷁	2	Khwan	Yin/yin	Earth	The receptive
䷂	3	Kun	Lunar/fire	Danger and obscurity	Difficulty at the beginning
䷃	4	Mang	Earth/lunar	Youth and ignorance	Youthful folly
䷄	5	Hsu	Lunar/yang	Waiting, sincerity	Waiting
䷅	6	Sung	Yang/lunar	Contention, opposition, strength in peril	Conflict
䷆	7	Sze	Yin/lunar	Multitude, age and experience	The army
䷇	8	Pi	Lunar/yin	Help	Holding together
䷈	9	Hsiao Khu	Air/yang	Small restraint	Small taming
䷉	10	Li	Yang/water	Pleasure, satisfaction, attachment to, a shoe	Treading (conduct)
䷊	11	Thai	Yin/yang	Spring, tree course	Peace
䷋	12	Phi	Yang/yin	Decay, patience, obedience, autumn, shutting up, restriction	Standstill

HEXAGRAM	NUMBER	NAME	NATURE	CROWLEY	WILHELM
	13	Thung Zan	Yang/solar	Union (of men)	Fellowship
	14	Ta Yu	Solar/yang	Great havings	Great possession
	15	Khien	Yin/earth	Humility	Modesty
	16	Yu	Fire/yin	Harmony and satisfaction	Enthusiasm
	17	Sui	Water/fire	Following	Following
	18	Ku	Earth/air	Troublesome services, arrest of decay, hard work	Work on the decayed
	19	Lin	Yin/water	Approach of authority, inspect, comfort	Approach
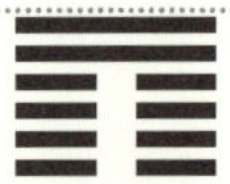	20	Kwan	Air/yin	Manipulation, contemplation	Contemplation
	21	Shih Ho	Solar/fire	Union, legal constraint	Biting through
	22	PÎ	Water/solar	Ornament, free will	Grace
	23	Po	Earth/yin	Overthrow, couch	Splitting apart
	24	Fu	Yin/fire	Return, visit from friends	Return
	25	Wu Wang	Yang/fire	Simplicity and sincerity earnestness,	Innocence

HEXAGRAM	NUMBER	NAME	NATURE	CROWLEY	WILHELM
	26	Ta Khu	Earth/yang	Great accumulation	Great taming
	27	I	Earth/fire	Nourishment, upper jaw	Mouth corners
	28	Ta Kwo	Water/air	Great carefulness, weak beam	Great preponderance
	29	Khan	Lunar/lunar	Pit, defile, peril	The abysmal water
	30	Li	Solar/solar	Inherent in, attached to, docility	The clinging
	31	Hsien	Water/earth	Influencing action, all, jointly	Influence
	32	Haong	Fire/air	Perseverance, keeping to the path	Duration
	33	Thun	Yang/earth	Returning, avoiding, retirement	Retreat
	34	Ta Kwang	Fire/yang	Violence, the great ram	Great power
	35	Zin	Solar/yin	To advance (good)	Progress
	36	Ming I	Yin/solar	Intelligence, wound	Darkening of the light
	37	Kia Zan	Air/solar	Household, wifely duty	The family
	38	Khwei	Solar/water	Disunion, family discord	Opposition

HEXAGRAM	NUMBER	NAME	NATURE	CROWLEY	WILHELM
䷦	39	Kien	Lunar/earth	Lameness, immobility, difficulty	Obstruction
䷧	40	Kieh	Fire/solar	Unravelling	Deliverance
䷨	41	Sun	Earth/fire	Diminution	Decrease
䷩	42	Yi	Air/fire	Addition, increase	Increase
䷪	43	Kwai	Water/yang	Displacing, strength, complacency, tact	Breakthrough
䷫	44	Kau	Yang/air	Unexpected event, a bold woman	Coming to meet
䷬	45	Zhui	Water/yin	Collectedness, docility	Gathering together
䷭	46	Shang	Yin/air	Advance and ascent	Pushing upwards
䷮	47	Khwan	Water/lunar	Straightened, distress, restricted growth	Oppression
䷯	48	Zing	Lunar/air	A well, self-cultivation	The well
䷰	49	Ko	Water/solar	Change	Revolution
䷱	50	Ting	Solar/air	A cauldron, a concubine, flexibility, quick ear and eye	The cauldron
䷲	51	Kan	Fire/fire	Ease, development, moving power, thunder	Arousing

HEXAGRAM	NUMBER	NAME	NATURE	CROWLEY	WILHELM
	52	Kan	Earth/earth	Peace, a mountain	The keeping still
	53	Kien	Air/earth	Fortunate marriage, gradual advance, goose	Development
	54	Kwei Mei	Fire/water	Unfortunate marriage (of a younger sister before the elder)	The marrying maiden
	55	Fang	Fire/solar	Largeness, abundance, progress	Abundance
	56	Lu	Solar/earth	Strangers	The wanderer
	57	Sun	Air/air	Flexibility, penetration, vacillation, wind, wood	The gentle
	58	Tui	Water/water	Pleasure, help from friends still water,	The joyous
	59	Hwan	Air/lunar	Dissipation, dispersion, turning to evil	Dispersion
	60	Kieh	Air/air	Joints of the body, regular division	Limitation
	61	Kung Fu	Air/lunar	Inmost sincerity	Inner truth
	62	Hsiao Kwo	Fire/earth	Non-essential, success of trifles, a wounded bird, small divergences	Small preponderance
	63	Ki Zi	Lunar/solar	Help attained, complete success	After completion
	64	Wei Zi	Solar/lunar	Help attained, complete success	Before completion

16

APPENDIX

PLANT CORRESPONDENCES

Nicholas Culpeper, the physician, herbalist and astrologer (see Chapter 8), writing in the 17th century, produced an extensive list of plants and their astrological associations, which are given below alongside contemporary plant correspondences, where these exist.

Plant Correspondences Ancient and Modern

CULPEPER'S PLANT	RULING PLANET / SIGN	CONTEMPORARY CORRESPONDENCES
Adder's tongue	Moon, Cancer	Healing
Agrimony	Jupiter, Cancer	Protection, sleep
Agrimony (water)	Jupiter, Cancer	–
Alder tree (black)	Venus, Cancer	–
Alder tree (common)	Venus, Pisces	–
Alehoof	Venus	–
Alexander	Jupiter	–
Alkanet	Venus	Purification, prosperity
All-heal	Mars	–
Amaranthus	Saturn	Healing, protection, invisibility
Anemone	Mars	–
Angelica	Sun, Leo	Exorcism, protection, healing, visions
Archangel	Venus	–
Arrach (garden)	Moon	–
Arrach (wild and stinking)	Venus, Scorpio	–
Arssmart	Mars	–
Artichokes	Moon	–
Asarabacca	Mars	–
Ash tree	Sun	Protection, prosperity, sea rituals, health
Asparagus	Jupiter	–
Avens	Jupiter	–
Balm	Jupiter, Cancer	Love, success, healing
Barberry	Mars	–

CULPEPER'S PLANT	RULING PLANET / SIGN	CONTEMPORARY CORRESPONDENCES
Barley	Saturn	Love, healing, protection
Basil (garden)	Venus	Love, exorcism, wealth, flying, protection
Bastard rhubarb	Mars	–
Bay tree	Sun, Leo	Protection, psychic powers, healing, purification, strength
Beans	Venus	Protection, wart, charm, potency, love
Beans (French)	Venus	–
Bedstraw (lady's)	Venus	–
Beech tree	Saturn	–
Beet (red)	Saturn	Love
Beet (white)	Jupiter	Love
Betony (water)	Jupiter, Cancer	–
Betony (wood)	Jupiter, Aries	–
Bifoil	Saturn	–
Bilberry	Jupiter	–
Birch tree	Venus	–
Bird's-foot	Saturn	–
Bishop's weed	Venus	–
Bistort	Saturn	Psychic powers, fertility
Bittersweet	Mercury	Protection, healing
Black hellebore	Saturn	–
Blites	Venus	–
Bluebottle	Saturn	–
Borage	Jupiter, Leo	Courage, psychic powers
Bramble	Venus, Aries	Healing, money, protection
Brank ursine (acanthus)	Moon	–
Briony	Mars	Image magic, money, protection
Brook lime	Mars	–
Broom	Mars	Purification, protection, wind spells, divination
Buckshorn	Saturn	–
Buckshorn plantain	Saturn	–

CULPEPER'S PLANT	RULING PLANET / SIGN	CONTEMPORARY CORRESPONDENCES
Bugle	Venus	–
Burdock	Venus	Protection, healing
Burnet	Sun	–
Burnet saxifrage	Moon	–
Butcher's broom	Mars	–
Butterbur	Sun	–
Cabbage	Moon	Luck
Calamint	Mercury	–
Caltrops (water)	Moon	–
Chamomile	Sun	Money, sleep, love, purification
Campion (wild)	Sun	–
Caraway	Mercury	Protection, lust, health, anti-theft, mental powers
Carduus Benedictus	Mars	–
Carrot (wild)	Mercury	Fertility, lust
Celandine (great)	Sun	Protection, escape, happiness, legal matters
Celandine (lesser)	Mars	Protection, escape, happiness, legal matters
Centaury (small)	Sun	Snake-removing
Cherry tree	Venus	Love, divination
Cherry (winter)	Venus	Love, divination
Chervil	Jupiter	–
Chestnut (earth)	Venus	Love
Chestnut tree	Venus	Love
Chickpea	Venus	–
Chickweed	Moon	Fertility, love
Cinquefoil	Jupiter	Money, protection, prophetic dreams, sleep
Chives	Mars	–
Clary (garden)	Moon	–
Clary (wild)	Moon	–
Cleavers	Moon	–
Clown's woundwort	Saturn	–
Cock's head	Venus	–
Colewort (sea)	Moon	–
Coltsfoot	Venus	Love, visions

CULPEPER'S PLANT	RULING PLANET / SIGN	CONTEMPORARY CORRESPONDENCES
Columbine	Venus	Courage, love
Comfrey	Saturn	Safety during travel, money
Coralwort	Moon	–
Costmary	Jupiter	–
Cowslip	Venus	Healing, youth, treasure-finding
Crab's claw	Venus	–
Cress (black)	Mars	–
Cress (sciatica)	Saturn	–
Cress (water)	Moon	–
Crosswort	Saturn	–
Crowfoot	Mars	–
Cuckoo pint	Mars	–
Cucumber	Moon	Chastity, healing, fertility
Cudweed	Venus	–
Daisy	Venus, Cancer	Lust, luck
Dandelion	Jupiter	Divination, wishes, calling spirits
Darnel	Saturn	–
Devil's bit	Venus	Exorcism, love, protection, lust
Dill	Mercury	Protection, money, lust, luck
Dock	Jupiter	Healing, fertility, money
Dog mercury	Venus	–
Dog's grass	Jupiter	–
Dove's foot	Mars	–
Dragon's blood	Mars	Love, protection, exorcism, potency
Elecampane	Mercury	Love, protection, psychic powers
Elm tree	Saturn	Love
Endive	Venus	Lust, love
English tobacco	Mars	–
Eryngo	Venus	Traveller's luck, peace, lust, love
Eyebright	Sun	Mental powers, psychic power
Fennel	Mercury, Virgo	Protection, healing, purification
Fennel (hog's)	Mercury	Protection, healing, purification

CULPEPER'S PLANT	RULING PLANET / SIGN	CONTEMPORARY CORRESPONDENCES
Fern (male)	Mercury	Rain-making, protection, luck, riches, eternal youth, health, exorcism
Fern (water)	Saturn	Rain-making, protection, luck, riches, eternal youth, health, exorcism
Figwort	Venus	Health, protection
Filipendula	Venus	–
Flaxweed	Mars	–
Fleawort	Saturn	–
Fluellin	Moon	–
Foxglove	Venus	Protection
French mercury	Venus	–
Fuller's thistle	Venus	–
Fumitory	Saturn	Money, exorcism
Furze bush	Mars	–
Garden patience	Mars	–
Garden rue	Sun, Leo	Healing, health, mental powers, exorcism, love
Garden tansy	Venus	–
Garden valerian	Mercury	–
Garlic	Mars	Protection, healing, exorcism, lust, anti-theft
Gentian	Mars	Love, power
Germander	Mercury	–
Gilliflower	Jupiter	–
Golden maidenhair	Mercury	–
Goldenrod	Venus	Money, divination
Gooseberry bush	Venus	–
Goutwort	Saturn	–
Gromwell	Venus	–
Ground ivy	Venus	Divination
Ground pine	Mars	–
Groundsel	Venus	Health, healing
Hart's tongue	Jupiter	–
Hawkweed	Saturn	–
Hawthorn	Mars	Fertility, chastity, fishing magic, happiness

CULPEPER'S PLANT	RULING PLANET / SIGN	CONTEMPORARY CORRESPONDENCES
Hazelnut	Mercury	Luck, fertility, anti-lightning, protection, wishes
Heartsease	Saturn	–
Heart trefoil	Sun	–
Hedge hyssop	Mars	–
Hedge mustard	Mars	–
Hemlock	Saturn	Destroys sexual drives, hemlock is deadly poisonous
Hemp	Saturn	Healing, love, vision, meditation
Henbane	Saturn	Henbane is deadly poisonous
Herb robert	Venus	–
Herb true-love	Venus	–
Holly holm	Saturn	–
Honeysuckle	Mercury	Money, psychic powers, protection
Hops	Mars	Healing, sleep
Horehound	Mercury	Protection, mental powers, exorcism, healing
Horsetail	Saturn	Snake-charming, fertility
Hound's tongue	Mercury	Tying dogs' tongues
Houseleek	Jupiter	Luck, protection, love
Hyssop	Jupiter	Purification, protection
Ivy	Saturn	Protection, healing
Juniper bush	Sun	Protection, anti-theft, love, exorcism, health
Kidneywort	Venus	–
Knapweed	Saturn	–
Knotgrass	Saturn	Binding, health
Lady's mantle	Venus	Love
Lady's smock	Moon	–
Lady's thistle	Jupiter	–
Lavender	Mercury	Love, protection, sleep, chastity, longevity, purification, happiness, peace
Lavender (cotton)	Mercury	–
Lettuce	Moon	Chastity, protection, love, divination, sleep
Lily-of-the-valley	Mercury	Mental powers, happiness
Liquorice	Mercury	Love, lust, fidelity

CULPEPER'S PLANT	RULING PLANET / SIGN	CONTEMPORARY CORRESPONDENCES
Liverwort	Jupiter, Cancer	Protection, love
Loosestrife	Moon, Cancer	Peace, protection
Lovage	Sun	Love
Lungwort	Jupiter	–
Madder	Mars	–
Mallow	Venus	Love, protection, exorcism
Maple tree	Jupiter	Love, longevity, protection
Marigold	Sun, Leo	Protection, prophetic dreams, legal matters, psychic powers
Masterwort	Mars	Strength, courage, protection
Medlar	Saturn	–
Melancholy thistle	Capricorn, Saturn, Mars	–
Mellilot	Mercury	–
Mint	Venus	Money, love, lust, healing, exorcism, travel, protection
Mistletoe	Sun	Protection, love, hunting, fertility, health, exorcism
Moneywort	Venus	–
Moonwort	Moon	Money, love
Moss	Saturn	Luck, money
Motherwort	Venus	–
Mouse ear	Moon	–
Mugwort	Venus	Strength, psychic powers, protection, prophetic dreams, healing, astral projection
Mulberry tree	Mercury	Protection, strength
Mullein	Saturn	Courage, protection, health, love, divination, exorcism
Mustard	Mars	Fertility, protection, mental powers
Nailwort	Mars	–
Nep	Venus	–
Nettle	Mars	Exorcism, protection, healing, lust
Nightshade	Saturn	Nightshade is deadly poison.
Oak	Jupiter	Protection, health, money, healing, potency, fertility, luck
One blade	Sun	–
One leaf	Sun	–
Onion	Mars	Protection, exorcism, healing, prophetic dreams

CULPEPER'S PLANT	RULING PLANET / SIGN	CONTEMPORARY CORRESPONDENCES
Orchis	Venus	–
Orpine	Moon	–
Parsley	Mercury	Love, protection, purification
Parsnip	Venus	–
Peach tree	Venus	Love, exorcism, longevity, fertility, wishes
Pear tree	Venus	Lust, love
Pearl trefoil	Moon	–
Pellitory of Spain	Mercury	
Pellitory of the wall	Mercury	–
Pennyroyal	Venus	Strength, protection, peace
Peony	Sun	Protection, exorcism
Pepperwort	Mars	–
Periwinkle	Venus	Love, lust, mental powers, money, protection
Pimpernel	Sun	Protection, health
Plaintain	Mars	Protection, strength, snake-repelling
Plum	Venus	Healing
Polypody	Saturn	–
Poplar tree	Saturn	Money, flying
Poppy	Moon	Fertility, love, sleep, money, luck, invisibility
Primrose	Venus	Protection, love
Privet	Moon	–
Purslane	Moon	Sleep, love, luck, protection, happiness
Queen of the meadow	Venus	–
Quince tree	Saturn	Protection, love, happiness
Radish	Mars	Protection, lust
Ragwort	Venus	Protection
Rattle grass	Moon	–
Rest harrow	Mars	–
Rhubarb	Mars	Protection, fidelity
Rocket	Mars	
Rosa solis	Sun	–
Rose	Venus/Moon	Love, psychic powers, healing, divination, luck

CULPEPER'S PLANT	RULING PLANET / SIGN	CONTEMPORARY CORRESPONDENCES
Rosemary	Sun	Protection, love, lust, mental powers, purification, healing, sleep, youth
Rupturewort	Saturn	–
Saffron	Sun	Love, healing, happiness, wind-raising, lust, strength, psychic powers
Sage	Jupiter	Immortality, longevity, wisdom, protection, wishes
St John's wort	Sun	Health, power, protection, strength, love, divination
Samphire	Jupiter	–
Sanicle	Venus	–
Saracen's confound	Saturn	–
Sauce alone	Mercury	–
Savine	Mars	–
Savory	Mercury	Mental powers
Scabious	Mercury	–
Scurvy grass	Jupiter	–
Selfheal	Venus	–
Service tree	Saturn	–
Shepherd's purse	Saturn	–
Smallage	Mercury	–
Soapwort	Venus	–
Solomon's seal	Saturn	Protection, exorcism
Sorrel	Venus	Healing, health
Southern wood	Mercury	Love, lust, protection
Sow thistle	Mercury	–
Spignel	Venus	–
Spleenwort	Saturn	–
Star thistle	Mars	–
Stinking gladwin	Saturn	–
Stonecrop	Moon	–
Strawberry	Venus	Love, luck
Succory	Jupiter	–
Sweet marjoram	Mercury	–
Tamarisk tree	Saturn	Exorcism, protection

CULPEPER'S PLANT	RULING PLANET / SIGN	CONTEMPORARY CORRESPONDENCES
Thistle (cotton)	Mars	Strength, protection, hex-breaking, healing
Thyme	Venus	Health, healing, sleep, psychic powers, love, purification, courage
Tormentil	Sun	–
Treacle mustard	Mars	–
Turnsole	Sun	–
Tutsan	Sun	–
Vervain	Venus	Love, protection, purification, peace, money, youth, chastity, sleep, healing
Vine	Venus	–
Violet	Venus	Protection, luck, love, lust, wishes, peace, healing
Viper's bugloss	Sun	–
Wallflower	Moon	–
Walnut tree	Sun	–
Water flag	Venus	–
Water lily	Moon	–
Wheat	Venus	Fertility, money
White lily	Moon	–
White saxifrage	Moon	–
Wild marjoram	Mercury	–
Wild thyme	Venus	–
Willow tree	Moon	Love, divination, protection, healing
Wintergreen	Saturn	Protection, healing, hex-breaking
Winter rocket	Venus	–
Woad	Saturn	–
Wold	Mars	–
Woodbine	Mercury	–
Wood sage	Venus	–
Wood sorrel	Venus	–
Woollen thistle	Mars	–
Wormwood	Mars	Psychic powers, protection
Yarrow	Venus	Courage, love, psychic powers, exorcism

ENDNOTES

1 *The Confessions of Aleister Crowley*, Bantam Books, 1970, page 110

2 *The Old Sod* by Alan Richardson and Marcus Claridge, Ignotus, 2003, page 10

3 Kenneth Grant, who was Crowley's pupil and in some ways his successor, argued that there is no such thing as the *Un*conscious, and that the *Sub*conscious was the more accurate term

4 *Lords of Light* by W E Butler, Destiny Books, 1990, page 138

5 *Please Understand Me II: Temperament, Character, Intelligence* by David Keirsey, Prometheus Book Co., 1998

6 Adapted from https://en.wikipedia.org/wiki/Humorism#Four_humors

7 *Magical Ritual Methods* by William G Gray, Helios Books, 1999

8 *Magick in Theory and Practice* by Aleister Crowley, 1929

9 From unpublished papers given to the author

10 Arranged by, and used with the permission of, Dr Kelley Ross

11 *Liber 777* by Aleister Crowley, published privately by the author, 1908

12 Flying Roll XII, *Telesmatic Images & Adonai* by G H Frater, DDCF [Mathers]; the Flying Rolls were Knowledge Papers circulated among members of the Golden Dawn

13 Ibid.

14 Flying Roll XIV by Frater D D C F [Mathers], 15 January 1893

15 *Magical Ritual Methods* by William G Gray, Helios, 1969

16 Gray used the Waite/Rider deck of cards

17 Flying Roll IV, *An Example of Mode of Attaining to Spirit Vision* by S S D D and F

18 Flying Roll XIV, *Talismans and Flashing Tablets* by Frater Sapere Aude

19 Ibid.

20 *The Orion Mystery* by Robert Bauval and Adrian Gilbert, Heinemann, 1994

21 *Uriel's Machine* by Christopher Knight and Robert Lomas, Arrow, 2000

22 *Egyptian Birth Signs* by Storm Constantine, Thorsons, 2002

23 *The Astrology Bible* by Judy Hall, Godsfield, 2005

24 *The Aryan Christ* by Richard Noll, Random House, 1997

25 www.alchemylab.com

26 *Handbook of Chinese Horoscopes* by Theodora Lau, Souvenir Press, 1995

27 The dates given relate to the northern hemisphere; they are approximately six months later in the southern hemisphere

28 www.alchemylab.com

29 *Chakras* by Naomi Ozaniec, Element Books, 2000

30 Ibid.

31 From *Liber 777* by Aleister Crowley, 1908, XXXIX

32 *British Herbal and Family Physician* by Nicholas Culpeper, 1652

33 From *Liber 777* by Aleister Crowley, 1908, XLII

34 From *Liber 777* by Aleister Crowley, 1908, XXXVIII

35 'Translated from a valuable Latin manuscript by Francis Barrett' in *The Magus*, Book II, by Francis Barrett, London, 1801

36 From *Info-Psychology* by Dr Timothy Leary, New Falcon Publications, 1994

37 From *The Game of Life* by Dr Timothy Leary, New Falcon Publications, 1994

38 From *The Tree of Evil* by William G Gray, Helios, 1974

39 From Sebastien Michaelis's *Histoire admirable de la possession et conversion d'une penitente*, 1613

40 From *Liber 777* by Aleister Crowley, 1908

41 From Sebastien Michaelis's *Histoire admirable de la possession et conversion d'une penitente*, 1613

42 From Collin De Plancy's *Dictionnaire Infernale*, 1863

43 Francis Barrett's *The Magus*, London, 1801

44 From the *Grimoire of Pope Honorius*, Trident Books, 2000

45 Johan Weyer's *Hierarchy of Hell*, MRTS, 1991

46 Richard Dukante's *Hierarchy. Modern Demonolatry*, 1963

47 Ibid.

48 Ibid.

49 From miscellaneous medieval hierarchies

50 *Ancient Signs: The Alphabet and the Origins of Writing* by Andis Kaulins, 2012

51 *Hebet En Ba, The Book of Rites* by Khiron, from www.spirit-alembic.com/egyptian.html

52 www.maat.sofiatopia.org/ten_keys.htm

53 Ibid.

54 Based on www.touregypt.net/featurestories/nomes.htm

55 From *Merlin's Chess* by Mike Harris, Ritemagic, 2005

56 Based on information provided by Mike Harris

57 Ibid.

58 Ibid.

59 Based on https://britishfairies.wordpress.com/

60 From Michael Viscoli, *The Celtic Tree Calendar*, Souvenir Press, 1999; the dates given relate to the northern hemisphere; they are approximately six months later in the southern hemisphere

61 *Merlin's Chess* by Mike Harris, Ritemagic, 2005

62 www.imbas.org/articles/elements_duile.html

63 Adapted with kind permission from http://blueroebuck.com/index.html

64 www.magickcourse.com/runereadings/Rune%20Postures.html

65 www.omniglot.com/writing/futhorc.htm

66 From *Futhark – A Handbook of Rune Magic* by Edred Thorsson, Weiser, 1983

67 From *Rune Magic* by Donald Tyson, Llewellyn, 1999

68 www.magickcourse.com/runereadings/Rune%20Postures.html

69 Richard Wilhelm (1873–1930) translated the *I Ching* and *The Secret of the Golden Flower*, on which he collaborated with Carl Jung

ACKNOWLEDGEMENTS

A lot of people inspired this work and I have built upon their ideas and inspiration, and sometimes came to them like a thief in the night: Will Parfitt, Deanne Quarrie, Mike Harris, Naomi Ozaniec, Wim van den Dungen, Dr Kelley Ross, Kitty Staples, Theodora Lau, Vivienne O'Regan, Judith Page and the late, great Billie Walker-John. Hearty thanks to all of them for coming out of the mists of cyberspace and helping me, a stranger. Special thanks to the late Judy Hall, old friend and friend-of-a-friend, who showed me a way. And to Margaret, for being the brightest of souls, capable of dispersing any mist.

PICTURE CREDITS

iStock/duncan1890 6, 8, 9, 10, 12, 18, 20b, 27b, 28a, 28b, 30, 33b, 36a, 37, 38a, 50c, 50b, 60a, 61b, 69, 70, 83b, 85, 96, 97, 100a, 103b, 138b, 142a, 143b, 148a, 154, 157b, 159, 162, 171c, 171b, 176l, 176r, 181, 187b, 198, 208a, 211, 236b; ilbusca 157a; kovalto1 56; Man_Half-tube 1; Nastasic 150; ZU_09 28; Vladayoung 27c; Library of Congress, Music Division 20; Public domain CC0/31a 107c; Duncan's Masonic Ritual and Monitor of Freemasony, Malcolm C Duncan, 1866 (CC0) 38; Rawpixel/60c, 61a, 121, 188a; Art Institute of Chicago 168; Clark Art Institute 61c; Minneapolis Institute of Art 83al, 83r; New York Public Library 93, 187a, 191; The National Gallery of Art, Washington DC 64, 122; The Walters Art Museum 109c; Wellcome Collection 16, 25, 54a, 142b, 171a; University of Michigan Library Digital Collections 88; Wikipedia/Alchemy and Mysticism, Jakob Böhme, Hermetic Library (CC0) 15; Deutsche Fotothek of the Saxon State Library/State and University Library Dresden (SLUB) (CC0) 17; Fuzzypeg (CC0) 74; Lucretius *De rerum natura*, published in Bresica by Tommaso Ferrando (1472) 27a.

INDEX

A

Abaddon 178, 179
Abenragel 123
Adonis 88
aether 14, 27
Agni 94
Agrippa, Cornelius 6
  Agrippa's phases of the Moon 133–7
  De occulta philosophia 16, 123
Air 42, 44–5
Aires/Aethyrs 20, 171–3
Akashic Records 19, 188, 189
Akhenaten of Egypt 187
alchemy 116
  correspondences of physiological alchemy 147
alphabets
  Egyptian 186
  Hebrew 55
  number/alphabet correspondences 71
  runic 222–7
  Theban 73
Amentohep IV of Egypt 187
Amoun 94
Amoun-Ra 94
Amphitrite 89
amulets 68
Amun 108, 184, 194
Amun-Re 96
Anael 164–7
Andjety 184, 192
Andras 178
angels 162, 171, 208
  angels of the planets, days and hours 163, 164–7
  first hierarchy 163
  monthly correspondences 167
Anglo-Saxons 24, 222
  Futhorc 223
animals 159
  Hall's metal, animal and gemstone correspondences 112–13
  table of animals (real or imaginary) 159
ankh 60, 68
Ankh-f-n-Khonsu 184
Ankt 184
Anti 184
Anu 204
Anubis 94, 108, 184, 195
Anuket 184
Anukis 194
Apep 184
Aphrodite 88, 89
Apis 185, 192
Apollo/Apollon 88, 89
apple trees 212
Aquarius 42, 74
  correspondences 111, 113, 115, 116, 118
  glyph or symbol 110
  medical astrology 145
Aquinas, Thomas 116
Arabic lunar astrology 123, 126–31
Arathron 169, 170
Arawn 204
Arbatel de magia veterum 168

archangels 36, 37, 59
Ares 88, 89
Arianrhod 204
Aries 42, 75
  correspondences 111, 112, 114, 116, 118
  glyph or symbol 110
  medical astrology 145
Aristotle 28, 29
Artemis 88, 89
Arthur, King 14–15, 61, 84, 200
  Arthurian tradition 85, 198, 201
as above, so below 14, 40, 191
Asar 94
Asclepius 14, 24, 89
Aset 185
ash trees 212
Asmodeus 178, 179
Asrais 208
Assiah 64, 100, 102
Astaroth 178, 179
astral flight 188
  invocation of astral flight 189
astral portals 67
astrological associations 42
  Air 42
  Earth 43
  Fire 42
  Water 43
astrology 106
  Chinese astrology 118–19
  correspondences of astrology and numerology 116
  Egyptian astrology 107–8
  Hindu astrology 117
  lunar astrology 120–39
  talisman figures 74–5
  Western Zodiac 109–15
Aten 185, 187, 195
Athena 88, 89
Atum 96, 185, 192, 193
Atum-Re Stah 96
Atziluth 64, 100, 101
Auriel 36, 37
axis mundi 24–5

B

Baal 24, 179
Baalberith/Balberith/Baal-beryth 178, 179, 180
Babylon 106
Bacon, Roger 116
balancing the elements 26
  elemental attributions 27
  table of the quarters 27
Banebdjedet 193
Barguest 208
Barrett, Francis 6, 124–5, 178
  The Magus, or Celestial Intelligencer 16, 17, 73, 123, 163
Bast 193
Bastet 185
Bat 194
Bean Sidhe 208
Bean Tighe 208
Bean-Fionn 208
beech trees 211
Beelzebub 178, 179
Behemoth 178
Beliel/Belial 178, 179
Beltaine 121
Benben stone, Egypt 24
Bendith y Mamau 208
Bennu 185
Bes 185
Bethor 168–70
Bhavani 94
Binah 57, 58, 64, 65
  pathworking associations 84
birch trees 211
Black Pullet 16
Blackwood, Algernon 17
Blavatsky, Helena 46
Bloddeuwedd 204
Böhme, Jakob Signatura Rerum 15
Book of Changes see I Ching
Book of the Sacred Magic of Abramelin the Mage 16, 18
Brahe, Tycho 116
Brahma 94
Bran 200, 204
Branwen 204
Briah 64, 100, 101
Brigid 121, 184, 205
Brodie-Innes, J W 17
Browne, Thomas 116
Buchis 194
Buddhism 24
  Buddhist elements and associations 48–9
  chakras 148
  Van den Dungen's Buddhist correspondences 97
Budge, E A Wallace 17
Butler, W E 25

C

Cailleach Bhuer 120, 208
Caldwell, Tony 176
Cancer 43, 75
  correspondences 111, 112, 114, 116, 118
  glyph or symbol 110

medical astrology 145
Capricorn 43, 74
correspondences 111, 113, 115, 116, 118
glyph or symbol 110
medical astrology 145
Cassiel 164–7
cedar trees 212
Celtic tradition 12, 198
Celtic deities 93, 184, 204–7
correspondences of the *Dúile* 215
faery correspondences 208–10
festivals 120–1
figures from Celtic myth 200–3
Harris's three worlds and the three faces of the goddess 199
holy cities of Ireland 213
Moon 139
royal treasures of the isle of Britain 214
treasures and elements 213–15
tree lore 211–12
working with Celtic symbolism 215
Ceres 88
Ceridwen 205
chakras 25, 148
basic chakra associations 149
body systems and the Tree of life 146, 151
chakras and deity correspondences 150
interior star associations 150
petals, colours, yantras and elements 149
Chandra 94
Chesed 57, 58, 64, 65
pathworking associations 84
chestnut trees 212
Chinese astrology 118
ascendant hours 119
Circle of Conflict 119
Earth Branches and Western correspondences 118
Triangles of Affinity 119
Chinese elements 46
cycle of elements 46
elements and associations 47
elements and seasons 46
five elements of Chinese tradition 46
Chiron 91
Chnum 185
Chockmah 57, 58, 64, 65
pathworking associations 84
Chomse 94
Chons 185
Christianity 12, 21, 24, 61, 68, 121, 162, 168, 181, 208
Circe 89
Circle of Conflict 119
Clement of Alexandria 14
Clurichauns 208
Coblynau 209
collective unconscious 15
tapping into the collective unconscious 60–7
colour scales 100
colours of the Emperor and Empress scales 102
colours of the King and Queen scales 101
flashing colours 103
concept association 12
creating order out of chaos 12–13
Doctrine of Signatures 15–16
grimoires 16
Hermeticism 14
Kabbalah 16–17
neters 13–14
Welsh Triads 14–15
correspondences 6–7
concept association 12–18
finding your own correspondences 19–21
what are magical correspondences? 10–11
Cronos 90
Crowley, Aleister 11, 17, 25, 40, 88, 106, 158, 171, 176–7, 198, 213, 236
Book of Law 184
Egyptian and Hindu deities 93, 94, 184
I Ching 238–43
Liber 777 6, 11, 17–18, 19–20, 54, 56, 154, 184
Tarot 78–80
Cube of Space 25
Cu Chulainn 200
Culpeper, Nicholas 142–3, 145
Culpeper's correspondences 156, 157
plant correspondences ancient and modern 246–54
Culwch 200
Cybele 88
cypress trees 212

D

Daghdha 205
Danish Futhark 222
Danu 205
days 108
angels of the planets, days and hours 163–7
De Plancy, Colin *Dictionnaire Infernale* 178
Dee, John 6, 20, 116, 168, 171, 174
Dee's synopsis of the 30 Aires or Aethyrs 172–3
deities
Celtic deities 93, 184, 204–7
Egyptian and Hindu deities 93–7
Greek and Roman deities 88–92
Norse deities 229–31
Demeter 88, 90
demons 176–80, 208
devils 176–7

arch demons of Hell 180
arch she-demons of Hell 180
Barrett's devil rankings 178
De Plancy's devil rankings 178
demons listed by purpose and rulership 180
Dukante's devil rankings 179
Honorius's devil rankings 179
Michaelis's devil rankings 178
Qlipoth 176–7
seven princes of Hell 180
Weyer's devil rankings 179
Diana 88
Dionysus 90
directions 25, 228
Doctrine of Signatures 15–16, 142
Donn 205
Drakes 209
Druids 12, 35
Druidic festivals and the eight sabbats of modern witches 120
dúile 35, 213, 215
Duamutef 187
Dukante, Richard *Hierarchy: Modern Demonolatry* 179

E

Earth 43, 44–5
Egypt 13–14, 24, 187–8
Hebet En Ba (Book of Rites) 187–8
invocation of astral flight 189
invocation of soul memory 189
neters 13–14, 106, 187–8, 213
nomes 107, 191, 208
nomes of Lower Egypt and their associations 192–3
nomes of Upper Egypt and their associations 194–5
Van den Dungen's ritual postures 190
Egyptian alphabet 186
Egyptian astrology 107
correspondences for the monthly signs of Egyptian astrology 108
Egyptian extra days 108
Egyptian deities 93, 184
Crowley's correspondences for major Egyptian and Hindu deities 94
major Egyptian deities 184–5
Van den Dungen's Egyptian mysteries 96
Eileithyia 90
Elder Futhark 222, 224–7
elements 26–7, 30
astrological associations 42–3
Buddhist elements and associations 48–9
chakras 149, 150
Chinese elements 46–7
complete table of the elements 44–5
Dúile 35
elemental attributions 27
elemental correspondences 32
elemental correspondences and the Kabbalah 34
gemstones 50
Indigenous American elemental correspondences 35
Kabbalistic associations 33–4
plants 50
tattwas and their symbols 51
Elen 200
Elizabeth I 171
Ellyllons 209
elm trees 212
Enoch, First Book of 13
equinoxes 107, 109, 120, 121, 211
Erinyes 90
Ernutet 185
Eros 90
essential oils 157
Crowley's and modern Wiccan correspondences 158

F

faery 208
faery correspondences 208–10
Farr, Florence 17, 83–4
fig trees 212
Fin/Fintan 205
finding your own correspondences 19–20
creating your own Magick 21
using magical tables 20–1
what is magic? 21
Fionn 200
Fir Darrigs 209
Fire 42, 44–5
Fireesin 209
food, herb and place correspondences 114–15
Formors 209
Fortune, Dion 59, 198
fourfold patterns 28
Aristotle's four sources of happiness 29
Galen's four temperaments 29
Hippocrates' system of humours 29, 142
Paracelsus's order of elemental spirits 29
Plato's correspondences 29
Frater Achad *see* Jones, Charles Stansfield
Frater Sapere Aude *see* Westcott, W Wynn
Fraternity of the Inner Light 59, 198
Frazer, Sir James *The Golden Bough* 12
Freemasonry 17, 38
Fu Hsi 236
Futhorc 223

G

Gabriel 36, 37, 164–7
Galen 28
Ganesha 94, 95
Geancanach 209
Geb 96, 185
Geburah 57, 58, 59, 64, 65, 159
Gemini 42, 75
correspondences 111, 112, 114, 116, 118
glyph or symbol 110
medical astrology 145
gemstones 154
elements, gemstones and plants 50
Hall's metal, animal and gemstone correspondences 112–13
Tree of Life and gemstone correspondences 155
Ghillie Dhu 209
Glaistig, The 209
Glashtin 209
Gnosticism 13, 181
aeon I and aeon II 181
god-forms 36
archangels of the quarters 37
four god-forms 37
Native British associations 37
Goewin 201
Gofannon 205
Goibhniu 205
Golden Dawn (GD) *see* Hermetic Order of the Golden Dawn
Gonne, Maude 17, 198
Gope girls 94
Grand Grimoire 16
Graves, Robert *The White Goddess* 211, 218
Gray, William G 6, 11, 19, 65, 67, 78–9, 81–2, 84, 176
Magical Ritual Methods 74
working the circle 41
Greater Key of Solomon 16, 18, 123
Greek and Roman deities 88
Tree of Life associations 88
wider associations 89–92
Gressil 178
Griffith 209
grimoires 16, 68, 168
Gronw 206
Gwenhwyfar 14–15, 201
Gwydion 206
Gwyllion 209

H

Ha 192
Hades 88, 90
Hagith 168–70
Hall, Judy *The Astrology Bible* 109, 112–15, 146
Hallowe'en 120
Hammemit 94
Hanuman/Hanumat 94, 95
Hapi 187
Harachte 185
Harris, Mike *Merlin's Chess* 198, 199
Hartley, Christine 109
The Western Mystery Tradition 198
Hathor 94, 108, 185, 192, 194, 195
Hatmehyt 193
hazel trees 212
Hebrew 54–5
Hecate 88, 90
Helios 91
Hephaistos 91
Heqet 185
Hera 88, 91
Herakles 91
herbs 142
Hall's place, herb and food correspondences 114–15
Hermes 14, 88, 91
Hermes Trismegistus 14
Hermetic Order of the Golden Dawn 6, 17, 18, 25, 46, 59, 65, 93, 109, 168, 184
Flying Rolls 73
lesser banishing ritual of the pentagram 40–1
magical images 61, 63
Tarot and pathworking 83–4
Hermeticism 14, 25, 39, 43, 191
Heru-pa-Kraath 94
Heryshef 195
Hestia 91
Hildegard of Bingen *Liber Simplicis Medicinae* 142
Hindu astrology 117
lunar astrology 123, 126–31
Navagraha 117
Seven Rays 117
Hindu deities 93
chakras and deity correspondences 150
Crowley's correspondences for major Egyptian and Hindu deities 94
Van den Dungen's Hindu correspondences 95
Hinduism 24
chakras 148
Hippocrates 28, 29, 142
Hod 57, 58, 59, 64, 65, 66, 159
Honorius, Sworn Book of 168, 179
Hoor par Kraat 185
Hormakhu 94
hornbeam trees 212
Horniman, Annie 17
Horus 94, 96, 108, 185, 192, 193, 194

hours 122–3
angels of the planets, days and hours 163–7
ascendant hours 119
magical names of the hours 132
Hours, The 92
humours 29, 142
humours and their correspondences 143

I

I Ching 7, 236
Crowley's and Wilhelm's hexagrams of the *I Ching* 239–43
Crowley's trigrams of the *I Ching* 238
generating hexagrams 237
hexagram lines 237
Imbolc 121
Imsety 187
incenses 157
Crowley's and modern Wiccan correspondences 158
Indigenous Americans 12–13, 16, 24, 35
elemental correspondences 35
Indra 94, 95
internet 6–7, 19, 162
Isaac the Blind 54
Ishvara 95
Isis 13, 60, 184, 185, 194
Islam 24

J

Jesus 61, 121, 181
Jones, Charles Stansfield 78–9
Judaism 16, 24, 54, 162
Jung, Carl 15, 30, 116, 236
Juno 88
Jupiter (god) 88
Jupiter (planet) 69, 70, 106
angels of 164–7
medical astrology 144, 146
Navagraha 117
Olympic spirit 169
planetary symbol 72, 110
plant correspondences 246–54
Seven Rays 17

K

ka posture 38–9
Kabbalah 7, 16–17
astral portals 67
Four Worlds 33–4, 64
elemental correspondences and the Kabbalah 34
left-to-right ordering 54–5
modern Kabbalah 66
tapping into the collective unconscious 60–7
Tree of Life 56–9
values of the Hebrew alphabet 55
Kabbalah Unveiled, The 18
kameas see magic squares
Kelley, Edward 171
Kelly, Gerard 17
Kelpies 209
Kether 57, 58, 59, 64, 65
pathworking associations 84
Khamael 59
Kheiron 91
Khentamentin 194
Kherty 192
Khiron 188
Khnum 185, 194, 195
Khons 194
Klippoth 176–7
Knight, Christopher *Uriel's Machine* 106
Korrigans 209
Krishna 94, 95
Kundalini 94, 95

L

Lakshmi 94, 95
Lalita 94
Leary, Timothy 174
Chapel Perilous 175
eight circuits of the nervous system 174
Game of Life, The 174
observations from *The Game of Life* 175
Leo 42, 75
correspondences 111, 112, 114, 116, 118
glyph or symbol 110
medical astrology 145
Leprechauns 209
Lesser Key of Solomon (*Lemegeton*) 16, 18
Leto 91
Leviathan 178, 179, 180
Libra 42, 75
correspondences 111, 113, 115, 116, 118
glyph or symbol 110
medical astrology 145
lime trees 212
Lingam 94
Lleu/Llew 206
Lomas, Robert *Uriel's Machine* 106
Lucifer 176, 179
Lugh 206
Lughnasadh 121
Lunantisidhe 209
lunar astrology 120–39

lusaas 193
Lutins 209
Ly Erg 210

M

Máahes 185
Maat 94, 185
Mab Darogan 201
Mac ind Og 201
Machen, Arthur 17
Macsen Wledig 201
magic circle 25
magic squares (*kameas*) 68
  kamea of Jupiter 69
  kamea of Luna (Moon) 70
  kamea of Mars 69
  kamea of Mercury 70
  kamea of Saturn 69
  kamea of Sol (Sun) 69
  kamea of Venus 69
magical weapons 30
  Cup 31
  Pentacle 31
  Spear or Rod 31
  Sword 31
Magick 21, 27
magickal directions 228
Malkuth 57, 58, 64, 65, 66
  pathworking associations 84
Mammon 178, 179, 180
mana 14, 27
Manannan mac Lir 206
maple trees 212
Mars (god) 88
Mars (planet) 10, 69, 106
  angels of 164–7
  medical astrology 144, 146
  Navagraha 117
  Olympic spirit 169
  planetary symbol 72, 110
  plant correspondences 246–54
  Seven Rays 117
Maruts 94
Mathers, Samuel Liddell MacGregor 6, 18, 61, 65, 184
  Greater Key of Solomon (transl.) 18, 123
  Mather's talisman figures in a square and circle 73
Matholwch 201
Mau 94
Medhbh of Connacht 206
medical astrology 143
  astrological influences 144
  Culpeper's Zodiac sign body correspondences 145
  humours and their correspondences 143
  table of significance of the houses in astrology 145
medical correspondences 146
  body systems and the Tree of life 146, 151
  chakras 148–51
  correspondences of physiological alchemy 147
  Hall's musical correspondences 146
medieval medicine 142
  Culpeper's astrological influences and effects 142–3
  use of herbs 142
Medrawd 206
megalithic sites 106
Mercury (god) 88
Mercury (planet) 70, 106
  angels of 164-7
  medical astrology 144, 146
  Navagraha 17
  Olympic spirit 169
  planetary symbol 72, 110
  plant correspondences 246–54
  Seven Rays 117
Meret 185
Merihim 178, 180
Merlin 202
Merrows 210
Merti 94
Michael 36, 37, 164–7
Michaelis, Sebastien *Admirable History* 176, 178
microcosm and macrocosm 14, 40
Mihos 193, 194
Min 194
Minerva 88
Mnevis 193
Modron 202
Mont 94
Montu 194
Moon 70, 106, 120
  Agrippa's phases of the Moon 133–7
  angels of 164–7
  Arabic and Hindu associations 123
  Barrett's four quarters of the Moon 124–5
  expanded Celtic correspondences 139
  magical names of the hours 132
  Mathers' and Agrippa's correspondences 123
  medical astrology 144, 146
  Navagraha 117
  Olympic spirit 169
  phases of the Moon 122–3
  plant correspondences 246–54
  Seven Rays 117
  Sidonius' correspondences 126–31
  symbol planetary symbol 72, 110
  Wiccan Moon names 138
Morgan le Fay 210
Mormyrus 195

Morrighan 206
Moses de Leon 55
Murdhuachas 210
Muses 92
music
  Hall's musical correspondences 146
Mut 185, 194

N

Nag Hammadi Library, Egypt 13
Native Americans *see* Indigenous Americans
Navagraha 117
Neith 185, 192, 194
Nekhbet 194
Nemhedh 207
Nemty 194, 195
Neoplatonism 16
Nephthys 94, 96, 108, 185
Neptune (god) 88
Neptune (planet) 110, 144
neters 13–14, 93, 187–8, 213
Netzach 57, 58, 59, 64, 65
  pathworking associations 84
Neuberg, Victor 171
New Age 17, 21
Newton, Isaac 15, 116
Niall 202
Nicholas of Cusa 16
Nirgun Brahman 95
Nodens 207
nomes 107, 191–5, 208
Norse deities 229–31
Norwegian Futhark 222
Nuadha 207
Nucklelavees 210
Nuit 94
numerology 54–5
  correspondences of astrology and numerology 116
  number/alphabet correspondences 71
Nun 96
Nut/Nuit 185

O

O'Dubhain, Searles 213
oak trees 211
Och 168–70
Odin 61, 229
'Odindis' 228
Oenghus 207
Ogdoad 195
ogham 13, 218
  ogham associations 218–19
Oghma 207
olive trees 211
Olwen 202
Olympic spirits 168
  seven Olympic planetary spirits 169
  Waite's analyses of the planetary spirits 170
omphalos 24
Onuris 193, 194
Opet 185
Ophiel 168–70
Orai 92
Osiris 13, 94, 96, 108, 185, 192, 194
Ossian 202
otz chaim see Tree of Life
Owain 202
Ozaniec, Naomi *Chakras* 150

P

pagan festivals 121–2
  Druidic festivals and the eight sabbats of modern witches 120
  festival associations 121
paganism 21
Pakhet 195
Pan 88
pan-animism 154
Parabrahm 94
Paracelsus 28, 29
Peck, William 17
pentagram, lesser banishing ritual of the 40
  Wiccan adaptations 41
perfumes 157
  Crowley's and modern Wiccan correspondences 158
Persephone 88, 92
Phaleg 168–70
phlogiston 14, 27
Phoenix 108
Phookas 210
Phul 169, 170
Phynnodderees 210
pine trees 212
Pisces 43, 74
  correspondences 111, 113, 115, 116, 118
  glyph or symbol 110
  medical astrology 145
Piskies 210
place, herb and food correspondences 114–15
planets 68–70, 106
  angels of the planets, days and hours 163–7
  chakras 150
  medical astrology 143, 144
  Navagraha 117
  Olympic spirits 168–70

plant correspondences 246–54
symbols of the planets 72, 110
talisman figures under the planets and signs 74–5
plants 25, 154
Culpeper's and modern Wiccan correspondences 156
elements, gemstones and plants 50
plant correspondences ancient and modern 246–54
Tree of Life and plant associations 155
Plato 14, 28, 29
Pluto 110, 144
pneuma 14, 27
poplar trees 212
Poseidon 88, 92
postures 38–9
runic ritual body postures 232–3
Van den Dungen's ritual postures 190
prana 14, 27
Prometheus 92
Proust, Marcel 39
Pryderi 202
Psyche 88
Ptah 94, 185, 192
Pwyll 202
Pytho 178

Q

Qebehseneuf 187
Qlipoth 176
Crowley's Qlipothic correspondences 177
Quarrie, Deanne 218

R

Ra 94, 185
Raphael 37, 164–7
Re 96, 192
Red Cap 210
Rhea 88, 92
Rhiannon 207
Robin Goodfellow 210
Roman deities *see* Greek and Roman deities
Ronwe 178, 179
Rosicrucianism 17
Rosicrucian cross 74
rowan trees 212
ruah 14, 27
runes 222
Danish Futhark 222
Elder Futhark 222
Elder Futhark, first aett 224
Elder Futhark, second aett 225
Elder Futhark, third aett 226
Futhorc 223
magickal directions 228
Norse deities 230–1
ritual body postures 232–3
Swedish-Norwegian Futhark/short-twig/röx runes 222
Thorsson's Futhark correspondences 227
Tyson's deity associations 229

S

Sachiel 164–7
Sagittarius 43, 74
correspondences 111, 113, 115, 116, 118
glyph or symbol 110
medical astrology 145
Sakti 94
Samael 164–7
Samhain 120
Satan 178, 179
Satis 194
Saturn 69, 106
angels of 164–7
medical astrology 144, 146
Navagraha 117
Olympic spirit 169
plant correspondences 246–54
Seven Rays 117
symbol planetary symbol 72, 110
Schimeon Ben Jochai 54
Scorpio 43, 75
correspondences 111, 113, 115, 116, 118
glyph or symbol 110
medical astrology 145
Sekhmet 108, 185
Selkies 210
Seneferu 195
Sepher Yetzirah 55
sephiroth 57, 78
Four Worlds and the sephiroth 64
sephiroth and the elements 65
updated version of the sephiroth and the elements 66
Seshet 185
Seth/Set 94, 108, 185, 193, 194, 195
Seven Directions 25
Seven Rays 117
shamanism 35, 38
Shang dynasty, China 236
Shellycoats 210
Shiva 94, 95
Shu 94, 96, 108, 193
Sidhe 208
Sidonius, Dorotheus 123

signs and sigils 71
Simpson, Elaine 83–4
Sobek 94, 194
Sokar 24, 185, 192
solstices 120, 211
Sonneilon 178, 179
Sopdu 193
Sothis 185
soul memory 188
  invocation of soul memory 189
Soyga, The Book of 168
Sphinx 108
Spriggans 210
spruce trees 212
St Patrick 12
Sulis 207
Sun 69
  angels of 164–7
  medical astrology 144, 146
  Olympic spirit 169
  plant correspondences 246–54
  Seven Rays 117
  symbol planetary symbol 72, 110
Swedish Futhark 222
sympathetic magic 12–13

T

tables of correspondences 24
  astrological associations 42–3
  balancing the elements 26–7
  Buddhist elements and associations 48–9
  Chinese elements 46–7
  Druidic and other shamanic systems 35
  elements, gemstones and plants 50
  four god-forms 36–7
  fourfold patterns 28–9
  Kabbalistic associations 33–4
  key concepts 24–5
  lesser banishing ritual of the pentagram 40–1
  postures 38–9
  tattwas and their symbols 51
  twentieth-century analyses 30–1
Taliesin 203
talismanic Magick 68
  flashing colours 103
  Flying Rolls 73
  magic squares (*kameas*) 68–70
  Mather's talisman figures in a square and circle 73
  number/alphabet correspondences 71
  Rosicrucian cross 74
  signs and sigils 71
  symbols of the planets 72
  talisman figures under the planets and signs 74–5
  talismans 68
  Theban alphabet 73
Taoism 148
Tarot 78–9
  Crowley's attributions for the Tarot pack 80
  differing path attributions 79
  Gray's attributions for the court cards 81
  Gray's attributions for the suits 81
  Gray's expanded associations 82
  pathworking 83–4
  pathworking associations 84
  Thorsson's Futhark correspondences 227
  Tree of Life 78
tattwas 51, 65, 67, 83, 191
  working with the *tattwas* 51
Taurus 43, 75
  correspondences 111, 112, 114, 116, 118
  glyph or symbol 110
  medical astrology 145
Tefnut 96, 193
Temple of Hathor, Denderah 107
Tetragrammaton 68
Theosophical Society 46, 117
Thoth 14, 185, 193, 195
Three Faces of the Goddess 199
Three Worlds 199
Tiphereth 57, 58, 61, 64, 65
  pathworking associations 84
tree lore 211
  Viscoli's trees of equinox and solstice 211
  Viscoli's trees of spring and autumn 212
  Viscoli's trees of summer and winter 212
Tree of Life 56, 60, 191
  Arthurian tradition 85
  body systems and the Tree of life 146, 151
  colour scales and the Tree of Life 100–2
  Four Worlds and the sephiroth 64
  Four Worlds on the Tree 64
  Gray's anglicization of the Tree of Life 67
  Gray's Tree of Evil 176
  Gray's Tree of Life 176
  Greek and Roman deities 88
  learning to use the tree 59
  magical images 61
  magical images associated with the paths 63
  origins 56
  paths and spheres 78
  pillars 57
  sephiroth and the elements 65
  sequence of the spheres 59
  sphere associations 58
  spheres 57
  spheres and paths of the Tree of Life 62
  Tree and the elements 65

Tree of Life and gemstone correspondences 155
Tree of Life and plant associations 155
updated version of the sephiroth and the elements 66
vowel sonics 65
trees 25
Triangles of Affinity 119
Trithemius, Johannes 163
Trotula of Salerno 142
Trows 210
Tuatha de Danann 203
Turner, Robert *Arbatel of Magick* 168
twentieth-century analyses 30
different world views 30
magical weapons 30–1
Twlwwyth Tegs 210
Twylth Teg 203
Tyson, Donald 229

U

Uranus 110, 144
Urisks 210
Urobach 178
Uther Pendraig 203

V

Van den Dungen, Wim 93, 95, 97, 190
Varuna 95
Venus (goddess) 60, 88
Venus (planet) 69, 70, 106
angels of 164–7
medical astrology 144, 146
Navagraha 117
Olympic spirit 169
planetary symbol 72, 110
plant correspondences 246–54
Seven Rays 17
Verrine 178, 179
virgin queen *see* Gwenhwyfar
Virgo 43, 75
correspondences 111, 113, 114, 116, 118
glyph or symbol 110
medical astrology 145
Viscoli, Michael 211–12
Vishnu 94, 95
vowel sonics 65

W

Wadjet 108, 185, 193
Waite, A E 17
Book of Black Magic and Ceremonial Magic 168, 170
walnut trees 212
Water 43, 44–5
Welsh Triads 14–15
Welz, Karl Hans 222, 232
Wepwawet 195
Westcott, W. Wynn 6, 103
Weyer, Johan *Hierarchy of Hell* 179
Wicca 25, 39, 43, 156, 158
Druidic festivals and the eight sabbats of modern witches 20
handfasting 121
Wiccan Moon names 138
working the circle 41
Wilde, Constance 17
Wilhelm, Richard *I Ching and the Secret of the Golden Flower* 239–43
willow trees 212

Y

Yama 94
yantras 148, 149
Yeats, W B 17, 18, 198
Yesod 57, 58, 59, 64, 65, 66
pathworking associations 84
Yetzirah 64, 100, 102
Ygraine 207
yin and yang 46, 237
yoga 38
Taoist yoga 148
Yoni 94

Z

Zeus 24, 88, 92
Zodiac 106, 107, 109
Hall's metal, animal and gemstone correspondences 112–13
Hall's place, herb and food correspondences 114–15
medical astrology 143, 145
talisman figures under the planets and signs 74–5
wider associations 111
Zodiac signs and planetary symbols 110
Zohar 54, 55